Toxic Nursery

CARLIE MARTECE

Published by Castle Mindscape

ISBN: 978-0-9928716-0-4

This story is based on a true disaster.

It is dedicated to the sad girls with dreams,
The mad girls with nightmares,
And the badgers with insomnia.

CONTENTS

CHAPTER 1

(Constructed Sanity Falls to Nothing)

Lost upon a scarred landscape, two fractured girls stumble towards an uncertain future. Their throats are dry: one of them hoarse from lunatic screaming, the other dehydrated by her favourite poison. The sky is bruise purple, flickering with a light that illuminates their pale, broken skin, while the dry ground beneath them writhes with glinting glass and mangled mechanisms. It's all incredibly tragic. Like death. Like poverty. Like losing your favourite kitten, in a junkyard, on acid, at Christmas.

They both have high cheekbones, and their hazel eyes are ringed with smudged, charcoal make-up, although one of them walks with her vision glazed over, willingly smothered by a perpetual delusion, while the other girl's vicious glance is like a death threat.

Honeysuckle teeters ahead on spikes that barely support her. She hopes that one day someone will catch her before she falls, and she's chosen an outfit to match that trite ambition. Her tight dress is desperately short, and she has forgotten her coat. Goosebumps molest her bare limbs despite the lack of breeze in the stale, dusty air.

Her angry twin, Alicia, has dressed in the more practical manner of a haunted renegade. Her shape is hidden by thick, dark layers, and her heavy boots treat each grudging step upon the earth like an attack upon a fallen enemy.

Honeysuckle looks back at her furious sister. "If we write it, will they come?" she asks, with a tone of sly suggestion. This theatrical girl is a real dream, a fantasy reality, the ultimate oxymoron, with a smile like a saccharine hallucination.

"If they come near me, I'll stab them," snarls Alicia. This one just wants to stab and set fire to people.

It's good to have hobbies.

Honeysuckle giggles. "You're never going to actually stab anyone though are you?" her coquettish voice enquires, as her bare ankles strain their tendons with the effort of keeping her upright in inappropriate footwear.

Alicia shoots her a lightning-fast shark's grin.

"I stabbed you didn't I?"

Alicia is the adrenaline surge that makes you punch your life in the face, and one day this might stand for something.

Honeysuckle ignores her, and continues to walk her attempted model's walk, so optimistic and vulnerable. "I don't want people to feel sorry for me," she says.

"Nobody will. You're disgusting," replies Alicia. Of all the people she despises, she fears Honeysuckle the most. It's bad enough having a small frame and skinny arms, without having a masochistic twin who opens the door to strangers. It takes veins full of nitro-glycerine and hatred just to counterbalance the incessant invitation to violation.

"And besides," she continues, with a glare of bitter mistrust, "there are already so many stories about girls like us. Harrowing accounts of courage and survival against all the odds. The kind of pity-me tale we let you read in women's magazines while you sit in doctors' reception rooms waiting for someone to help you, something that could have been just two pages of misery if it weren't for some attention-seeking bint with too much time on her hands who's turned it into a supposed work of literature."

Honeysuckle laughs, a hyper-feminine giggle that's both grating and baiting. "If you're not an attention-seeking bint with too much time on her hands, then what are you?" she asks the angry one, looking back over her shoulder with the flash of a salacious smile.

"I'm your goddamn spine, bitch," retorts Alicia, as she kicks her in the back, leaving a dusty boot print on the thin fabric of her hopeful dress. Honeysuckle falls to her knees, again, blood and dirt on her smooth, bare legs. She bursts into tears as her sister kicks her once more.

Feeling nothing but contempt for the fallen wretch before her, Alicia continues her ranting. "You call me 'attention seeking' when you dress like that?" she splutters. "Showing off your pasty flesh to anyone who wants to letch on you? You may as well be stood in a window with a price sign round your neck. Always begging, 'pick me, pick me,' and never for one second stopping to care about how your behaviour reflects upon the rest of us."

Honeysuckle glares up at her beloved enemy through the black lightning shapes of mascara-streaked tears. "What about *you* making us look like a psycho?" she asks. "Driving everyone away so that nobody will ever love us?"

Alicia glares with remorseless repulsion at her fallen twin. "That's right, bitch, some tears for the camera... ever the little actress. You're going to really enjoy this, aren't you? People will finally understand your pain. Everything you 'went through as a child', how 'brave' you've been, because what the world really needs is another tragic tale, another 'fucked up, middle class, white girl' biography. Bored, middle-aged housewives read that crap so they can discuss it with their friends over a nice cup of tea. 'Oh, isn't it awful?' they say, but really they're loving it, and they can't wait to get to the bit where the heroine reveals how she was abused as a child, to read the sick little details in all their glory. They're salivating over what a fascinating soap opera life can be, and all those sordid little stories serve to alleviate the tedium of their pointless domestic existence. 'Oh, doesn't it make you think?' they say."

Alicia clenches her fists and takes a deep breath before continuing, trying not to explode. "'Make you think.' Really. Is that because you don't 'think' usually as part of your daily routine? Is it a novel concept to you? 'Well, I was going to just automate through the day like some kind of pre-programmed mediocrity machine, but now that I've been reminded that some people get molested and end up mental, I thought I'd do a spot of *thinking* instead.' Oh well done. Maybe if you're genuinely ignorant enough to believe that we all grew up behind white picket fences, and nothing truly disturbing ever happens except for in the movies, then yeah, I guess it would 'make you think'. Although perhaps if people walked through life with their eyes open rather than being eternally spoon-fed a societal fallacy then it wouldn't take some made-for-TV, housewife special to *make them think*."

Seething with frustrated outrage, Alicia surveys the mindscape before her. Everything here is broken. The sky leaks as easily as Honeysuckle's face, with an acidic rain that corrodes all exposed flesh beneath it. There is desolation in every direction, with so many shadowed, uncharted territories filled with twisted demons and dismembered dolls. Nothing grows in the barren soil and everything they try to build turns to rust.

It wasn't always like this. Before the terror, corruption and downright cynicism, this was a lush dreamland populated by delicate butterflies and mystical creatures: a place of hope, wonder and grand adventure. There were meadows where Clairey used to play and vast woodlands where Katie used to hide. The two little girls had a happy home here, a safe haven from the outside world. Skies were a non-threatening shade of pastel blue, and light from the ever-present sunshine would be refracted through prisms that hung in the treetops, painting intricate rainbows across innocent faces. There was magic, laughter, and a constant sense that something wonderful was about to happen.

Everything has to end. The sun went down indefinitely, the children were put to sleep, and pretty flowers turned rotten, dropping faded petals onto a land now littered with sharp debris and broken bones. Alicia burned down the forests while Honeysuckle poisoned the streams. They now spend their time wandering lost and deranged in a hell they helped create, looking for an exit that doesn't yet exist.

Alicia looms over Honeysuckle in the ruins of their home. She is too overwhelmed by the white hot adrenaline surge of the moment to have any past regrets. "And another thing," she snaps, her eyes glaring out over jagged rocks, "I could never quite grasp the supposed connection between suffering and courage. It would be a little patronising, don't you think, to go round a hospital ward full of terminally ill patients and start telling people how 'brave' they are? As if they chose their situation. As if that's any consolation, when their lives are about to end, to be thinking, 'Well, at least contracting a terminal illness gave me the chance to show everyone how brave I am.' As though given the option, they wouldn't rather be less 'brave', and not about to die."

"The same goes for child abuse survival," she continues. "'Oh, aren't you brave!' they say. 'Brave'. Really. As though as a child I thought, 'I know, I'll get me some abuse. It'll fuck with my head in later life, but right now it will give me the chance to show some *courage.*'"

Alicia can contain her fury no longer and it explodes out of her. She grabs a fistful of Honeysuckle's hair with one hand, and uses the other to repeatedly punch her in the face. One punch for the domestic violence that was all her fault. One punch for the sexual abuse that she made happen. One for the homelessness. One for the hopelessness. One for her drug addiction. One for all the psychologically abusive relationships she kept crying out for, and one more for luck, just because her face looks so damn punchable.

Honeysuckle goes limp, like a discarded ragdoll, and takes it. She takes it because she deserves it and because she knows that she will heal. She is like a sickly weed growing up through a crack in the concrete, trodden on repeatedly but still refusing to die. She takes it because despite it all, she still has an endless capacity for love, and she loves Alicia... poor, terrified, crippled Alicia.

Alicia is the paraffin that sets your future on fire, but like everything else, she will fall to nothing.

Honeysuckle gazes up at her sad sister through blood, tears and ruined make-up. "So how do we begin this?" she asks her, lisping with a voice that rattles through shattered teeth.

The glare in Alicia's eyes dims to something murky and unfathomable, staring at Honeysuckle, staring back at herself, lost to the ages.

"Oh," she whispers, "I think we've begun already."

CHAPTER 2

(Angelic Tragedy Hits the Shore)

On a cracked screen by Alicia's feet, the movie begins, all hazy and indistinct, like one of those old analogue devices with inadequate reception. We're going to rewind to the start of the Reality Show, a program recorded live from the optical nerve of our physical vessel, so you can see how we got to this point in our existence. You may want popcorn, or you might require a box of tissues. That would depend entirely upon what you're into. You may simply wish to change the channel, rather than watch this pathetically poetic joke of a documentary. We swear by whichever celebrated immortal is deity of the week that we will play back our truth, and nothing but our truth.

Memory begins on the hippy traveller circuit, and the main things that we recall are drugs and colours. There were none of your modern narcotics, the kind made from crisp, white powders like bitter candy drifts of snowy delirium. There were just plants and hallucinogenic fungus, gifts from Mother Earth for those spiritualized vagrants who choose to worship the Goddess.

We celebrated our fourth birthday in a tent in a foreign country. We were encased within the shell of a scrawny little creature with shy eyes and self-conscious mannerisms. Our parental units bought us Lego and some cake.

The tent was blue, as were the skies in both reality and the mindscape. Despite the physical beauty of our external surroundings, we existed mostly in the imaginary realm, because life made more sense there and had a certain structure. We would either be manic Clairey or timid Katie, the morning would begin with a quest, various new territories would be explored throughout the afternoon, and by bedtime the mission would be fulfilled. It is important to have a routine. The most crucial aspect was that whoever we were, we had control, we were our own leader, and we could choose our destination. Also, we could choose to be surrounded by people other than unwashed narcissists with names like Solstice and Moonbeam.

The car was green. Our days were usually spent sat on the back seat, stuck next to the piles of colourful rags made from organic fibres that our parents referred to as "clothing". We would sit there drawing pictures. Being no child prodigy, our artistic output consisted mostly of stick figures and basic cartoon animals. They were the type of drawings that a well-meaning mother would blatantly lie about by pretending they weren't dreadful, her parental delusion attaching some inexplicable merit to them as she stuck them to the fridge.

It was a shame we didn't have a fridge.

We love being lied to.

The sand was yellow. We were already familiar with sand from when we lived by the beach with Father #1. It came in these miniscule pieces and you could build things out of it, just like memories, squashing tiny wet fragments together in an attempt to make a coherent structure.

The sunsets were orange. There would be orange flame across the sky before nightfall, as tiny orange sparks floated in the fog of hippy herb smoke. That smoke could give you crazy dreams. You might dream that you will grow up to be an alien, leaving earthly boundaries behind as you zoom off to join an intergalactic battle across the stars. You might dream of mysterious, ancient forces that choose to project you into the future as a sentient being and give you latent powers that activate as you take your adult form, creating a post-human entity with the ability to deconstruct a mediocre reality.

You might dream that you'll become a troubled young woman with a debilitating mental health condition who is unable to hold down a job because she can't function as a productive human being.

It's good to have something to aspire to.

Back then, our hands were red, smothered by a liquid that shone with the vivid scarlet shade that evokes both passion and terror. Our mother's hands and feet were red and everyone was laughing. In the tiny village of sand that we had drifted into, they didn't get many Caucasian visitors, and they were fascinated by the menacing stain that their henna made upon our skin, a shocking crimson both hilarious and hypnotic.

Somebody would later become obsessed with that morbid hue, for the usual tragic reasons.

The final shade was the hazy purple of twilight. Countless evenings floated by in a delirious haze, as garbled conversations made only the slightest flicker of sense. When the smoke wasn't enough for us to lose ourselves, people drank mushroom tea, the fungus writhing like worms within the murk of a filthy glass. Some hippies once gave us a sip of their poison, just for a joke. It wasn't enough for the full-blown hallucinatory effect, but it served to temporarily make the daily miasma of passive smoke more philosophically profound than usual.

The next day, realising that everyone dies alone, no matter what you achieve you will one day be forgotten, and we are but a tiny speck of dust in an ever expanding universe that will one day no longer exist, we cried almost constantly from breakfast until bedtime. Even making a polychrome house out of Lego bricks failed to cheer us up.

The colours of those early days all swirled together, creating a psychedelic effect, like the patterns on our tie-dyed T-shirts. We were trying to pretend that we would never die.

The fact is, however, that we are all mortal, and no drug, guru, belief system, New Age philosophy or bowl of lentil soup is going to make things otherwise. Burning up diesel as you race from one sacred energy spot to the next is never going to save the Earth. Meditating cross-legged under a blanket may make you think that you are connecting with the divine spirit within, but it also makes you look like a multi-coloured ghost, crouching like a psychedelic blot on the landscape while your children play in the dust.

Living in your own bubble of positive energy can also dampen your natural instinct for self-preservation. The time that we pulled up to a ferry port in a car that reeked of marijuana, the authorities didn't look too impressed. They led Father #2 away to one holding area while ourselves and Mother were marched to another, and stern gazes observed us both like insects as they strip-searched Mother, and then patted our infant physical vessel down to make sure our cartoon T-shirt wasn't stuffed with heroin and there was no crack cocaine in our faded blue underwear.

They were eventually convinced that we weren't international drug-smuggling terrorists, and let us go. By this time, we had missed our ferry and had to wait for the next one. Our parental units found this terribly inconvenient.

When this anecdote was repeated to fellow travellers, their suntanned faces offered forlorn frowns of sympathy as marijuana was shared in friendly commiseration. Embarking on an international, free-spirited drug binge with a four year old child was just a far out, radical way to live. The square, authority types who tried to control our minds were so uncool for not getting that.

"They want to put us all in boxes, man."

"They add fluoride to toothpaste to calcify our third eye."

"They want you to raise your child within the confines of consumerism so you'll keep buying their products and she'll learn how to conform."

"Man, I don't think I can stand up."

We were left in the care of many enlightened individuals, passed from one stoner group to another like an oblivious, angelic tragedy. We learned all about the mystical creatures that roamed the Earth before the rise of mankind. Dragons and fairies and elves, oh my. There is no evidence that such beings ever existed, but sometimes you need to free your imagination from the restrictive confines of science. Perhaps Gaia stole the dragon fossils to test your faith.

We were beginning to think she'd created the hippies to test our faith, as the days went by without sober company, a roof over our head or food that didn't taste of soil. However, there was one element of the traveller lifestyle that oddly appealed to us, and that was the lack of hygiene.

Even before embarking on our toxic escapade, we had been petrified of washing. Getting changed was manageable enough. If we were changing by the bed we could just hide under the sheets, and in the bathroom there was usually a large towel that we could utilise as a shield from prying eyes. Even without adequate cover, there were still methods to keep ourselves concealed. We could change our T-shirt by putting the second one on before taking the first one off, which was easily done with a minimum of tangled arm acrobatics. The same could be done with skirts. Shorts and trousers were a little more difficult, but we could usually cover our body sufficiently with the remainder of our clothing if we stayed sitting down.

It was bath times that were terrifying, and whoever invented the shower was a perverted creep. At least, getting into the bath, you only had to be naked for the few seconds that it took you to get into the water, and then you could cover yourself with washcloths to preserve your modesty in front of the cameras. In the shower, these attempts at privacy were virtually impossible. To our great distress, we were never allowed to wear a swimsuit or even sit down. We had to stand up while we tried to get clean, unable to cover our body with washcloths, left with no way to preserve our dignity. Life on the road was a noxious fiasco, but it at least brought relief from the horror of regular washing.

There were Clairey days of running around manically, making peculiar noises, and Katie days of curling up and finding a safe place to hide with our toys. Sometimes, we would be left in the car for hours on end. On one such occasion, Clairey opened her window wide, letting in fresh air, sunshine and whatever magical fantasies were floating on the breeze. While sitting alone through the eternal hours, she was on an exciting quest in her mind. The friendly grown-ups who wandered past merely smiled at her as she smiled at them, everybody so delightfully complicit in her grand adventure. There was so much to daydream about, no matter how long she was left alone, she could never get bored.

Mother was furious when she returned.

"Don't you ever open that window when we're gone, do you hear me? Anybody could just come along and take you. We'd come back and there'd be no more Carlie."

This was the sound advice that nearly led to our asphyxiation. Dogs die in hot cars. Luckily, we are not a dog, which meant that we didn't need special biscuits, nobody had to take us for a walk, and we managed not to suffocate whilst sitting on the threadbare upholstery. Alone in the car, we could no longer be Clairey, with windows open, enjoying the fresh air on our face and embracing the world around us. We had to be Katie, curled up, with windows closed, hiding from the unfamiliar.

It got so hot one day that the air was like soup. The car was parked in a dusty mirage of a town, under the midday sun, and the atmosphere contained waves of fatigue and luminous blotches. The unknown people that our parents had warned us about were gathered all around, tapping on the windows, trying to make us open them.

We were not going to be taken. We merely slid down further in our seat to drown in the stale radiance, with our cares floating away as our limbs and eyelids became heavier, weak but contented, slipping under without a fuss.

Close your eyes like a good girl.

We were nearly unconscious when our parents found us. They had not meant to be gone so long. They had just been smoking something outlandish and overpowering and had gotten confused.

Parenting.

You're doing it wrong.

This experience was actually not that terrible. It had just felt like sinking into a nice warm sleep.

The worst time was when we needed the toilet and they failed to return in time. The car was parked in a supermarket car park after sunset, so the air was cool and breathable, although we ended up longing for unconsciousness, anything to take the edge off reality. We needed to go to the bathroom but we weren't supposed to leave the car, and besides, we had trouble undoing our seatbelt without help, our door had a child safety lock, and outside was just a jumble of strangers and streetlights.

We thought that if we cried, they would come back for us. The hours passed, they did not return, the situation became desperate, and we started screaming. This time, there was nobody tapping on the windows, just people hurrying past, heads down, ignoring the screaming child in the foreign car.

By the time our supposedly responsible adults returned, we were mired in piss and shit, but our screaming had at least subsided due to overwhelming shame and a lack of energy. Father #2 yelled and slapped us in the face because we had made his car smell disgusting. There is nothing quite like leaving a neglected child in your car long enough for them to soil themselves to make it lose that new car smell. Unfortunately, he didn't have one of those charming air fresheners in the shape of a tree to give the vehicle an odour of summer meadows.

Mother said that we should have left the car to find a toilet. Of course, nothing sinister ever happened to a small child wandering around a car park in a foreign country at night.

We were Katie for several days after this, hiding, crying and feeling hideously unclean. It was the kind of miserable anecdote that we would later present to various therapists for their analysis.

Little Katie had many sad stories. It became easier to access the memory files once we found a therapist who was able to help us rebuild our brain and gain control from the adult level. Fortunately, there were always three "alters" who retained approximately the same age as the physical vessel. Two of them were initially found hovering above the mindscape on an ethereal plane that existed somewhere beyond space and time. When discovered, Estella and Morgana were both in their twenties, and each wore their opposing, arrogant lunacies with pride.

Morgana believes that every religion is a path to God. Estella believes that she, herself, is God. Morgana cares for everyone, gushing compassion from a bleeding heart. Estella cares for nobody but herself, crushing the sympathies of her fellow alters, seeking to make us all as emotionless as her so we won't hold her back next time she wants to destroy someone. These two psychotic ladies are able to view our wretched past through strange eyes that claim to transcend the present and foretell the future.

Morgana took on the role of Katie's guardian angel, reaching back to every diseased recollection to take the pitiful girl into her arms. "Don't worry Katie, one day you will be clean again," she soothed, with her ever-comforting outpouring of kindness.

While her physical vessel sat in the cramped back seat of a rusty car, Katie disappeared into the mindscape, where she could hide her face in Morgana's tear-stained breast and cry the tears of a traumatised infant.

Estella merely looked down on them with a smirk, narrowing her eyes in cold appraisal, ready to grace us all with the final word.

"But first you need to get over your phobia of washing," she informed her, in a voice tainted by cruel laughter.

"That would help."

CHAPTER 3

(A Beautiful Car Crash Takes Me Wanting)

We first presented our teenage temptress in a spectacularly one-sided fight scene with her sadistic twin sister. Now we move on to her first sex scene, and the debut starring role of Honeysuckle Jane Martece, as a broken lesbian in the shower. Telling you about this right now means jumping forward nearly twenty years, which will seriously mess with the chronology. However, it will be a while until we get to properly meet our precocious little diva, and she's the type of girl who can't go too long without attention, so we'll indulge her.

One copy of the pseudo-pornographic music video, Honeysuckle Blue, still exists somewhere beneath stacks of white paper in the cramped studio of an unknown visual artist. Preserved on a cheap, re-writable compact disc, with its name written on the front in childlike print in permanent marker, the film is presently hiding from a world that would happily tear its vulnerable starlet to pieces. The scratched, plastic casing contains a clumsily fitted front cover, a still image from the film printed on low grade photo paper. You can see the peachy flesh tones of naked girl skin. You can see one of Honeysuckle's downcast eyes, all smoky green eye shadow and numb oblivion.

Play the film, and you get a seven second intro, where the black screen morphs into a world of slow motion lesbianism, to the sound of static noise. For a moment you might think this is some kind of conceptual art piece, until the song starts playing and you realise it's more like an amateur music video that somebody has made to express their inner pain. You're then treated to eleven seconds of heartfelt imagery. Lucky you. There's a disposable razorblade being dismantled, a thigh being cut open, and some handheld footage of a night-time walk towards an overpass. Images flicker in and out of each other, slightly in time with the music, but not really in time with anything.

It wasn't exactly what Honeysuckle had in mind.

She was going to be a porn star. She thought it was something she could do to make money, seeing as every attempt to hold down a regular job had led to either Alicia ruining everything by smashing stuff up and cutting us open, or Terra, the most terrified alter, being a hyperventilating, gibbering wreck, curled up in a corner and rocking. We are clearly too crazy to do the work that normal people do, and we can't live off benefits forever because too many people will think we are parasitic scum.

"I'll make us some money," declared Honeysuckle. "I don't mind being naked in front of a camera. There's always money for women who don't mind being naked in front of a camera."

The problem with Honeysuckle is that she burns herself too easily. She can't even be trusted to make a cup of tea, let alone make important life choices, without ending up scalded and blistered.

At eighteen seconds in, just as the vocals are beginning, the film cuts back to Honeysuckle in the shower. This was back when she used to braid ribbons into long, messy curls, giving her the look of a doped up ragdoll. Her face resembles a typical drunken blur of bargain make-up and desperate aspiration. The footage was obtained halfway through a party, so the foundation that she'd bought from the market had already worn off to reveal the shiny skin of her angular features. The emerald eye shadow, which was chosen to bring out the faint shimmer of green in her light brown eyes, was still somewhat in place. Her low-priced mascara, however, was an absurd choice for filming bathroom footage, as it generally ended up making jagged lines down her face from just a few tears, so it was hardly likely to survive a shower scene intact. She just doesn't think these things through.

Honeysuckle smiles at her girlfriend as though there isn't a camera.

She knows the camera's there.

She had always known the camera was there, for as long as she could remember. She had always been watched. We all have. All our lives, we have been infuriated by the incessant violation of our privacy. The main difference between the rest of us and Honeysuckle is that she doesn't believe in privacy and doesn't mind feeling violated. She would have made far worse films than this if we'd let her.

Basically, she got this ludicrous notion that she was going to make pornographic films and we needed to find some way of indulging her ourselves before we lost her to the predatory vultures.

We think she got the idea from that creepy guy we met on holiday in our late teens. We are not sure whether he saw the vulnerable glimmer of Honeysuckle in our eyes, or just spotted an opportunity because we were alone, but he stopped us in the street to offer us work on a film he was making. Most of us weren't sure what he was talking about, he was so enthusiastically vague.

Honeysuckle knew full well what he was talking about, and she felt vaguely enthusiastic in her usual ambiguous, clueless way. We didn't like his lecherous eyes or his cheap suit, so we told him to go away.

Honeysuckle never forgave us for limiting her career options like that, which is how we ended up, five years later, placating her by letting her film amateur lesbian pornography with her girlfriend in our mate's bathroom. We need to take control of the situations she gets herself into. We thought, this way, at least we get to edit the footage. It won't be like before. It's always reassuring to know where the camera is.

We knew where the camera was, because we had set it up before handing over to Honeysuckle and getting into the shower with her co-star, whom we will now refer to as Girlfriend #3. This was the one who always made us feel so guilty about our bisexuality, as though our former involvement with men had left us contaminated in some way. She often boasted about how much gayer than us she was.

"I don't sleep with men," she said

"I'll never sleep with a man. Ever," she insisted. "I'm a proper lesbian." As though it was some sort of competition.

It did make us laugh when, after we split up, she went off to sleep around, as many people do, and accidently got pregnant. Nothing says failed lesbianism quite like an accidental pregnancy.

Regardless, she wasn't pregnant at the time of filming. She looked scrawny next to Honeysuckle, who had spent the past three years taking anti-psychotic medication. The meds had never made us any saner, just sleepier, twitchier and fatter. We eventually replaced them with amphetamines to give Honeysuckle the lifestyle she'd always wanted, of sex, drugs and digital video.

It was just a shame we didn't wait longer between coming off the anti-psychotics and filming this footage. We should have at least been to the gym a few times. We're in much better shape now that we take care of our health, but at the time of filming there was an unfortunate tyre of disgusting flab around our gut. Thankfully, we edited it out as best as possible, mainly focusing on shots where Honeysuckle was breathing in, with her back arched, giving her a more aesthetically pleasing silhouette. She at least had a much better posture than her girlfriend. The abrasive creature she was dating spent most of the film slouched in a way that was extremely unflattering. This is the problem with not growing up naked under prying eyes. She lacked the self-consciousness that would have made her carry herself attractively. She clearly wasn't accustomed to being watched.

This whole experience was basically Honeysuckle's way of turning her difficult past to her advantage. When life gives you lemons, make digitally filmed lesbianism.

The film was mainly mixed on three different visual tracks. There were two death tracks and one sex track. Nobody actually dies in the melodramatically named "death tracks", they just show imagery that symbolically portrays Honeysuckle's profoundly disturbed nature and her occasional wish to die. She likes to express her feelings.

Death Track One is essentially a remix of one of the weird, introspective films that we made in the final year of our conceptual art degree. It gives a serious impression of building up towards a suicide. Disposable razorblades are dismantled against a variety of backgrounds, their plastic casing pried open by a metal nail file in order to free that useful little blade. There's also a point of view shot of someone walking by a main city road at night. They are on a narrow pavement, with the road to their left, a fence to their right, and the sickly orange glow of sodium streetlights shining off glistening metal and cold concrete. Up ahead, the road becomes an overpass. This depressive imagery is bizarrely mixed in with shots of Honeysuckle applying her make-up. She lines her eyes with the dark shades of the misunderstood and applies lip gloss in the face of tragedy.

Death Track Two is less varied. It shows Honeysuckle's pale thighs, slightly open, with some artwork resting in her lap. We had once painstakingly drawn a biro picture of a teddy bear but left the background unfinished. This creation from our past is now glued onto some cardboard so it can rest upon her legs without bending. The camera is held in her left hand as her right hand cuts her thigh open with a tiny blade and then dips delicate fingertips with short-cropped nails into the resulting wound. The crimson liquid is then smeared onto the white background of the teddy bear drawing. It's all very moving.

There is nothing in this film that hasn't already been shared a million times on the internet.

Disturbing childhood imagery... because what Daddy did will always hurt.

Self-harm... because you wanted to make the pain real.

An overpass... because life just passes over you.

Razorblades... because you're not very sharp.

Lesbianism... because, breasts.

Except, the mammarally challenged young ladies in

this film could both seriously do with boob jobs if they wish to make money out of this. Girlfriend #3 is almost totally flat from taking too much speed, whereas Honeysuckle's breasts don't stick out much further than the stomach fat she had acquired from taking major tranquilisers.

At least they've both bothered shaving. Our sad little starlet is still disturbed enough to feel nauseous when she sees pubic hair, while her girlfriend got into the shaved look the usual way, through watching pornography.

The original footage of the sex track would probably be classed as pornographic. Two women in their early twenties get into the shower together and start kissing and groping, then playing with each other's clits and sticking their fingers inside each other. Some people like that sort of thing. At least it's something to watch if you're bored. There are four breasts, if you could call them that. There are definitely two twats.

Unfortunately for Honeysuckle, and for certain fans of homemade lesbian video, there are only about three seconds in the whole film that show a clear view of the sex track.

The three different visual tracks are layered so that they all show simultaneously with varying degrees of transparency. The opacity of each track dips and jumps in a steady flicker that begins all smooth and dreamlike but gradually builds to an aesthetic stutter that's harsh and jarring. It's almost hypnotic. Images of misery compete with glowing pixels from the gutter for the chance to pester your eye sockets and irritate your skull. It took hours of frame by frame editing to compose that dull, clichéd footage into such mesmerising wreckage.

Emotional nudity... because naked people have feelings

too.

Death Track One twists twice. It doesn't matter if we spoil the ending because you will probably never see this film. If she was left to her own devices, she might be dumb enough to post it on the internet, but she is usually carefully supervised by people who would never allow such stupidity. At three minutes and six seconds, there is a conclusion to the suicide build-up of razorblades and a gradually approaching overpass. Neither is used to actually kill anybody. This is relatively obvious, seeing as this film would be illegal if the leading actress was to literally die at the end. We simply cannot allow such things in these draconian times of political correctness, which is probably for the best, because if she had died then we wouldn't be here to write this.

The first twist is the razorblades being dropped from the overpass and onto the underlying asphalt. This initial revelation, if you can still focus despite all the fluctuating flesh shots, is the sight of a hand held out over the railing, palm upwards, holding a collection of tiny blade strips. One by one, these are discarded into the night air, where they flutter down to fall upon the light traffic of the ring road below. This takes all of eighteen seconds.

At three minutes and twenty four seconds the last razor falls, and you then get ninety frames of none-layered footage, where fans of mediocre lesbian video get to finally watch their favourite subject matter without superimposed levels of histrionic botheration.

At three minutes and twenty seven seconds, Death Track One returns, and the final twist is Alicia cutting Honeysuckle's face open.

More specifically, she had already cut it open before we picked up the camera, and what you are shown is the aftermath. There's a mutilated face, on top of the intoxicated shower scene, on top of the scab-stained teddy bear. It's the full-on optical assault of a psychological disaster.

Attention seeking... because there aren't enough people with real problems, and we're all so concerned about your personal trauma.

The flickering slows down as the film approaches its merciful conclusion. At three minutes forty three, with five seconds to spare, the static noise returns, and the penultimate shot is of a pale hand smearing blood across a lacerated thigh.

The final shot is Honeysuckle's orgasm face before the screen fades to black.

CHAPTER 4

(My Dull Reality Knows No More)

We were seven years old when the aliens landed. They beamed down to the imaginary world inside our skull at a time when it was still predominantly a glorious paradise. The sun was shining and Clairey was playing with her animal friends amongst the vibrant flowers, basking in her latest daydream. Her little twin, Katie, had been missing for a while. There were parts of the nearby woodland that had become strange and overgrown, with weird, thick shadows where there had once been dappled rainbow sunlight. Katie had last been seen heading towards the shade, called by peculiar voices, and Clairey had not seen her since. She didn't want to go searching for her because she didn't want to be frightened. It was easier to just forget. She was only four. Clairey and Katie were the initial personality, split into two before memory began, and had stopped growing at four years old, deciding to stay that age forever.

Clairey had been obliviously enjoying the bright sunshine of an eternal summer when the five otherworldly beings appeared before her. "Who are these people?" she wondered, gazing up at them with wide eyed curiosity.

They looked human apart from their colouring. Three were adults, one was adolescent and one was an older child. Of the three adults, the eldest was tall and entirely white, her skin, hair and clothing all shining a sun-bleached radiance, with just the slightest flecks of shimmering silver around the pupils of her eyes. The second eldest was composed of the most stunning hues of purple, and looked vaguely familiar. Her skin was a smooth, gleaming lilac while her hair fell in violet waves. The third held every varying tint of green, like a personification of nature but with just the slightest hint of rot and sickly poison if you saw her from the corner of your eye. The child accompanying them was at least twice Clairey's age. She glowed with the amber and gold of buttercups and beaches.

However, it was undoubtedly the adolescent alien who most arrested Clairey's attention. She looked the way Clairey could imagine herself looking if she was teenage and blue. Defiant, electric eyes shone from pale, icy skin beneath tousled, indigo ringlets. She fixed Clairey right in the eye and spoke firmly yet respectfully, as though addressing an equal.

"We've come to take you away," she said. "Soon, it will no longer be safe for you here."

"Why won't it be safe?" asked Clairey. Even as she spoke, with her mousey little voice, she realised that a missing part of her knew the answer to this particular question. Just thinking about Katie seemed to dull the sunshine. She could almost hear that uncanny noise rustling through the tangled branches.

"It's better that you don't know why," the extra-terrestrial replied.

So this is how Clairey ended up flying a spaceship of childhood escapism through a galaxy of chemically induced brain damage. She was completely obsessed with her new otherworldly companion, who soon became her idol, her imaginary friend and her future. She never pictured herself becoming a regular, adult human being, because she was convinced that one day she would actually become the intergalactic warrior princess.

The constant sense of being watched was still embarrassing, but it had a less sinister edge now that Clairey suspected her alien comrades were probably just monitoring her important mission. While her family settled down into domestic suburbia, she was soaring through space. While her classmates learned their multiplication tables, she was fighting battles across the stars. While her peers were learning early life lessons, she was becoming someone who would never be able to handle reality.

We blame Jesus.

We were, in fact, baptised as a Catholic... which is something that Honeysuckle now finds hilariously ironic. Luckily we didn't have any of the follow-up ceremonies where you get a magic name. We have plenty of names already without the need for religious embellishment.

When the alien delusion began, Clairey initially assumed that everyone on Earth had their own alternate existence within another realm. She didn't think she was special. She would ask casual acquaintances who their alien friends were and what their home planet was like, but most of them either wouldn't say, or would just describe characters and scenarios from cartoons and computer games. Most people seemed to be incredibly secretive about their other lives. Maybe they were spies from the red planets and that's why they were trying not to give too much away. It was hard to know whom to trust.

The months went slowly past, and she gradually came to realise that most people didn't want to hear about her tales of extra-terrestrial adventure, and actually, many people thought she was lying. The only alternate land that most residents of suburbia were even willing to talk about was the one from the Christianity story. You know, that one where the main character is three different people.

The vicar came to our school once a week to tell everyone about his favourite imaginary friend. It was different to when Clairey spoke about her visitors from space, in that most of the audience seemed to genuinely believe him. Unfortunately, most tales from the Bible were dull compared to the sights that Clairey had seen, with spaceships, lasers, and weirdly coloured beings. Although, apparently, the crucifix guy was a different colour to most people in our village, which made the prevailing attitude towards a certain local family more than a little hypocritical.

We endured several of the vicar's visits without hearing a single tale of interest, until one occasion when his rambling monologue seemed to be building towards an interesting conclusion. Having finally got our attention for once, he ended his story on a cliff-hanger. Jesus had been cornered by non-believers who were demanding explanations.

"And then," the vicar concluded, "Jesus said something very clever."

He then paused with a kindly, smug smile.

"But you will have to wait until next week to find out what it was, because that's all I've got time to tell you today."

The Jesus story was put on hold just as we had started to care. Clairey liked a bit of mystery. Depending on how it had turned out, there was a chance she might have paid more attention to this curious land of religion in future, and devoted less time to her intergalactic world. It would have been nice to be part of a belief system that other humans were involved in. She might have felt less isolated.

The vicar returned a week later, and told us he had a very inspiring story to tell, about Jesus. He then proceeded to repeat the exact same parable he had regaled us with on his previous visit, word for word. As he plodded through the now familiar story, the teachers all glanced nervously at each other, all realising what was happening but nobody wanting to say anything, in case they appeared impolite. After several awkward minutes, we arrived back at that same pesky cliff-hanger.

"And then, Jesus said something very clever..." he told us, again.

"But you will have to wait until next week to find out what it was, because that's all I've got time to tell you today," was the last thing he said, with his vacantly benign smile.

What was it that Jesus said?? The suspense felt like it was killing us by this point, and now we had to wait yet another week.

However, when we sat for assembly the next day, the teacher had some unhappy news.

"I'm sorry to say that the vicar won't be coming to talk to you anymore, children. He died last night from a heart attack."

His timing was impeccable.

The cliff-hanger plot was thwarted and the accompanying revelations died with him. We would never know how the story was supposed to end, and that clever response from a cornered Jesus was destined to forever elude us.

Clairey realised the ridiculousness of this situation,

and ended up getting some seriously judgemental looks from the children around her as she struggled to adequately stifle her laughter.

Really, from this point on, everything that happens is Jesus' fault.

CHAPTER 5

(Doll Eyes Flickering Wake the Fallen)

Between the ages of seven and ten, while Clairey was up in space enjoying a flying saucer ride she refused to disbelieve, the mindscape beneath her was transforming into something ghastly.

Katie had been left behind. For her, the alien dreams would never be real, because she was ensnared in a place of nightmares. Following a strange noise and a cryptic impulse, she had been lured into the darkest part of the forest when the violence began. She ended up being trapped in the gloom for years with nobody to look after her. Her little limbs couldn't move. Slimy things that scuttled on vicious legs would crawl over her in her misery. She cried the tears of the forgotten, as her dress was lifted up and she was covered in dirt.

She had already survived so much filth without breaking, but now there was violence instead, angry blows to a delicate face, and there was no longer any escape from the devastating dementia. For the next twenty years she would belong to the monsters.

A piece of her soul was knocked away, and this fragment was called Terra, named after a mispronunciation of "terror". Even to this day, when she takes consciousness, the mindscape is a place of noise and chaos and we all fall blindly around in the monochrome hailstorm of electrical static. Sensory information gets jumbled by faulty wiring. The fear becomes something physical, and our skin crawls with it as nerve endings jangle painfully. Everything is terrifying;

every person, sound, inanimate object, and thought. Our initial response is to try and minimize the horror by shutting out the external world as much as possible. This usually means curling up in a ball under a blanket and covering our eyes. Glimpses of disgusting memories flicker in and out of view as we cling on to what remains of our sanity.

Right from the beginning, the fear that radiated from this horrified creature was enough to uproot trees, crumble distant mountains and crack the earth apart. Brilliant crystalline structures that once hung from treetops came falling down in splintered pieces to slice open innocent skin.

Another lost child plummeted to the ground.

While Terra had been breaking off from Katie, little Clairey was also losing part of herself to the continued fracture, although she was far too busy with her intergalactic adventures to notice. Something dreadful fell away from her, and never really stopped falling, tumbling eternally from a suicide precipice. This was Terra's twin, the tragic Fuchsia.

Terra is incredibly, painfully aware of all there is to be frightened of. Fuchsia is oblivious. She will wander into danger, stumble off cliff tops, and spend a lifetime falling deliriously into disaster, all the while intoxicated by a malevolent daydream.

While Clairey explored her own special galaxy, Fuchsia, Terra and Katie suffered in a decaying mindscape with just one other companion. This girl was the core processing unit of our psychological structure. She kept to herself and would always be the only one without a twin, remaining perpetually in the centre, living her life on the dividing line that the rest of us have arranged ourselves around.

They never knew Serena existed. This thoughtful creature was always as quiet with people in real life as she was with her fractured sisters, and only made her presence felt when it was time to learn something new. Clairey's psychotic conviction that she was an alien from another planet would never be seen as a sign of a demented mind so long as Serena was excelling at school. Clairey prattled mindlessly about her imaginary life, while Serena worked hard and got brilliant grades, and they both ignored the shadows that surrounded their thoughts, losing themselves to either fantasy delusions or intellectual development.

In the first term of junior school, studious little Serena was the first pupil in her year group to receive a certificate of merit for academic excellence. She was that much of an over-achiever. It was just a shame that her achievements never seemed to be enough to stop Father #2 from begrudging her existence.

"Carlie's teacher has been very impressed with her work," said Mother one time after arriving back from parents' evening.

Father #2 carried on reading his newspaper, ignoring her as she sang our praises.

"She's top of the class at English, and Maths!" Mother beamingly enthused.

"There is one problem though..." she said, prompting Father #2 to finally look up from his newspaper as our stomach sank.

"Her handwriting is almost perfect, apart from the fact that she keeps writing the letter 'n' back to front."

Father #2's face was suddenly filled with indignant fury. "Can't you even fucking write properly, you stupid little bitch?" he roared, leaping up from his chair and lurching towards us.

He grabbed our arm and yanked us across the room, gouging nail marks into the fragile skin of our arm. We were dragged to the dining room table and given pen and paper by Father #2, who informed us in no uncertain terms that failure to write "n" correctly one hundred times would result in violent punishment and an evening without food.

We loathed being hit. He got away with calling each blow a "smack" because it was open palm, but a grown man putting his full body weight into striking a frail child's face was enough to send a girl stumbling across the room, one side of her head becoming a wall of pain while something scrambled itself, dizzy and disorientated, within her skull. On one occasion, he actually knocked us unconscious, but luckily we then hit our head on a table as we collapsed to the ground and this second blow seemed to wake us up again.

At least the table liked us.

To be fair, children who write the letter "n" backwards do need to be punished. Faultless handwriting is of the utmost importance in this digital future where nobody types anything, ever. Plus, your child may grow up to be a noxious, nutty narcissist and she might end up in a dramatic situation where the fate of the world depends upon her ability to immaculately handwrite the three words that most adequately describe herself, with death to all humanity being the wretched result of those letter "n"s being backwards. With this melodramatic, vindictive strop, Father #2 was clearly trying to prevent a future apocalypse. Either that, or he was just behaving like an absolute twat, we're not sure which.

"You mustn't make Daddy cross," Mother used to say.

This fantastic piece of advice might have been easier to adhere to if the man in question was not a paranoid stoner whose drug-induced psychosis often made him convinced that we were laughing at him. We weren't laughing. In retrospect, it is genuinely hilarious that someone would advocate peace between all nations while waging war upon their tiny stepchild, but at the time it was all rather depressing, as we had yet to find the humour in these situations.

"Get that look off your face, you ugly little rat!" he would yell.

It was true that the large teeth and pointed angles of our undeveloped features did appear fairly rodent-like, but we were never sure which facial expression he was referring to when he launched into a violent temper. It seemed to be our smile that he despised the most. Terra decided to stay out of trouble by not smiling, but she soon learned from his angry blows that it wasn't polite to look too obviously unhappy either, so she mastered a kind of dead eyed, slack jawed, vacant expression that seemed to incite the least indignation. It wasn't remotely attractive. It was no wonder the boys at school made fun of us, as most guys seem to prefer females whose faces show emotion. You can't generally get away with that hollow, empty look unless you are wearing very expensive clothing or you have really large breasts.

"Nobody asked you to speak, you ugly little bitch!" he would shout at us.

He had a point. Whenever children open their mouths to speak, it's generally to provide a rather annoying addition to the conversation. Their inane, irksome voices have been known to grate like the sound of chalk on a blackboard.

Children.

You can't live with them.

You can't kill them off without the sensationalist tabloid newspapers making a massive fuss.

It was probably for the best that we were classically conditioned not to speak or smile, like Pavlovian bitches with silent misery instead of salivation. Although, according to various relatives' New Age philosophies, it wasn't behavioural programming with strategic domestic violence that made us cry all the time and never smile, it was our lack of "positive energy" and the fact that we didn't have faith in the healing power of the universe. Upsetting things only happened to us because we were too busy dwelling on the negatives. We needed to "trust in life".

Meal times were the worst. We couldn't help but do something wrong, whether it was eating too noisily, forgetting that we weren't supposed to speak, or using our cutlery incorrectly. No matter how much we timidly and self-consciously tried to perfect our mannerisms and etiquette, we were still bound to do something despicable that would result in a hand or a ruler to the face. Despite the futility of our efforts, we always tried our utmost to eat our plate of vegetables and grain in a way that wasn't majorly infuriating, but with limited success.

Mother and Father #2 both kept to a vegetarian, almost vegan diet. That's because all living creatures are precious and must be protected from harm. Of course, unwanted stepchildren don't really count as living creatures. They are more like unwanted items of furniture you can't get rid of from your house, like a hideously coloured footstool or a wonky spice rack.

Luckily, the aliens were coming for us soon. Clairey became increasingly convinced of this after their signals started coming through stronger and more frequently. Occasionally their bizarre messages could be heard with our physical ears in reality and not just in the mindscape. It was almost time to go, and she was so excited about her upcoming abduction and our physical return to her spiritual home.

It was such a pity that their plans for us fell through.

Clairey's hallucinations and delusions continued to sustain us, until her ability to live separately from reality was lost during a serious physical illness, and we developed the unfortunate handicap of knowing that we were mad, which nearly destroyed everything. It was clearly safer to fly with the aliens than to be ensnared in the Venus girl trap of brutal dolls and broken mirrors. Our downfall occurred following a summer holiday in the van.

The van was pastel purple and sky blue, with patches and patterns of yellow, red and green. Our family liked to camp by the side of the road, like gypsies, to save money, which was fine because the van worked as a self-contained home, providing you weren't fussy about hygiene or personal space. Some people enjoy escaping from the consumer culture of capitalist utilities, domestic shelter and pre-packaged roofs.

It was when we were camped in the mountains that Clairey first saw the unholy one. She had gone off walking by herself, needing to clear her head after spending hours sitting on floral cushions and breathing air that tasted of marijuana, mould and diesel. Her feet decided to move of their own accord. Following a mesmerised impulse, she was lured over a rocky path through the trees towards the base of a cliff, her mind filled with a sense of curious destiny. Despite the glorious sunshine, she suddenly had that feeling of apprehension that comes when the sky clouds over, yet she could not stop walking.

Having reached the cliff, with its pale stones and light waterfalls, the little girl froze in her tracks at the sight of something terrifying, a nightmare brought to life. There was an opening in the rocks halfway up the side of the largest waterfall, and he was standing there, looking out over the wilderness. Clairey was the first to view the demonic entity that would haunt us for the next thirteen years. There was a feeling of being drawn into sinister events that we really didn't want to be part of. We had walked all this way looking out from the back of our head while our feet had taken us to a place of fate and sacrifice.

Katie suddenly took control of the physical vessel, turning to run away as fast as her fear of demons would carry her.

We never walked by ourselves after that, preferring to stick with our family, our fellow travellers, who on this holiday were Mother, Father #2, Grandfather, Brother and Sister #1. We explored the mountains and forests and avoided Satan. Our walks were continuously blessed by the bubbling presence of clear mountain streams, and Grandfather kept encouraging us to drink out of them, saying that this was the cleanest water in the world. We believed him. We didn't need corporate water out of carcinogenic bottles when everything we needed was provided by nature.

It took us three months to fully recover from the

Hepatitis A that nature chose to grace our liver with. Apparently, drinking non-chlorinated water that something might have pissed or died in can be dangerous to your health. Who knew? We spent considerable time being yellow and vomiting before gradually turning white again as we slid into a post-viral depression.

This is when Clairey's three year space adventure officially ended. Reality became real. We wouldn't grow up to be an alien. We would instead become one of those terrible creatures, the adult human. We would soon be going to secondary school, not into space. That constant sense of being watched wasn't our alien friends monitoring us at all; it was probably cameras, those horrific, manmade constructs, placed in every room to mockingly observe our descent into human adulthood.

In the mindscape, the neurochemical trauma of physical illness interfered with the navigation equipment on Clairey's spaceship, and she came hurtling down to ground level consciousness as her ship began to disintegrate. She tumbled out of a hatch, grazed and bemused, still only four years old. The wasteland she now found herself in was more terrifying than her most suffocating nightmares.

CHAPTER 6

(Demonic Hauntings Tumble Free)

It's time for a final flash-forward, to tell you about one of Alicia's movies. It's the audiovisual equivalent to having an infant pyromaniac defecate in your head, but it helpfully sums up what we had to put up with when Little Miss Hatred was at her most deluded.

We first presented our frustrated teenage firecracker in a spectacularly one-sided fight scene with her masochistic twin sister. Honeysuckle's problem was that she just wanted people to fancy her, but she was often too much of a deranged, drug addled mess to be particularly attractive. Alicia's problem was that she just wanted people to fear her, but she was too much of a frail, cowardly little girl to be even remotely frightening. Her short film is in three parts and will hereby be known as the Fail Trilogy.

A digital copy of this pseudo-psychopathic video still exists, but nobody ever watches it. The first instalment is called Forsaken, and begins with a point of view shot of someone walking slowly into a cave, as sunlight glares off the chalky rocks that surround the emptiness within. This is probably meant to be symbolic. Various psychotherapeutic interpretations of walking into a cave include exploring the unconscious mind, a process of self-discovery, the seeking of refuge, or a return to the womb.

She always was a bit gay.

"I'm gonna burn you," says a creepy, feminine voice, followed by a burst of canned sitcom laughter.

"I'm gonna cover you in petrol..."

This was an obsessive thought that ran through Alicia's mind on one tormented loop, but never came close to being acted upon, apart from that one time...

"I can't take it anymore," she says, as the view switches to the gloomy basement of her student abode. She constructed this pitiful tribute to her own insanity for her finals at university. After spending two years making self-absorbed mixed media compositions and taking emotional photographs, we learned to combine our interests within the medium of film, enabling us to assemble captured images into time-based collages that were a testament to our lunacy.

"I have to do something about it, which is why I'm gonna kill you," she says, in her faux-scary, childlike voice. This auditory track was recorded in the bathtub of Home #6. We had lost our fear of bath times by this point, thanks to a certain young lady's thoughtful assistance, and we had always noticed how eerily our voice echoed in the filthy, damp bathroom, making it the ideal location for capturing a vocal death threat.

"Because you're a bad person... and you treated me like shit... and you told me you loved me, but you were lying, you never loved me."

While the voice-over says this, you can see the wraithlike Terra stumbling blindly around in the basement room, her face a pallid green oval under the infra-red photography. Alicia sent her down there with the aim of capturing a sense of foreboding. The imagery is supposed to look as though it's building towards a murder, just like Honeysuckle's film increasingly threatened to end with suicide. Unfortunately, Alicia's attempts to portray fear completely fail at scaring the audience because the only person she ever really terrifies is herself. She's a demon-haunted girl.

There are endless days where she doesn't know who she is. Clairey's spaceship adventure was tame and unobtrusive compared to the noxious alternative dimensions the teenagers constructed for themselves. Alicia's conviction that she will one day be a murderer is sometimes so overpowering that she believes it's already happened; there's red evidence of death all over her hands, rotting bodies in the cupboard beneath the stairs, and every police siren is a death knell to her current freedom.

As the film continues in an unlit bedroom, trembling fingers light a match under an infra-red light that has been digitally tinted a monochrome scarlet.

"They'll say I'm mad. Everyone always says, "Oh, Carlie's crazy". I don't care. You're gonna die... there's nothing you can do about it... and then everything will be ok..."

The video cuts back to the basement room, with a first person shot of someone staggering over abandoned junk as they walk towards a cardboard box. This footage was mostly gathered together on one visual track, so there aren't many layered scenes, just a great deal of cutting from one image to the next. She always was fond of cutting. She cuts confusion to bleed clarity, cuts the deck to bleed hearts, and one day the veil will be lifted and she'll cut the bullshit to bleed reality. However, right now there's just cut footage and another visual jump, this time to a candlelit scene with a toy bunny and a severed doll's hand on the bedroom floor.

The only people she ever came close to killing were the magician and his girlfriend. He made us completely dependent on him by bandaging our wounds with toxic dreams and pretty lies, and then he killed himself but didn't die. This was when the fire had risen.

Back in the dilapidated, green-tinted basement, the cardboard box is opened to reveal an abandoned china doll. The track then cuts back to the cherry-tinted bedroom, and the sound of a heartbeat accompanies a camera sweep across a gathering of discarded playthings.

"I don't care if I end up in prison, I'm gonna burn you."

She sets fire to a doll at this point.

"I'm not evil… it's just Alicia that's evil. She's a psycho. I hate… I hate… I hate her…"

This is the part of the narration that we don't understand. We were convinced that Alicia made this film, as it contains all the hallmarks of her personality, with the death threats, creepy dolls and intense fixation with immolation, so why is she now referenced in the third person by the voice-over if it's not her that's speaking?

Is the narration someone else's voice? Alicia does generally sound far more vehement and caustic than this whingeing drivel. However, this was not always the case, and there were days of being a sad little apology for herself when she may well have pretended to be somebody else. It's no wonder that so many people suspect those with dissociative conditions of using their illness as some sort of lame excuse.

Speaking of lame excuses, there's always the possibility that this could actually be Honeysuckle. There is certainly a breathless femininity to the rambling, echoing declaration of murderous intent. What's perplexing though, is the fact that Honeysuckle is generally more known for her love letters than her death threats.

Love letters... are often not appreciated when they're from a demented young lady you'd cross the street to avoid.

Death threats... are all fun and games until you receive one yourself... then they're fucking hilarious.

Petrol... is for putting in cars, not on people, you dickhead.

This film was generated at the peak of our insanity, and will probably never make sense. With a few seconds to spare, a scrawny figure lies down on the thin carpet of a sparsely furnished bedroom.

"Burn," says the mystery voice-over, as the screen flashes up a can of lighter fluid.

"Die," it then helpfully suggests, as the ludicrous young lady on the floor begins to pour the aforementioned lighter fluid onto her T-shirt.

"I know you can hear me. There's no use in trying to ignore me. I can read your thoughts. I know where you live. I always know where you are. I always know exactly where to find you. You can't tell anyone, 'cause no one will believe you."

The first part of the story ends with a lit match being calmly lowered towards her fuel-soaked stomach.

This is when things get really weird.

Just before the match hits flammable fabric, the scene cuts to the abandoned basement room. "That's why I need to kill you, to get you out of my head," she says, her voice echoing out from the gangrenous hues. The film doesn't remain long enough in one room to have any coherence. Our personality doesn't remain long enough as one person to have any coherence. We had always hoped that our life wouldn't stay long enough in one dimension to have any coherence, just so we wouldn't get bored.

Up to a point, we had lived our lives in an uncomfortable middle ground. We were unstable enough to be unemployable and socially repellent, but sane enough to want more from life than to sit laughing to ourselves, naked, in a padded cell, with faeces smeared on the walls. We also had enough volatility to repeatedly sabotage all chances of happiness, but had too strong a grip on reality to completely lose ourselves in a glowing delusion that could alleviate our inner trauma. There was an overwhelming urge to step away from the borderline, to choose a side, the side of genuine madness rather than this lonely, mediocre purgatory.

He exploited that. He re-opened paths to an alternate universe, a place of magic and redemption, a place of strange powers and mystical beings. He taught Clairey to fly again. He raised our "spiritual" aspects, Morgana and Estella, high on glorious pedestals, just so he could knock them hurtling to the ground and laugh horribly at their fall.

This is why Alicia needed to burn him.

Her film was made after the fire as she languished in the smothering embers.

The second part is called Forgotten, and makes repeated suggestions of kidnapping and murder, beginning with the camera in the basement zooming towards a photo of our physical vessel as a child, stood in a park by the swings. The shot gets close enough to lose focus, an incomprehensible, sickly miasma, and then there's the hiss and flicker of superimposed static followed by monochrome footage of those same swings being used by a different child while the grating notes of a brass band play on an irritating loop.

There is more static, a walk through a sinister valley at night, lit by nervously darting torchlight, and then more static. The haze of snow that bothers analogue televisions is partly caused by cosmic microwave background radiation. The nebula of noise that bothers our head is more the result of very early drug abuse and a lack of focus or psychological consistency. Each of those tiny dots is a potential thought that got lost before it could lead to worthwhile action.

"Not too far away in the future where what we'll be able to do is replace dysfunctional brain mechanisms with microchips," says a male voice cut from a random documentary as the camera shows elegant hands buttering bread in a mouldy kitchen.

Cut back to the valley, and the torchlight darts across an abandoned picnic blanket littered with food, drink and crockery.

Drift back into the noise, with a glimmer of saccharine childhood imagery, an advertisement for a toy truck.

Fade back to the sound of the brass band and the greyscale imagery of a child playing on the swings.

More static.

A toy rabbit.

More static.

Morph back to domesticity, a young woman's hands, cutting cheese for her sandwiches in that grim, magnolia kitchen.

"And it raises an important moral and ethical question in society, do we intervene with psychop..."

Cut, mid word, back to the nocturnal valley, with a

child's cardigan caught in the branches of a tree.

"I think the phrase, 'a walking time bomb' is very indicative. Victims, in my experience are people who happen to be in the wrong place at the wrong time," the pilfered documentary voice-over informs us, with clipped pronunciation and hollow tonality.

The second part of Alicia's film ends with a crimson hand pushing open a door to reveal a dim bedroom, with drawn curtains hiding the daylight and a deserted computer screen flickering a sapphire glow. Walking closer to the machine, we notice that somebody has been browsing various hunting knife stores on the internet.

Her greatest obsession, after petrol, was the idea of slitting someone's throat. She was all about the immolation and the stabbery. She also likes roses, hexagons, and bubble wrap... especially when these things are on fire.

"I'm gonna burn you. I'm gonna cover you in petrol, while you're asleep, and then just as you wake up, I'm gonna light a match," she calmly informs the viewer. If there was an award for Unconvincing Psychopath of the Year, Alicia would definitely win it.

"Burn in hell, I'll meet you there soon," is the last word from our little hatemonger, as the third film begins and everything starts to combust.

There is a Barbie burning on a television screen, her limbs scorched to a smoky charcoal that jarringly contrasts with the Technicolor print on what's left of her smouldering dress.

There are the blistering remains of a china doll. She has been placed with her arms open on a crucifix of bricks while the fire dances around her and tangerine flames flicker within her empty eye sockets. The only part of her that survives the incineration is her price tag, which was bizarrely untouched by the petrol splash and now glows pale orange next to the light from her burning chest.

Over these repetitive visuals of dolls on fire is a collage of various voices from angry music saying "burn". Well done, Alicia. This is exactly the kind of soundtrack that a real murderer would make. Also popular, are renditions of people saying "stab" while a ragdoll get pins stuck into her, or the word "drown" accompanying a rubber ducky's head being pushed under water while a toy boat looks on in horror.

This whole fiasco was supposedly intended as an exercise in catharsis. She believed that there would be some release from communicating her feelings and making people understand her rage. It was just a shame she couldn't direct all that anger towards worthier targets. Some angry young people fight for their favourite political issues, oppose their local council, take on the government and try to change the world. Alicia just wanted to kill anyone who had the audacity to abandon her. Her film was carelessly constructed and lacked any genuine sense of foreboding or malice, but this wasn't why it was a failure. It failed because it didn't make her feel any better. The Honeysuckle movie at least exorcised a few subconscious demons, but all the Alicia movie did was inadvertently parade her demons around in silly hats while simultaneously neglecting to remove their claws from her throat. Alicia always thought that she was so superior to Honeysuckle, but the unfortunate truth is that her film is nowhere near as good as hers.

Clearly, fucked up girls make much better videos when they're naked.

CHAPTER 7

(Jagged Glinting Eats the Solemn)

Between the ages of ten and fourteen, we were mostly mute in reality, shuffling our meagre form along crowded corridors and suffering in a waking coma. Despite an almost autistic lack of social development, we remained in the top classes due to Serena's amazing grades. There was very little academic subject matter she didn't understand, and she often got frustrated with the slow pace of most classes, slipping in and out of reality due to a lack of stimulation. A quiet, timid intellectual, she was always painfully shy, preferring to listen than to speak, keeping her knowledge to herself, cushioning herself from the terrors of the mindscape with the reams of information that surrounded her. Basically, she believed that it wouldn't matter if she was mental, so long as she knew things.

For four year old Katie, there was no such escape from the nightmares of our internal world. The entire forest was now pitch black and filled with demons, grinning things that clawed at her bare arms, with red eyes glinting through tangled branches. Her twin, Clairey, had become an absolute fruitcake. Katie's crying and screaming were a logical reaction to the fiendish horror of her surroundings. Clairey's reaction, of skipping around the ghastly monsters, randomly giggling and shouting "Yaaayy!" at them, was slightly more disturbing.

The two little girls were both completely ignored by their older sisters, Serena, Terra and Fuchsia, who were all aging in line with the physical vessel up to this point.

Terra was mostly to blame for our continued silence, living her life in a state of perpetual anxiety, her whole existence being one long panic attack. Fuchsia was also socially vacant, dwelling within the poisonous fantasy of an eternal dream of suicide. Not one of us could be described as a "people person".

Secondary school was horrific. There was continued pressure to become an adult human, and we had never prepared for this, having planned to become an alien warrior princess before primary school was over. Classroom banter took on a newly flirtatious quality that made us feel physically sick. Our frequent lack of spoken communication, rather than making us inconspicuous, actually caused us to be the primary target of abuse from boys, their lechery turning to derision at the sight of our expressionless countenance. Certain experiences can make a person age at an inhuman rate. Bypassing the teenage years, young adulthood and middle age, fragments of our psyche hurtled forwards through the aging process, becoming sad, lonely old women.

At age two, a forgotten nightmare had split our inner child into Clairey and Katie. At age seven, domestic violence had knocked Terra out of Katie and bashed Fuchsia out of Clairey. At age eleven, the horror of pubescent social pressures beat Rose out of Clairey and Katherine out of Katie, further pieces of our personality breaking off to become lost in the dark for years.

Rose was aged in a way that felt used up and rotten, whereas Katherine's antiquity had a quality that was more innocent and desolate. Unfortunately, they did none of the fun things associated with being elderly, such as cross stitch, going to the cinema in the daytime or deliberately scaring small children. These withered, ancient creatures merely limped through a life that was already over, crying constantly and mumbling beneath their shallow breath.

Most of the time, we were all entirely self-absorbed and unaware of each other's existence, apart from Serena. External continuity was achieved by her keeping constant notes on all our behaviour, both in and out of reality, and then scurrying around the mindscape like a nervous secretary, trying to make sure that whoever was projecting to the outside world had access to sufficient information to understand how she reached her present context. Her hard work behind the scenes prevented the amnesia that would have made our dissociative condition more obvious to the outside observer.

What people saw when they looked at us was an ungrateful wretch, lucky enough to be born and raised in the First World, and yet she cried continuously, barely spoke, and was always cutting herself. If you smiled at her, she didn't smile back, just lowered her eyes to gawk at the floor with slack-jawed misery. If you tried to talk to her, she would not reply. On the few occasions that she did make a vocal response, it was in the irritating voice of a nutty infant, like a schizophrenic on helium, lacking even a basic grasp of the rules of conversation. Everybody knows that the best way to deal with a bitch like that is to spit at her, kick her and push her over. It's fantastic, you can do what you want and she probably won't say anything, or if she does, it will be in such a timid, mousey voice that nobody cares.

"Did you know she used to think she was an alien?"

"I hope she gets deported."

"She wasn't born round here anyway, and her Mum's foreign."

"She's always hanging around with that rich girl who

lives in that massive house."

"They're probably lesbians."

We had no sexuality at this age, but people got the impression we were gay because we were so terrified of anyone male that when we did speak it was only ever to females. When we weren't curled up in a ball, rocking, we were mostly hanging around with our nasty best friend, who lived in the biggest residence in the village. We sometimes got on well with her due to a similar morbid humour and social awkwardness, but most of the time she was just hanging around with us to feel better about herself. There is nothing quite like comparing yourself to a frequently crying, half-mute child abuse victim to make you realise how awesome you are. Her bullying of us was generally verbal and psychological rather than physical. She was like a cruel character out of an old-fashioned children's novel, all freckles, frizzy hair, incessant verbal lashings and drowning kittens in ginger beer.

There were now so many abusers in our life, we should have been getting really angry by this point. It would have been considered a logical reaction to the endless harassment, and most people wouldn't have blamed us if we had just turned around and punched our next tormentor in the face. Unfortunately, there were three things preventing this from happening.

Firstly, we had an under-developed muscular system from being raised by hippies on a low-fat, low-protein diet that mostly consisted of acidic tasting vegetables that made us want to vomit. We're still not sure which to begrudge the most, the fact that we were abused, or the fact that we were denied bacon. Despite having long since rebelled against this enforced vegetarianism, to this day, about ninety per cent of people who meet us think we're a vegetarian until we tell them otherwise. Perhaps the diet we were raised on had a long term effect on our appearance... or perhaps it's just because we're skinny, weird and a bit of a lesbian.

Anyhow, the second reason for our lack of aggression was that most of our early abusers were so much bigger than us. We had been trained to believe that any counterattack would be pointless, and it was better to retreat from abuse with the numb acceptance of a bleak depression than to invite further violence by trying to retaliate against it.

The third reason was, we were all just a bit lame.

There was anger though. There were furtive thoughts of burning, stabbing, and driving over hippies, crushing them beneath the wheels of their own brightly painted camper vans. There was so much rage, held back and trapped underground where it festered into something deranged and ridiculous.

This was how Alicia was born.

In the mindscape, something was stirred up out of the smouldering embers between cracks in the earth, a scorched entity, all jagged and molten. She deliberately and mercilessly attached herself to every dream of murder that ever haunted our shadowed thoughts. She felt as miserable as Katherine, as disturbed as Katie and as fearful as Terra. Alicia came into existence when the vessel was thirteen, and it would be a long time before she became much older. We created her to defend us from the demons, by becoming a monster. She was supposed to do our bidding and protect us from our enemies, but she soon turned against us for not being strong enough. Her eternal, exploding revulsion made us scream and shatter, burning everything in sight, and for years there was nobody to protect us from her incendiary lunacy.

She looks the way the rest of us would look if we were a coke addled ragdoll with a knife to your throat.

At first, nobody except Serena knew she existed. There was a constant sense of being attacked from within, but everything was so dim and clouded, we could never quite perceive who was stabbing us or setting fire to our surroundings. In those early years, she would occasionally externalise by taking control of our right hand to gouge the skin on our left hand open with talon-like fingernails. There was an ongoing feeling of otherness, of observing behaviour in third person that we had no comprehension of or control over.

In art class, one of us painted an underground world, where glowing demon eyes shone clumsily in a hidden void beneath a landscape surface of sunshine and cartoon flowers. It was not particularly impressive. It took years to hone our artistic talents so that our output was as professionally presented and aesthetically pleasing as it was batshit insane.

CHAPTER 8

(Like All the Stars You'll Never Be)

We were at our nasty best friend's house one day, when she had the malicious idea of sending a death threat to somebody we'd both recently fallen out with. Some of us were horrified at the thought, but Alicia was impressed and glad to be of help. Our friend handed across some scissors and some teen magazines, which Alicia accepted eagerly, keen to cut out the letters for our first ever sinister collage.

An "I" from "Is He the One?"

An "m" from "How to Stay Slim".

A "G" from "Get the Body You've Always Wanted".

An "o" from "Flawless Foundation".

An "i" from "This Season's Must-Have Hairstyles".

An "n" from "Banish Those Blemishes".

A "g" from "Fighting the First Signs of Age".

A "T" from "Get the Perfect Tan".

An "o" from "Grow those Nails".

A "K" from "Exercises for Killer Abs".

An "i" from "Lose inches from your waist with these ten essential diet tips".

An "l" from "Cellulite, be gone!"

An "l" from "7 Deadly Diet Sins".

A "Y" from "You'll never be famous."

An "o" from "Why are you still reading this?"

A "u" from "You'll never be anything other than a dumb, suburban wannabe."

After Alicia had finished helping assemble the paper construction, complete with empty threat and splashings of scarlet nail varnish, we got a crisis of conscience and asked our friend not to post it. She responded by laughing.

She ended up posting it by first class post on the day before our fourteenth birthday. Apparently, she was timetabled for a full day of classes with our victim on that date, and she was relishing the opportunity to make a detailed study of her reaction.

Even though the whole thing was our friend's idea and all Alicia really did was help with a few cuttings, everyone in school still blamed us for the letter. People could see the look of murderous distrust in our narrowed eyes and knew that we were trouble. To be honest, this event didn't make a great deal of difference to our reputation, because most people didn't like us anyway. All it meant was that our fourteenth birthday was ruined by the police coming to our house.

We'd already had a dreadful day at school. The class had been set a maths assignment that we couldn't quite grasp due to the illogical phrasing of the question, so we had spent the lesson gouging our fingernails repeatedly from our cheekbone to our jawline while everyone glared at us in disgust. The teacher ignored our behaviour and concentrated on helping the pupils who didn't have swollen welts of freshly grazed skin on their left cheek. Helping us with trigonometry was never going to stop us from bleeding.

A police officer was waiting for us when we got home, brandishing the death threat and a barrage of questions, but we denied everything. Our class had recently been given some job interview advice in our Personal and Social Education lessons, where we had been told never to hide our hands, because it makes it look as though you're a dishonest person. Bearing this in mind, we kept our scarred hands on the dining room table all through the questioning. It was just a shame we couldn't stop them from shaking.

After the policeman had left, we tried to play the new computer game that we'd been given for our birthday, but it turned out to be a cheap, pirate copy, and it didn't work. We then tried to have a nice bath, but someone had used up most of the hot water, so instead we just sat and watched television and tried not to feel anything. Our fifteenth year wasn't off to the best start.

This was the year that Father #1 tried to get custody.

We had been sent down to stay with him and his girlfriend for the Easter holidays. Their house was absolutely freezing, so most of the time we had to cover up by keeping our coat on indoors. Except for our winter coat, the only clothes we wore outside of school were fitted jeans and crop tops. It was important to show off our tiny waist, so that people could see how thin we were and want to love us. At this age, we were still dressing as mainstream as possible in an effort to be accepted. It wasn't working. We didn't need to dye our hair the colour of obsidian, wear unusual clothing or listen to loud, angry music in order to be the local freak or a social outcast. We did that with our personality.

That Easter, it was becoming apparent that something was not quite right with Father #1, and he was giving us the creeps. One day, the sun came out and we were able to go without our coat, showing the world our emaciated beauty as we walked down the street.

"You'll soon fill out, won't you," observed Father #1, as we caught him staring at our chest.

He was wrong to say that.

We have been flat chested all our life, apart from when we were on anti-psychotics.

"Come along, little bottom," he said, as he patted the back of our jeans. Our bottom was indeed "little". All of our body was. At an age where most kids start seriously growing, we had begun to shrink.

We made the mistake of telling Father #1 about the domestic violence, and he responded by telling us that we could move in permanently with him and his partner. We weren't comfortable with this prospect because it would mean leaving behind a mother we loved, and although Father #1 never hit us there was still something oddly unsettling about his manner towards us.

Despite our requests to the contrary, he filed for custody, and we received an official letter summoning us to a hearing. We were terrified because we thought he might mention the domestic violence to his lawyers, and then Father #2 might get in trouble with the authorities. Mother was really protective of her husband, and we were scared that she might stop speaking to us if we betrayed him like that.

At the hearing, we covered our battered hands with long sleeves and pretended to be the sanest girl in the village. There is a way of talking to people if you want them to think that you're really normal. Read a variety of glossy magazines aimed at your gender and age demographic, and start to communicate with the outside world using the exact same vapid language that their journalists use. Stop pretending to be a real person with opinions, hopes and homicidal dreams, and just be what the magazines tell you to be. Become the girl on the shiny front cover. Shut out all political thought, and learn to genuinely care about the state of your pores. If you have immaculate cuticles and exquisitely plucked eyebrows, it won't matter that your stepdad hits you. Use the correct conditioner for preventing split ends, and when the boys at school spit on you, it will just mean they're trying to get your attention, because they fancy you.

"I don't want to live with my dad, he's really weird," stated the vile, shallow entity we were pretending to be, wrinkling her perfectly made-up features with an exaggerated grimace.

"Like, he doesn't even have a television."

In all seriousness, this was actually a problem, because everyone but Serena was infatuated with that glowing box of dreams. For the children, it was a curiously hypnotising source of comfort. The elderly women were too tired and defeated to want anything more from life than to stare at that square of mediocrity. The soulless machine was a friend to Fuchsia in her suicidal loneliness and a cotton wool cocoon in which Terra could take refuge from the fear. Regardless of the show's title, meaning or content, its ceaseless transmissions were numbly reassuring. Only Alicia chose her programs selectively, finding a certain cathartic release in glaring at morbid subject matter and destructive imagery, anything with death or violence.

Father #1 didn't get custody. We chose the mother who nurtured us and the father who scared us instead of the father who made us weirdly uncomfortable.

It was around this time that we became possessed by the need to monitor our eating habits. At first, this fixation was just seen as a harmlessly normal part of our integration into the adult world. It is, after all, regarded as a typical womanly trait to be preoccupied with your figure, your diet, and knowing how many grams of fat are in a cheese salad sandwich. It's all some women ever talk about.

"Have you tried the one where you cut out carbohydrates, saturated fats and all foods beginning with the letter B?"

"Oh yes! I did, and I lost twelve pounds."

"Have you tried the one where you just eat green food on a Tuesday?"

"Yes, I lost all sense of perspective."

"Have you tried the one where you can only eat food once you've painted your entire face orange and read a celebrity gossip magazine?"

"Yes, I lost my dignity and individuality."

"Have you tried the one where you discuss all the mediocre details of your latest faddy diet with bored people in your office?"

"Yes, everyone around me lost several hours of their lives and the will to live, listening to me monologue about the calorie content of digestive biscuits."

We started off by just having a reduced calorie intake. As our meals got progressively smaller, so did our waist, our limbs and our sunken face, until eventually we were surviving off a light snack once a day and looking like a skeleton wrapped in teenage skin.

"I could never be anorexic, I love food too much," some girls would say as they stared at us with condescending disapproval.

Those girls were idiots. Nobody worships food more than the anorexic, just as no one thinks of water more than the thirsty, nobody is more sex obsessed than the repressed loner, and nobody craves money more than the financially destitute. Food was all we ever thought about, all we ever dreamed about, it was worth more than gold or precious stones, but we denied it to ourselves because we believed that we were worthless.

"I could never be anorexic, because I don't hate myself," is what they really should have said.

Never doubt an anorexic's obsession with pie.

Our school bag became an increasing struggle to lift onto our shoulders. Despite its receding mass, our body felt heavier due to the difficulty that our wasted muscles were having in dragging it around, and we had to set off earlier for school each morning to give ourselves longer to complete the progressively more gruelling walk. It soon became too much effort for anyone other than the slow, expressionless ancient ones to stay conscious. Serena would sleep through lessons, but as soon as we had broken our fast with our daily snack after the long walk home, she would use that sudden raise in energy levels to complete the work that she should have done in class, as well as her set homework, before passing out again and leaving Rose or Katherine to stare lifelessly at the television for the rest of the evening.

By this age, we should have been developing some kind of early sexuality, but this is difficult to do when you're an anorexic half-mute.

In the mindscape, something rose up out of the slime in the shadows, a twisted entity, all smooth and bleeding. She hopelessly and inexplicably attached herself to the fake social front that we had created out of fashion instructions and weight loss tips. She felt as empty as Rose, as deranged as Clairey and as masochistic as Fuchsia. Honeysuckle was created when the vessel was fourteen, and she would remain that age for some time. Before her later days of resembling a narcotic train wreck, she looked just like the rest of us, only prettier.

Alicia's age froze at fourteen so she could become Honeysuckle's twin, the psycho alter of an airhead bimbo, the thorns beneath her petals, the Chucky to her Barbie. This was the point at which Fuchsia and Terra also stopped aging, staying in their early teens until several years and several therapists later, when they finally gained a means of personal evolution.

Therapist #1 had an insinuating manner that made us acutely self-conscious. We had been referred to him on account of the muteness, the crying and the self-injury, and once our anorexia was added to that cheerful mix, he threatened to have us sectioned.

"You are a seriously screwed up individual," he told us, winning a prize for World's Most Perceptive Comment.

Mother decided that it would be better if we didn't attend his sessions anymore, and we were taken back to the doctors' for a new referral to a different mental health professional, which meant being placed on a waiting list, a situation we were to become frustratingly familiar with.

Our anorexia was eventually "cured" by Honeysuckle's shallow nature when she realised that our shapeless frame was sexually repulsive. She wanted to be beautiful, and beautiful people generally have fantastic muscle tone, so we were now required to exercise. Our shrunken vessel could only manage a few laps around the back garden at first. Luckily, this ten minute work-out earned us the right to a full cooked meal, so it was worth the effort of forcing our near-dead body to physical exertion. Before long, we could run a mile a day. This increased to six miles a day after two months of waking at half past six every morning to do our necessary exercise before school.

Our daily goal was to run four circuits of one and a half miles around the village, and we soon developed a system where each circuit was rewarded with a prize.

The completion of one circuit meant we could go all day without self-harming.

If we ran two circuits, we could go without cutting ourselves and we were allowed a cooked meal after school.

Three circuits meant no self-injury that day, a cooked meal in the evening and breakfast in the morning.

Four circuits were rewarded with the right to go all day without cutting ourselves, as well as the privilege of eating whatever we wanted.

We managed those four circuits almost every morning and spent our days feasting on pie and cake, now miraculously cured from our eating disorder and self-hatred. Honeysuckle had delivered us from starvation. Of course, she didn't ward off the scratching and fasting out of regard for herself or concern for her fellow alters. She did it all in the hope that making herself perfect would earn her the admiration she craved. Nobody wanted a shapeless girl with mutilated skin.

Our scars began to heal and our lower body developed shape from our newfound muscle tone. She even alleviated much of our silence, externalising as much as possible to talk to people other than our nasty best friend, and gradually learning to function as a social entity. Despite being shallow and self-serving and having very little of Serena's intellect, she bizarrely had a way with people. It was almost as though her feminine prattle had a certain charm.

Honeysuckle was also a great help when it came to dealing with the Watchers. They had always been there in one form or another, whether it was ghosts, monsters, aliens or cameras, there had always been somebody watching us. It used to be so painfully embarrassing, especially in bathrooms, because nobody wants to use the toilet or get undressed while being so cruelly scrutinised by prying eyes. Their constant viewing of our every move made our lives an excruciating misery. The children felt violated, Alicia displayed a typical, furious reaction, and even calm, rational Serena felt shamed by the incessant lack of privacy.

Honeysuckle adored it. Constant attention made our girl the eternal starlet. So long as she looked beautiful, nothing ever shamed her. We created Honeysuckle to defend us from the cameras by becoming our leading lady. She was intended to be our bewitching servant and enchant our demons into submission, but she soon turned against us for not being attractive enough. Her eternal, hollow hunger made us decay and bleed, poisoning everything in sight, and for years there was nobody to protect us from her melodramatic lunacy.

We could have forgiven her desperation if she had actually felt attraction, but she was dead inside for years, completely asexual, only wanting a boyfriend so she wouldn't have to be alone, craving a co-star in her life's never-ending drama. Regrettably, the years of being a mute self-harmer had taken its toll on our reputation, trapping us in a social rut it seemed impossible to break out of. No amount of sweetness or classical bone structure was going to make anybody want her. She would raid her parents' drinks cabinet to turn up drunk at school discos, but no matter how short her skirt was, boys would just make fun of her until she disappeared. She usually turned into Fuchsia by the end of the night, the falling, wretched girl who was becoming her own sad shadow.

Over the next two years, Honeysuckle gradually became a member of a small social group that included her nasty best friend and a few other girls from the top classes who were sympathetic enough to put up with her. Being on the edge of the school scene, they eventually decided to expand their social horizons by attending the teen disco in a nearby town.

Every girl in that dingy room had a short skirt, an apricot complexion and a dream of a less lonely tomorrow. Honeysuckle fit right in. The precocious dancers paraded themselves around in a deliberate effort to win Best in Show, flaunting their assets for the judges and clamouring for the ultimate prize of social acceptance. It was just as well those feminists of the past used to tie themselves to railings and throw themselves under horses so that we could now savour this kind of liberated freedom.

Our gang had politely met the required dress code of heavy make-up and hopeful hemlines. However, we were blatantly not "local". Most of the club's regulars were deeply prejudiced against anyone who didn't grow up on their street, and the fact that we had come from out of town meant that we may as well have been from a war-torn Third World nation.

"Where are you from?" they would ask us.

"Around here," we would lie.

The violence was bound to happen eventually.

Fuchsia was crying in the toilets one time because she was horrendously depressed, when some local girls decided that her distress was a matter for their investigation. We generally gave off train-wreck vibes that suggested potential strife, and the nightclub's charming clientele had the honed senses of pack animals, zoning in on the possibility of provocation.

"Why are you crying?" Are your mates giving you trouble?" they asked, tempering their eagerness for violence with a dangerous, false empathy.

Fuchsia wailed some demented drivel about nobody loving her, trapped in her own world of heartache and oblivious to the surrounding danger.

"We're gonna have words with your mates, love," they said, grinning at each other. The world suddenly changed from being a lonely place of shattered fantasies to being an over-crowded hell of implied threat and grim menace.

"No, please don't," requested Terra, as the walls closed in.

It was too late, as most of the pack was already heading out the door, leaving two delightful young ladies to stay with Terra and watch her.

"There's no need to talk to them," said Terra, with her shaking voice and haunted eyes.

"It'll be alright, hon," they said.

The rush of the pack returning was marked by the door slamming open and their anger bounding into the bleak, tiled room.

"That one with the frizzy hair just told me to fuck off!" one of them yelled with triumphant fury to her friends. Their eyes were on fire as Terra quaked in a room of externalised Alicias. There was going to be a fight, and it was all her fault for talking to strangers, for leaving the house to strut on a conveyor belt of vacuous dolls rather than staying at home with her homework and the television.

"I'm gonna kick her head in!" the local girl shouted, as her mates goaded her on with ecstatic rage.

"What's up with you?" somebody asked Terra, who was now hunched over slightly, rocking back and forth.

"They'll blame me if you hit her," said Terra.

"Don't worry about it, love. It's got nothing to do with you," they said.

Unfortunately, her friends thought it had everything to do with her. She was in the process of trying to appeal to whatever sense of rationality or compassion might stop these psychos from ruining her life, when one of her friends came to inform her that she was going to get her head kicked in when she returned to school on Monday. She just broke down at this point, with all exit doors slamming shut and a bitter haze clouding all reason.

The fact is that some people just really enjoy fighting. Alicia would probably relish fighting if we didn't hold her back with our guilt, but some people see no wrong in dismantling someone's face for their own amusement, turning a Mucha into a Picasso, treating a human being like a living Mr Potato Head, with a boot where their mouth should be. Appeals for no trouble are generally wasted on people who find facial rearrangement a source of entertainment.

In all honesty, this evening's misadventure could have been so much worse. With some fast running, our whole gang managed to eventually escape unscathed, apart from our nasty best friend who got into a fight and ended up with a black eye. Regardless, it was made clear that under no circumstances was Terra to return to school if she wanted to live.

The following Monday, nobody killed her, but she

received plenty of threats and verbal abuse because the word on the street was that she had deliberately sent a gang after one of her friends and had been throwing her weight around with her contacts from the ghetto. After the years spent crying, starving, cutting and barely speaking, people had always known she was bad news.

We were taken out of school. There were just a few months left before the final exams, so lessons were just about finished anyway. There was nothing left to teach, just endless reams of data to accumulate, forcing the curriculum into long-term memory until it could be regurgitated onto exam papers. We could do this at home. We have always worked better away from other people, authoritative atmospheres and the timetabled existence. Being alone all day would drive some people mad, but we were mad anyway.

Serena could externalise as much as possible because there was nobody around and plenty of memorising to do. This studious isolation was her ideal life. She threw her cognitive energy into continuous exam preparation, trying her hardest to pretend that the rest of us didn't exist.

Alicia burned beneath our surface but could never quite break through. She was chained to a rock in the mindscape, where she thrashed around, gnashing her teeth in frustrated fury. Honeysuckle was placed in a padded cell following a nervous breakdown, but she was known to melt through the walls and into reality, where she would do her utmost to die for the cameras. Her life was over, and now her viewers wished to watch her demise. She re-started our former hobby of self-injury, upgrading from fingernails on the back of the hand to razors against the wrists, but not in a way that counted.

At this point, she was still heading across the street rather than down the road.

The doctor finally managed to get us a few sessions with Therapist #2, who encouraged us to use art to express our feelings. We had no idea at the time how relevant that advice would later become.

Returning to school to sit our exams, we got pushed, kicked and spat on while walking into the exam halls, but we still managed to get straight As, mostly due to Serena's astounding memory. There was a place for us to study at sixth form college in preparation for university. Our chosen subjects were Art, English and Psychology, because we were obsessed with painting, writing and madness. Everything was going to be so much better with this new beginning; we would make heaps of new friends, get ourselves a boyfriend and be invited to loads of parties. Everyone would finally approve of us and life was going to be fabulous.

CHAPTER 9

(Secret Prisoners Find the Open)

We developed a meticulously obsessive way of drawing and painting, building up shade and colour gradually and paying painstaking attention to detail. The miniscule, repetitive dashes of our new technique delivered us to a calm, almost meditative state. So long as we completely focussed our attention on creating something flawless, our raging emotions could be relatively contained. Each picture was a tiny part of the world that we had control over, and we could ensure that not the slightest line was out of place while everything else seemed to crash and tumble around us.

Our most intense fixation was with childhood imagery. No matter what theme the teachers gave us to work with, we would somehow twist it around so we could draw our toys. For the topic "Rhythms from Animal Forms", most people drew their pets, but we made a detailed observational drawing of a Snoopy figurine. When the subject was "Artificial Illumination", we created drawings of a Glowbug, first positioning it under a lamp for a dramatic lighting effect, then spending about fifteen hours on each study, using precise but extreme shading to create the illusion of three dimensions. Our best drawings were in response to the brief, "Associated with Music". This topic gave our classmates the chance to show how "alternative" they were, with many of them drawing pictures of their guitars. We drew a toy puppy dog listening to music through some giant headphones and a stuffed bear doing some karaoke.

That bear was our most impressive achievement so far. We spent about twenty hours drawing him with his little karaoke machine and microphone. We never finished the background though, choosing instead to scan his image onto a photo-editing program and create a digital, Vasarely-style composition. The original drawing sat for five years gathering dust among our possessions, until later finding its way into a bizarre, self-mutilation themed, lesbian video project.

Our conscious energy was mostly divided between Serena's academic studies and Honeysuckle's lonely daydreams. Serena didn't have time for a social life because there were always notes to type up, essays to write, research projects to undertake and textbooks to read, and that was just in reality. In the mindscape, there were forces to be controlled if she wanted to ensure her continued survival.

She had no idea how to care for the children; their thoughts were too unformed and illogical for her to comprehend, so she put them to sleep. Their inert bodies cluttered an increasingly desolate ground while their academic sister concentrated on building her own internal library.

She needed to keep Alicia restrained and internalised to stop her from wreaking havoc. She built an elaborate, hexagonal labyrinth for her under the ground, using telekinetic powers to bend the substances around her to suit her purposes. We managed two years without self-injury while our angry teen was slicing up her enemies, gloriously ruling within the simulated mass-murder fantasy world that her big sister had constructed to contain her.

Honeysuckle was put under less restraint than Alicia because Serena thought she might be useful. She could presently be trusted not to self-mutilate, as she was desperate for acceptance, living in hope that noticeably restraining her own madness would eventually lead to social inclusion. All she did in the mindscape was harmlessly fabricate hackneyed illusions of popularity, romance and physical perfection. In the real world, she was the only one of us who vaguely knew how to talk to people. She had learnt about relationships from soap operas and about gossip from women's magazines. Serena didn't understand these things, and so the adolescent environment of sixth-form college made her feel bemused and isolated, which is why she pushed Honeysuckle forward to speak for her.

The daytimes saw Honeysuckle wandering the college's dusty hallways, hollow and lost, looking for approval and acceptance. Most of her peers remained within the same cliques they had occupied at school, so she was at a serious social disadvantage. Her former best friend didn't help matters by telling everyone about the time she caused gang warfare with her street contacts in the hood. However, she eventually managed to get herself a boyfriend.

Just after her seventeenth birthday a former classmate invited Honeysuckle for drinks at a local pub. She met a guy there who told her she was perfect. He somehow became Boyfriend #1, and she accidently lost her virginity to him one evening while semi-conscious on too much vodka. It was agonizing and disturbing, with something mocking in his eyes that reminded her of a devil from long ago. The aftermath brought a further fragmentation. It was almost as though it had become a hobby by this point, segments of our personality falling away like a kind of psychic leprosy.

Someone broke out of Honeysuckle's head and reached for the vodka bottle. She gulped the rancid spirit straight down, not caring if it tasted like paint thinner, not caring if it was paint thinner, only wondering how much she would need to swallow to reach her desired goal of complete oblivion. Jane was about thirty years older than the disturbed damsel whom she had ripped her way out of, but she still behaved like a teenager, only with a more haggard, world-weary aura of glittering hopelessness. Her lifestyle choices and lack of responsibility would keep her eternally young as she tore through life in a booze-drenched delirium. Jane would never really exist sober. She would externalise during rare social opportunities to take too much of everything and make the host regret ever inviting us.

Jane's twin was a stressed, screeching, hysterical woman called Kathy, who broke out of Alicia's head and clawed her way up from the underground prison to the surface of the mindscape, gaining torn fingernails and filthy cuticles that Honeysuckle would never approve of. She was the most useless aspect of rage, the smashed plate, the lunatic wail. This one had no vivid dreams of knives or arson, just a constant, panicky neurosis about how much there was to do and how difficult everything was. She carried enough of Alicia's furious energy to distract Serena from her studies, while being far harder than her progenitor to contain within a blood-soaked delusion. Kathy would henceforth externalise at times of high pressure and make everything worse.

Even though we were Jane less than one per cent of the time, it was still Jane's behaviour that socially defined us. She would kiss practically anybody, which is how we got a reputation for being a whore despite only having had sex on one occasion. It was a good job we had a split personality, or this would have been very confusing.

Jane was at the pub one evening, and everything was a blur of stale smoke, dingy walls and ancient furniture. The former Boyfriend #1 was there, kissing another girl while his friends made derogatory comments about Jane and laughed at her. This would have been bearable if there had been someone for her to kiss as well, but the main humiliation arose from the fact that nobody there was attracted to her. She decided to drink heavily. Of course, nothing depressing has ever happened to a young woman with esteem issues who has decided to get atrociously wasted.

Alcohol... because loss of verbal self-control is a great idea when you're already mental.

"All men are bastards," Jane slurred to the group of girls who had allowed her to tag along on their night out and were probably already lamenting that decision.

"My boyfriend's nice," one of them responded in defence of the male population.

This made Jane drink even faster in an attempt to keep from crying.

"You're a bastard," she said, to the next guy who innocently walked past her on his way to the bar.

The first one looked slightly scared by the weird, drunk girl and moved swiftly on.

"You're a bastard," she said, to the next one.

The second one appeared merely irritated.

"You're a bastard."

The third one was a mate of her ex-boyfriend's, who already thought she was a slag, and was pleased to respond to her provocation by throwing his drink in her face. Evidently, the drinks were on Jane.

We became Honeysuckle, who hurriedly staggered to the bathroom to survey the damage. Her foundation was ruined and she would have shiny skin for the rest of the evening, patches of oil glinting off her forehead and sharply pointed nose. It was a disaster. Somebody needed to invent a special waterproof mattifying powder suitable for belligerent young ladies who were prone to getting drinks thrown at them. Luckily, she had managed to close her eyes in time to prevent the kind of retinal irritation that causes that unsightly bloodshot look, and her mascara had just made a slight smear beneath the lower eyelid, which was easily fixed by a quick dab with the cheap, scratchy toilet tissue provided.

Her main problem, however, was her vest top. She had thoughtlessly chosen a material that got darker when wet, and there was now a hideous damp patch across the front. She wanted to dry it off using the hand dryer, but the damn thing was out of order. Luckily, the one in the men's room was working, so she used that to make herself presentable again. The place made her glad she wasn't a man. It stank in there.

We didn't go back to that pub again. Relentless social alienation meant that we barely went out at all, and nobody asked us to the prom because we were emotionally repulsive.

"I can't go to the prom, because nobody fancies me, it's not fair," sighed Honeysuckle in art class one day, working on an intricately shaded drawing of a soft toy in a room that reeked of paint and aspiration.

"Don't be silly, lots of people are going without dates. I was thinking of going, we could go together and just hang out with people, and dance," her classmate suggested, in an effort to cheer her up.

The well intentioned girl soon regretted her altruism when Jane turned up to the pre-drinks already drunk, kissed a random man in a tracksuit, and had to be carried to the venue, where she passed out in a toilet cubicle that ended up needing its door kicked in to ensure she was still breathing. Our reputation plummeted further.

A few lonely months went by, and only two people joined Honeysuckle for her night on the town to celebrate her official eighteenth birthday. The silly girl was still mentally only fourteen, and a complete loser. Luckily, she managed to pull somebody in the vile nightclub she had chosen to parade herself around in, which went some way to justify her existence. Who needs loads of friends, when you can let strangers take you to hotel rooms?

"This is what I do now," thought our vacuous birthday girl. If everyone thinks you're a slut and treats you accordingly, you may as well behave like one. You've done the time, so do the crime.

The only memorable thing about the guy who became Boyfriend #2 was that he had a car. He only liked Honeysuckle because she was young and slim, and threatened to dump her if she put on too much weight, but at least he could drive her places so she wasn't constantly stuck in that dull village.

For someone who resembled a fake-tanned, pink lipstick wearing abomination and spoke nothing but insecure drivel, Honeysuckle certainly surprised some people with her excellent exam results. Nobody realised that she was someone else in the exam hall. Studious Serena had devoted her life to learning; blinded by academic pressure, she became convinced that a decent education would save her. She honestly believed that the best jobs went to people who got the highest grades in college, regardless of their level of confidence or emotional stability.

Life sure had some treats in store for her.

CHAPTER 10

(Their Immorality Starts To Bleed)

Jane was hardly the first university student to wake up in her living room next to a puddle of vomit with an excruciating headache and no recollection of the previous evening. If she had known her life would be a book one day, she might have done something more interesting, such as had a piss on the toasted sandwich maker or taken a shit in the oven. Sadly, it appeared that all she had done was regurgitate a mixture of vodka and stomach lining onto the threadbare carpet before passing out in a plastic chair in the beige and magnolia living room she shared with her allocated flatmates.

"Good morning," said one of the girls we lived with, in a tone of forced politeness, as Jane opened her bloodshot eyes.

"What happened?" asked Jane, unfolding her aching and overly exposed limbs from their uncomfortable position on the acrylic chair that her skin had stuck to.

"Don't you remember?" asked her flatmate.

Jane could recall getting dumped by Boyfriend #2 over the phone, then drinking a foul cocktail of various spirits with a dash of lemonade out of a chipped ceramic mug. Everything after that was a blur of bright lights and awful music.

"You came back here without your key or your coat, tried kicking the door in, then when I came to let you in, you stormed past me and went to smash up the bathroom."

"Shit, I'm really sorry," said Jane, seeing flashes of

drunken abrasiveness on a screen in her head as Serena tried to play back corrupted memory files while patching up her disgraced underling.

"Offer to pay for the damages," Serena whispered to her poisoned little friend.

"I'll pay for all the damages," offered Jane, prompted by a voice of logical conscience she could barely comprehend. What she really wanted was to keep all her student loan to herself in order to buy more alcohol and forget everything again, but she sometimes felt this inexplicable urge to not behave like an absolute dick.

After we had been to get our coat back from the nightclub, Serena settled down to a day of studying, trying to ignore the cameras that were hidden in miniscule gaps in the walls and focus on the textbooks in front of her. It was quite difficult for her to concentrate because she kept losing her external presence to Honeysuckle, who wanted to spend her time staring out of the window, crying, probably because she had run out of lip gloss or broken a fingernail. Being the eternal tragic princess, this one often failed to achieve anything productive. Through a grimy window pane she could see bleached skies becoming overcast and the autumn trees dying. It was a shame she wasn't doing a degree in melodramatic Goth studies; she would have gotten first class honours.

The phone rang.

"How are you doing, Carlie?" our mother asked us.

Our empty girl wailed about how lonely she was, while Mother tried to placate her with the reassurance that she would soon settle in and make new friends.

"What are you talking to her for?" Father #2 yelled in the background.

Through the speaker of her mobile phone, Honeysuckle was fortunate enough to hear an argument between Mother and Father #2 regarding whether or not Mother should be spending her time talking to "that bitch", which was presumably a reference to us. Mother's defence of her bizarre urge to communicate with her distant offspring by telephone was brought short by a cry of pain and the sound of a door slamming.

"What happened?" asked Honeysuckle.

"He just kicked me," Mother cried.

"Please leave him," sobbed Honeysuckle, knowing full well that she wouldn't.

Our lives having become a mediocre teen drama, the return to self-injury was inevitable. Still heading across the stream rather than down the river, the miserable young madam added kitchen knives to her list of things to cut herself with, along with razors, fingernails and chunks of smashed glass. It is important for an artist to vary her repertoire. For her diary entry that day she painted a page with the contents of her capillaries. She had a square shaped sketchbook in which she produced a daily composition that visually expressed her feelings, and each completed page got added to an ever-expanding grid of paper and emotion that covered her bedroom wall. Most of her present angst was due to family problems and a lack of social acceptance. Her lack of social acceptance was partly the result of her insecurity, but also had a great deal to do with a furious alter ego of whom she was becoming dimly aware, someone who had always been there as a savage scream in her skull but was now starting to break through into reality.

She tried going out with her flatmates one time, drinking incredibly slowly in an attempt to avoid the alcoholic amnesia. One of the young ladies made a passing comment in a tone that implied they didn't like her.

It's the strangest feeling, the contradiction between an increasing irrationality of your thoughts and the fact that your physical senses tell you the world is becoming clearer. You get the energy to throw furniture but lack the strength to take an insult. You acquire the motivation to burn down the building you're in but lack the determination to save yourself from the inferno. Such destructive, distorted vision shouldn't seem so sharp.

Alicia stormed off before she could kill anyone.

"I should properly smash the place up this time," she fumed on her furious march home, "show those trendy fucks what they get for judging me."

"You shouldn't do that, it's not logical," said a calm voice in her head.

"What's illogical is blindly accepting social exclusion from an elitist clique of fashion-conscious fucktards who make me uncomfortable in my own home because I don't dress like a prostitute and can no longer listen to mass manufactured popular music without wanting to set fire to the radio," replied Alicia.

"Nobody's deliberately excluded you. In fact, you've excluded *yourself* with your pointlessly hostile behaviour. You may be surprised at how little respect most people have for teenagers who scream abuse at people for no reason and break things," Serena responded.

Torn between either succumbing to her immediate aggression or being guided by her dissociated intelligence, Alicia slammed back into the cramped apartment, livid and confused. She stomped into her room to slice open her arm with a kitchen knife, seeing as she wasn't already enough of a psycho teen cliché and she wanted to make her pain visible.

Over the next few days, she returned to cutting with a vengeance, re-joining her bimbo alter ego in the self-injury gang, both gouging their arms open because nobody understood them.

"Why do you behave like this?" Serena once tried asking her demented siblings in a bid to understand their irrational self-destruction.

"The urge to cut comes from the need to indulge the jagged delirium," explained Honeysuckle, "to give in to the madness and the chaos for one glorious moment of self-abusive clarity. It's an unfathomable glory that turns rupture into rapture, a way to die while resolving nothing, to drown in death today while still surviving for a tomorrow that just might make sense."

Alicia's response to the same question was slightly blunter.

"If I don't get some kind of release from this infuriating bullshit, I will definitely set fire to someone's face."

At this point in our lives, the mindscape was a miasmic world where frenzied females stumbled around blindly, like a badly lit city centre on a Friday night. They could sometimes glimpse each other in an occasional flicker of lightning. The only alter who could see everybody clearly was Serena, and she had to multi-task, always working on the accumulation and storage of internal knowledge but also keeping a constant watch over her alters and ensuring they were sufficiently updated about external occurrences to prevent memory loss. She watched the Reality Show on a little television she had previously constructed in her secret library. To her sightless sisters, she was an occasional voice in their head guiding them towards sanity, and the thread that held them all together.

She had noticed that there were major characters and minor characters within our personality system. The children, Clairey and Katie, had obviously shown considerable presence during our infancy, but Serena was presently managing to keep them both asleep. The two most potent aspects now were Honeysuckle and Alicia. They both took a solid form in the mindscape, and although they lacked Serena's awareness of or control over their surroundings, they had the strongest connection to our physical vessel when they externalised. An externalised alter would have white, clouded eyes in the mindscape as she took her place in reality.

The minor characters were Fuchsia, Jane and Rose, who had come to resemble shadows of Honeysuckle at various ages, and their opposites were Terra, Kathy and Katherine, respectively, who were like shades of Alicia. Sometimes the minor characters would become completely absorbed by the larger egos of Honeysuckle and Alicia, creating just one main bimbo/psycho dichotomy. At other times, they would acquire a presence of their own, despite being alters of alters, fragments of fragments. These entities took a translucent form in the mindscape, reflecting their status as mere nuances of a more dominant consciousness, but despite their lack of substance they still occasionally had the power to control our vessel within reality. These were the times when life most resembled a toxic dream or a shimmering nightmare, and nothing felt real.

In our more stable moments, we would all enter reality at once in an awkward hybrid and seem almost like a real person, but it only took the slightest knock to make us fracture on the surface and begin switching.

Serena had a master plan. It involved continuing her studies until her unstable alters had settled into a manageable pattern of behaviour, and then throwing her energy into building a career, perhaps finding a solace within corporate success that we could never seem to find within relationships. If we had a respectable career with an impressive salary, then it wouldn't matter that nobody liked us. We could buy friends. It's wonderful when people like you for your pay cheque rather than your personality. We would still be haunted by that constant, disconcerting feeling of being watched, but we could do some watching of our own on our giant television. Providing our bed was king-sized and our linen bed sheets had the highest possible thread count, it would be irrelevant that we woke up every morning with voices screaming in our head. Also, if we were lucky enough to afford a detached house with a garden in today's intimidating housing market, at least we would have our own land in which to bury the bodies.

She chose Business Management because it sounded like something that might impress prospective employers. There would surely be plenty of distractions for shallow Honeysuckle and the rising presence of angry Alicia within the university lifestyle without Serena having to choose an academic subject that would interest them. Personally, she could study anything, because she seriously enjoyed learning, so she thought she may as well go for a sensible qualification, seeing as she was the one who had to plan for the future.

Shut in her noisy, cupboard-like bedroom, Serena tried to focus on her economics text book, but she was losing her grip. She kept zoning out, and then coming round to find that she had covered her writing paper with intricate biro drawings of bleeding eyes and demented lines of poetry. With a dawning horror, she began to realise that it was no longer possible for her to study anything unless the people she shared a mind with were also interested in the subject. Buying an economics textbook had clearly been a waste of time. Honeysuckle was only interested in the economics of how much a decent eyeliner would cost, because she wanted to find one that would last throughout a hedonistic evening without leaving her with that untidy looking under-eye smudge, while Alicia wanted to burn down all the banks and offices and live in a blood-drenched world of anarchy.

We clearly fitted into the "disturbed teenager" demographic. Products that could be sold to us included angry music, dark clothing and razorblades. We should really have crossed over to the dark side years ago, but we had been far too busy trying to make the "normal" people like us. Now, Honeysuckle no longer wanted to wear pastel blue jeans, crop tops and fake tan to be like the girls in the magazines. She wanted to dye her jeans black, wash her skin back to its natural, sickly pale and put rips and safety pins in her tops just to show how different she was, before finding her way into nightclubs where everyone dressed just like she did and hoping that people would accept her.

As Serena's attempts to study became increasingly futile, she thought about quitting the course to get a job instead. However, she had no idea how she would control the volatile elements of her character out in the real world. Without her studies to focus on, she generally found it impossible to remain in reality at all, which meant no supervision whatsoever for her insane siblings.

She realised that all she had ever known was how to work towards the next qualification, and without the education system she would be lost. This meant that she needed to choose a subject where the rest of us would help rather than hinder her progress. The only subject she could imagine us all being able to focus on was art. Alicia could express her rage and find cathartic release by creating disturbing imagery, and Honeysuckle could depict images of tragic beauty to express the sadness of her existence.

Whether or not the world needed this kind of emotional drivel wasn't something we even stopped to consider.

CHAPTER 11

(New Delusions Heal the Broken)

"Yaaayy!!" yelled Clairey, literally skipping into her Art Foundation class.

"Yaaayy!! I get to paint a picture!!"

"Yaaayy!! I get to do some contextual research!!"

"Yaaayy!! I get to irritate every person in the room by being relentlessly happy at them until their ears bleed and they want to stab me in the face."

"Facial stabbings, yaaayy!!!"

The children were awake.

It is difficult to say why Serena lost her control over our infant aspects at this particular time. It would have made more sense if she had lost it during one of our later phases of heavy recreational drug use, because narcotics are not renowned for their usefulness in aiding self-restraint. However, while training for art school, we were stuck back at home with Mother and Father #2, leading a virtually friendless, sober life. We had started the foundation course six weeks late on account of our disastrous first university attempt, so there was plenty of catching up to do, which often required staying awake until four o'clock in the morning doing a backlog of coursework. Serena was in study nerd heaven, and had yet to endure the chemical barrage upon her consciousness that later years would bring.

Still, the children woke up.

When not externalised, Clairey would skip around a mindscape that now resembled a battered, barren wasteland, smiling at monsters and being enthusiastic at the dark. When taking her place in reality, she had no realistic notion of where she was, and believed she was taking part in an art-related television program. What else do you expect when you put a deluded infant in a room with cameras and paint? The cameras were so small she couldn't see them, but she knew they were there.

"Yaaayy!! I'm not allowed to believe in aliens anymore, so the only explanation for the cameras is that we're being secretly filmed for a reality television show about Art Foundation students. I'll be the viewer's favourite character because I'm so happy. Everybody likes cheerful people."

"Yaaayy!! Crayons!!!"

It would be nice to think that nobody would watch a pointless television show of unknown people sat in the same room every day, making amateur visual art and discussing the latest music news and social gossip, but the sad truth is that there have actually been successful programs with far less content than this. It was just a shame we had no idea who our viewers were. If we overcame our egos for just a minute, we had to admit that the cameras probably had nothing to do with the entertainment industry at all. They had more likely been planted everywhere by a government organisation that wished to spy on the general population.

Some of us were more suited to being in front of the camera than others. Honeysuckle, the world's most misunderstood starlet, now believed she was a poet, and when she wasn't precociously flouncing around for the viewers at home, she was stumbling around the mindscape, speaking in ridiculous rhymes and falling in love with her own tragedy.

"Broken knives and cold confusion, glowing with a

new delusion, twisted by a dark subversion, haunted by a sick perversion," she murmured sleepily into the emptiness. She also wrote a poem about a "beautiful car crash". If she was ever to write her memoirs, the lines of that poem would be used as the chapter headings due to how much they defined her mentality. The distasteful, eponymous phrase was clearly a metaphor. It was not that she admired road traffic accidents or wanted to be deliberately controversial, she was just infatuated with expressing her feelings. This is why people generally didn't like her.

"Hunted and haunted and dead inside, this is where we came to hide, with your knives at our throats and our screams in the air, may the suicide residue matt in your hair," she sighed, listlessly staggering in and out of reality. She decorated the starless gloom in her head by conjuring translucent delusions of love, desire and social inclusion, while simultaneously decorating her sketchbooks with self-obsessive collage of a low aesthetic standard. Most evenings saw her crying herself to sleep because nobody wanted to date her. Her continued friendlessness meant that there was no way for her to meet anybody, which was probably for the best because her self-esteem was so low she would probably pull from the dregs of society and end up destroyed by sadistic vultures or languishing as some crack dealer's concubine.

"Gutter whore, come shine for me; your taste has a bitter irony, and you know how much you torture me, with your poison-coated empathy."

Somebody needed to tell that girl there were far worse things than boredom. Unfortunately, there was very little communication within the mindscape since Serena lost her ability to converse with her alters. All she could do was hand the rest of us hastily written memory notes in a bid to maintain surface cohesion. Honeysuckle would read the latest update on real-world occurrences and burst into tears due to the lack of anybody falling in love with her. When Alicia was given her notes, she usually just set fire to them, and Katie also didn't want to read about the real world because she was frightened.

"Yaaayy! Reality notes!!" Clairey would say, before drawing on them with chunky crayons or folding the paper into the shape of a boat.

Serena tried making us view the Reality Show on various strategically placed, constructed televisions, but they were faulty and had the aforementioned tendencies to just show old re-runs of past misfortunes rather than give us the live feed from the present day.

"Who is afraid of a worthless whore? Who gives a fuck when I die anymore?" asked Honeysuckle.

Pertinent questions indeed. She had yet to learn that the ability to make sentences rhyme did not make tedious self-pity acceptable. She was sent for yet another psychiatric assessment in an effort to find professional help for her tribulations.

"I feel like I become someone else sometimes," she told the consultant psychiatrist, "a really angry girl who goes mental at people for no apparent reason and drives everyone away."

She was, of course, referring to her apoplectic twin, who was still sporadically externalising to have hysterical strops, cut her flesh open and smash inanimate objects.

"Do you ever lose time?" asked the psychiatrist.

Honeysuckle thought about it. She knew that she wasn't always herself, but there were no gaps in her memory, and she could look back clearly upon the angry behaviour of Alicia, the hyperactive adventures of Clairey and the terrified nightmare existence of Katie, even though she had no personal sense of identification with the other young ladies' actions.

"No, I don't," she responded.

Satisfied that we didn't have a dissociative condition, the consultant referred us to a therapist who was supposed to help us deal with our depression and anxiety. Honeysuckle was glad, because this provided an opportunity to whinge about her difficult childhood before moving onto more important matters, like her present lonely existence, with no dates, no parties and no one to live for. Alicia merely relished having an audience to whom she could vocalise her wish for Father #2 to die.

The first session appeared relatively promising, with Therapist #3 seeming to believe that he could help us. He set us a homework assignment of going to a local nightclub to try and make some friends. The club he recommended was one we used to frequent when we were trying to be one of the normal people, with the same saccharine disco tune on a repetitive loop, women who dressed like desperate dolls and men who probably watched football.

We didn't go.

We stayed in and self-harmed instead.

"The darkness fills my rotting brain, I poured my beauty down the drain," lamented our precious poet, holding her bloody arm over the sink.

Our therapist didn't like us after this.

"So, did you go to the nightclub?" he asked.

"No, I hate those sorts of places," snapped Alicia, before having a rant about the drunken, soulless, meat market vapidity of mainstream nightlife.

"Well, if you won't complete the assignments I give you, then I can't help you," the therapist informed us, casting a critical eye over the sliced-up top we had worn to match our lacerated limbs.

"Do you know," he continued, "I actually don't think you even want to be well, I think you just cut yourself to show how different from everyone else you are."

"I never wanted to be different," sobbed Honeysuckle, "I try to be like other people, but it doesn't work. Even around the other weird kids on my course, I don't fit in because people never like me and nothing I do is good enough."

"Well, if you wanted to change your situation, you'd have taken my advice and gone to that nightclub. I'm afraid if you won't listen to me, there's very little I can do for you."

We got re-referred to a different psychiatrist who put us on anti-depressants that made us overweight and made our sweat smell like cat's piss. Why just be depressed, when you can be depressed, fat and smelly? Badly designed medication is clearly the only option for young people who dislike the lecherous, booze-dripping, cheesy music-dancing, vomit stained misogyny of Friday nights in the trendy clubs where people only go to find a potential mate from a selection of alcoholic wankers.

Serena concentrated on her coursework, trying to ignore the cameras and yearning for a day when she could control the madness. Alicia tried to find catharsis by creating miserable, vicious imagery, yearning for a day when she could actually kill people without retribution. Honeysuckle continued to stumble through the role of tragic princess extraordinaire, dreaming of decadence and obliteration. "I died here," she said, on her scarlet stained sheets, "it was beautiful. You should have joined me."

Katie hid from the monsters, while Clairey skipped through yet another blood-soaked, paint-splattered day of art and insanity, shouting, "Yaaayy!"

CHAPTER 12

(As Toxic Cravings Wake and Feed)

Home #2 was a flat in one of the city's brand new student complexes, built to house the exploding population of eager young people keen to spend several thousand pounds on a three year hangover and a useless certificate. Having had no previous inhabitants, the bedroom couldn't possibly have been haunted, so we have absolutely no idea where the demon came from. It was possibly lured through the dimensions by Fuchsia's eternal masochistic naivety, her lonely, loving spirit marking her as a sacrificial victim.

The first thing we did was cover two of our walls in massive sheets of white paper. Our entire room was going to be a work of art, a gigantic collage of hearts, flowers and lunatic slogans.

The second thing we did was drink too much vodka, turn into Fuchsia, and slit our wrists. Some of us had started thinking that we were gay, and our tendencies for self-absorbed melodrama had temporarily made this a problem worth dying over. The ambulance men patched us up just fine and we were put on a waiting list for therapy, but we got an instant reputation as an utter nutcase which destroyed all chances of a fresh start and reinvention since we had cleverly bled all over our clean slate.

By this time, Serena had managed to get the children back to sleep, although they were still prone to waking at various inconvenient moments. We were mainly alternating between the sick poetry of Honeysuckle and the brutal reality of Alicia, neither of whom she had any control over. Honeysuckle humped the leg of desperation on the sofa of inappropriate behaviour, Alicia drove the tank of hatred through the latest arbitrary location of annoyance, and the teenagers each had a very different physical presence. Honeysuckle could be identified by the raised chest, tight stomach, arched back posture of a girl who always wanted to look her best. She breathed slowly and heavily, with her mouth usually open and heavy-lidded eyes prone to rolling upwards. If she generally looked wasted, it was because she usually was, although even when she was sober, there was always something noxiously delirious about her distorted grasp of reality. Alicia, her vicious opposite, lived in a high-tension state of hyper-consciousness. All sensory information was amplified, all muscles were tense, and she was furious. Her eyes blazed with ridiculous dreams of murder.

Honeysuckle had lesbian sex for the first time in freshers' week. She didn't manage to obtain any footage because she was too penniless to afford her own camera then, so the event was only witnessed by those hidden cameras which we couldn't control, the tormenting devices that only she could handle. Happy and hung over, Honeysuckle dragged herself across the courtyard the next morning, back to her own room, where she promptly told her flatmates that she was gay. The boys didn't mind, but the girls stopped speaking to her. Possibly they were afraid she wanted to rape them. They weren't really her type, so they needn't have worried.

Unfortunately, the main problem Honeysuckle had in those days was that she would pathetically fixate on the people she fell for. It probably wasn't a good idea for her to be jumping straight into bed with someone she hardly knew when she was so severely unstable. When her queer infatuation was not reciprocated, she started feeling heartbroken, abandoned and disposable, crying all the time and saying she was worthless and wanted to die. The possession incident was basically her wish almost coming true.

We already felt uncomfortable in our flat. At first we tried eating our tea downstairs, but it soon proved impossible because some of our co-inhabitants made Alicia feel physically sick. With the exception of one, with whom we had a rapport, they were basically the kind of wholesome, young middle class people whom you might see on an advertisement for bread or milk. They frequently made derogatory, bigoted comments about the people on the neighbouring council estate, without the slightest trace of irony. Alicia found it difficult to look at them without imagining them on fire.

"If I was in charge of this country, people would think I was a bit harsh, but I'd totally sort out the problem of people like that," one of our housemates declared, waving his fork in the direction of the offensive poverty zone.

"What do you mean?" asked Alicia, her own fork paused mid-air while a baked bean dropped onto her colourful plate.

"Well, in some countries, if you're caught stealing, you get your hand chopped off," he explained. "If we had that law here, it would massively reduce our crime rates. People aren't scared of prison. If there was a deterrent that people were actually afraid of, then they wouldn't steal."

"What about if a destitute parent falls through the cracks in the benefit system, ends up homeless and steals a loaf of bread to feed their family?" Alicia enquired, with a false calmness. "Surely you wouldn't chop their hand off then?"

"Yes. Yes I would," he proudly declared.

Alicia got into trouble with the accommodation office. Apparently, it's acceptable to despise the impoverished, but it is not acceptable to tell some over-privileged moron that you're going to slit his throat while he's sleeping. For the short remainder of our time in that flat, we mostly stayed in our room.

Our soulless cell had achromatic walls, plain furniture and a hollow sparseness from our meagre amount of personal belongings. It mainly differed from the other identikit bedrooms of the student block by the sanguinary insanity that covered the walls. It was just as well that no girl ever wanted a relationship with Honeysuckle. She could never bring anyone back here, since Alicia's antipathy now dominated the decor, her unhinged, patchwork mural making the place a shrine to her own glorious madness.

After dining alone one evening, Honeysuckle curled up with a book, indulging in classical literature on her leopard print bedspread and sipping water for the hangover that had plagued her since morning. She eventually drifted off to sleep, and the events that followed made her wonder if she would live to see the sunrise.

The horror began with a peculiar dream. We were walking along a path through a junkyard. The only light was a creepy, electric radiance that shone off scrap metal, and we were heading towards a gap in the fence ahead. It was when we saw the dog lying dead by the side of the dirt path that the nauseous feeling of dread arose in our stomach. Despite our innocence, there was an overwhelming sense of guilt, and the need to remove ourselves from the vicinity of this canine corpse immediately. This was when we heard the ticking. We awoke to see the Antichrist crouched by our bedside, holding an old fashioned alarm clock inches from our eyes.

"You've got no time," he laughed, as the battle for our soul commenced.

Basically, it began with Satan waving his clock in our face, and it all went downhill from there.

Afterwards, it was difficult to succinctly put the memory of abject horror into words. We tried painting and drawing it, eyes in the dark, shapes forming in the gloom, but nothing quite seemed to capture how alive and deadly our enemy felt. You go to sleep by yourself in a locked room, you wake up, and all your senses reliably inform you that something is in there with you, something unimaginably evil that wants you to die. You remember all the unlucky stories you have heard about healthy young people dying in their sleep, and you think, "this is it, this is happening to me now". There are certain people he watches over their whole lives, those with a certain quality within their souls that marks them for the taking, and when the time comes, he breaks through to claim them. His presence in the room was no less real than the MDF wardrobe, the stuffed Eeyore or the cheap laundry basket. He was there to kill us.

We blamed ourselves. Fuchsia in particular had been sending out her psychic self-annihilation wishes for days, deliriously dreaming of death and threatening to jump off the neighbouring multi-storey car park. According to certain belief systems, suicide is a sin that damns your immortal soul. Her Godless thoughts must have sent out a beacon to this demonic entity that had come to take us to hell.

He felt like the shadow of a stranger in the corner of your eye as the sky clouds over. He looked like the sound of the apocalypse. We had always thought that the highest level of terror was mortal fear, the dread of your life ending. This went beyond that. This was immortal fear, the horror of being taken to a place of fire and agony for all eternity.

Paralysed, unable to scream, our physical vessel was thrown around the room. Until sunrise, there was no imagination to retreat to, no fracture to absorb the trauma, just one mind, stripped down to something basic and primal, staring death in its ghastly face. We all remember that tortured crawl to the door, the cruel relief of nearly reaching an exit, then the sinking dread of turning back to look at the bed and seeing our body there, contorted and barely breathing while he hovered above it, followed by the hiss of being sucked back into that shell of suffocation.

As the sun rose, something pure broke out of our consciousness and prayed for our salvation. She surrendered herself to a benevolent higher power and pleaded for our soul. For the next several years, she would be a warrior for the light.

When he was gone and it was over, part of our skull was bruised from being thrown against the wall, and a few strands of our hair had somehow bleached themselves white. There is nothing quite like a battle with Beelzebub to cause the first signs of premature aging.

We are now comfortable accepting this whole episode as a combination of sleep paralysis and psychosis, but it has taken us a while to get this far. For years, we had thought that we'd spent this particular evening engaged in an immortal struggle on the spiritual plane. We honestly believed we were special.

Having temporarily learned our lesson about the holy perils of suicidal thinking, the next time one of us wanted to jump off the multi-storey car park, we went up there with a camcorder to document our feelings instead. Nobody likes a person whose talentless artistic output is an endless morbid obsession with their own misery, but then nobody wants their day ruined by watching someone plummet to their untimely demise, so we chose the better option of creation instead of destruction, of amateur video instead of actual blood splatter.

We tried to move on from dwelling upon how lonely we were and learn to concentrate on the positives. Although we occupied a hostile domestic environment - due to our flatmates being judgemental and us being just mental - at least we had food and shelter. We may have neglected our drawing skills in favour of emotional video projects, but we were working towards a university degree, so at least our lives had some direction, and we were incredibly lucky to have so much time to spend on these visual projects, regardless of their actual merit. The biggest improvement of all was that we now had something resembling a social life. Within mainstream culture we were often viewed as a freak, but there was an alternative subculture where nobody was fazed by our gayness or madness, and it was easier for us to enter this world now that we lived in a city.

We were out at a club once when a boy approached us.

"I don't know if you noticed, but I've been staring at

you for ages, and I thought I'd come to talk to you," he slurred with a drunken grin.

"Erm, ok," said Honeysuckle, with a polite smile. She was wearing her favourite baggy jeans and ripped T-shirt, and sitting this song out to knock back more vodka.

After a few minutes' awkward attempt at conversation, the boy said, "I've run out of things to say, so can I kiss you now?"

"I'm sorry, I prefer women," replied Honeysuckle, still convinced that she was a lesbian.

"Ha. So did my ex-girlfriend," the boy retorted.

The next time we were out clubbing, we were on a date with a girl we had met at a gig. There was dancing, vodka and kisses. Male attention towards public lesbianism had never bothered Honeysuckle, but it sometimes triggered Alicia's defences, making her verbally hostile to anyone caught staring. Pulling away from a kiss, she caught the boy who had previously been chatting up Honeysuckle gawping at her.

"What are you looking at?" she demanded.

"What are you doing with my ex-girlfriend?" he responded, bemused.

Oh, the hilarity. The alcoholic, Sapphic mentality. It was just a shame that there was no instant pay cheque for being in drunken situations that would later make vaguely amusing anecdotes, because we were useless at most other things, we had bills to pay, and our student loan was barely enough to live off. We needed to find work.

We'd had several attempts at employment that had ended in hysterical disaster as the walls between reality and other dimensions publicly crumbled. Serena has always worked hard within the mindscape to create a consistent stream of memories and to ensure a visible divide between sensory stimuli and our imaginary constructions. Even to this day, when control of her external situation is taken away, these internal tasks become increasingly difficult.

Job #7 was a call centre assignment through an agency, and we managed about three months of selling car insurance before the inevitable breakdown. We beat our sales targets every day, but could not quite manage to control our behaviour enough to adequately function within the workplace environment. It never takes us long to become the craziest girl in the office. Usually it's the livid ranting, the paranoid delusions and the rocking back and forth that give us away. Luckily, the wages from these three months, combined with our student loan, gave us enough money to pay the rent for a while, although it wasn't long before we had to move house, having been declared a danger to our housemates by the accommodation officials.

Home #3 was a room in a shared house that we heard of through friends. It was basically a hideously painted storage room with a mattress on the floor, a battered desk and an ancient wardrobe, but it meant sharing with people who had liberal views and a relaxed attitude towards mental health issues, so it seemed like an improvement on our previous situation. We had a housewarming party that was also a celebration of the physical vessel's twentieth birthday. Everyone smoked too much weed and one guest vomited into the bin.

Honeysuckle fractured spectacularly that evening due to the abnormally high level of tetrahydrocannabinol in what she was inhaling, and became Jane, her favourite shadow. Jane's new best friend was a boy she had met at university who was even more prone to being spectacularly wasted than she was, and who turned out to be evil. He arrived half way through the party, having apparently knocked on every other door on the street, trying to remember where we lived.

The problem with Jane was that she had a tendency to get us into certain precarious situations and then instantly disappear, the cold water splash of sobriety marking her sudden desertion. She should have been more careful about where she took us, especially when she had vulnerable child alters who occasionally woke up after their bedtime... but then, responsibility was never her strong point.

"I really like this song, but it's not as good as the stuff off their first album," said Jane, in all seriousness, to the beer bottle she was holding. Her addled brain had ascribed a level of psychic consciousness to this inanimate object that made it worth talking to. This is when half our guests left us.

"It's been quite a good party, I didn't think this many people would turn up," she later commented to a section of the wall. A particular patch of the paintwork had been looking at her in a way that implied enough conscious thought to make it a worthy conversational partner. Nearly all of the remaining guests left at this point, insulted that their hostess found them less interesting to talk to than a wall.

Jane doesn't recall passing out, but then she frequently doesn't. However, she does remember waking up as her clothing was being removed by a boy whose face kept changing. Jane doesn't react to danger because she doesn't care what happens to her. Katie reacts to danger and tries telling it to go away, but it sometimes takes people a while to respond to the fact that a girl has changed her mind, and the resulting pain feels like being stabbed. These days we tend not to leave the house, or see anyone at all, unless we are convinced that we can present a coherent social front with no sudden switches. It sadly took years for us to develop that sense of responsibility, or gain that level of control over our life.

After the party, Alicia found out about what happened to Katie, and there was a new number one target on her list of people to douse in petrol and set fire to.

We felt the need to change our physical appearance and become someone else. A dreadlocked girl from our university course offered to braid our hair for twenty pounds, and we thought this might make us slightly less recognisable, as people often commented on our natural curls. We visited her house and ended up being given a slightly altered aesthetic and our first ecstasy pill. With our uncontrollable mood switches, and that malevolent spirit haunting our soul, the move to Class A drugs was definitely a good idea at this point.

It was wonderful being happy.

We had spent the past few days being scared to attend our next group tutorial in case an uncontrollable force within us broke through to reality and stabbed Jane's former best friend in the face, but that didn't matter right now, because we were getting so many hugs. Our new housemates wanted us gone already because Fuchsia recently wrote "help me" on her door in blood, but that was now irrelevant because our skin had an intoxicating tingle and everything sparkled. Demonic beings stalked us through the dimensions and we were so incapable of socially acceptable behaviour that we often saw no future except in a solitary cell in an asylum, but at that present moment, a nice girl had given us glittery eye make-up and was playing "kiss the pretty lesbian", so we weren't really feeling the need to think that far ahead.

"I want to be on pills all the time," said Jane, and everybody laughed.

She wasn't joking.

Afterwards, back in the ugly bedroom that we couldn't leave for weeks because we were scared of getting attacked if we went outside, we returned to our previous fixation' with making intricate ballpoint pen drawings.

An immaculately shaded, disembodied teddy bear's head leaked stuffing from its neck, impaled upon a spike. A smooth lock of curly hair fell over an eye that was really a worm, as a crescent moon shone through a web that became a mouth containing a solitary, sharp tooth. A poison flower morphed into a snake that swallowed a teardrop. Twisted nothings peered out from their world of venom. A replica of a bleeding heart was stranded in a dreamscape of snakes and arteries. You could give her a reason to want to die, and her veins would be yours to open.

We had always thought that we were crazy.

The sad truth was, we hadn't been, but we were about to be.

CHAPTER 13

(The Darkness Burns through Resurrection)

Our housemates in Home #3 brought someone else with them to re-sign their rental contracts for the next academic year and didn't inform us until afterwards. We were soon to be homeless. We had to house hunt by ourselves and try to find a suitable spare room with strangers, which was a potentially frightening prospect for the strangers involved, because most people struggled to live with us on account of our admittedly volatile disposition. With regards to therapeutic treatment, we were still on a waiting list. Luckily, Fuchsia ended up crying outside a nightclub one evening because nobody loved her, as if desperation and infantile tears would rectify this matter, and the sympathetic girl who stopped to comfort her and talk her out of killing herself happened to be looking for an extra housemate.

"Trust in life," we told ourselves, basking in everything we had been raised to believe about a benevolent universe that took care of its blessed children, while we moved ourselves into a house that turned out to be cursed.

We were particularly sensitive to hexes and sinister energy vortexes because this was our personal era of developing a higher state of consciousness. The mindscape had levels. Most of us lived on the barren wastes of the ground level amongst the graveyards of forests, a place of rust and decay lit sporadically by a guttering light. On the lower level beneath the ground, there were labyrinthine, hexagonal prisons where Serena

kept attempting to contain Alicia, who would defy her by
clawing her way repeatedly to the surface, all blazing eyes
and jagged fingernails. There was also a higher level,
above the clouds. Clairey had spent time there when the
vessel was young, soaring gloriously in tune with forces
from a realm unseen by most mortal beings. Since her
spaceship crash landed, we didn't think anyone else had
been up that high. We were wrong.

Estella had been born from Alicia's malice and Katie's
mistrust at some point during the fiasco of our teenage
era. She had risen up from the unhinged animosity,
levitated by her own self-glorification, and had taken up
residence within the nebula, refusing to co-exist with
people she was better than.

Her twin, Morgana, had evolved from Honeysuckle's
love and Clairey's magical delusions and had also floated
upwards, high on meditative, spiritual aspirations.

According to Serena's memory files, Estella had
previously externalised on occasions when we'd felt
threatened, and enjoyed dealing with confrontational
situations by behaving like a narcissistic twat. Morgana
preferred fighting supernatural battles, and had initially
made her presence felt in the battle for our soul when the
demon first invaded our student bedroom. She was pure
altruism and forgiveness, and basked in the light from the
Christian God, the Pagan Goddess, the corporate Santa
Claus, the generous tooth fairy, and the sun that shines
out of the Easter Bunny's arse.

"Trust in life," she beamed to herself as she unpacked
her cheap possessions into the mouldy bedroom of
Home #4. This was a delightful example of shared
accommodation, with a kitchen the size of a cupboard, a
battered selection of films and computer games in the

cluttered living room, and a Magna Doodle attached to a wall in the landing for the housemates to communicate with each other using sporadic comedy catchphrases. We lasted there until the end of that summer, which in terms of weather, was one of this country's less depressing summers.

We might have enjoyed the sunshine if the outside world hadn't become so terrifying. Our surrogate family of dysfunctional housemates all developed some degree of agoraphobia, an affliction that can arise from smoking too much weed and not being able to walk down the garden path because you think the fence is laughing at you. We all tried going to the park once for a picnic, but it took most of the day to prepare the space cakes that were necessary for ingesting our favourite drug outdoors without attracting police attention. By the time we got outside, there were police patrols everywhere and we couldn't breathe. The fact that their black and white uniforms made them look a bit like penguins if you squinted made us feel no less guilty or confused.

Within a few days, the girl on the top floor made a major suicide attempt and needed to return permanently to her family home to be looked after by her parents. Our student residence now needed a new addition to its collection of vulnerable misfits, which is how we ended up living with the magician, who Alicia nearly murdered in his sleep. She still claims he deserved it.

The magician was a housemate's friend from school who needed a place to live after his fiancée, the mother of his child, dumped him and kicked him out of the home they shared. When he was present, events seemed to happen that made no scientific sense, which he could somehow explain in ways that seemed both fascinating and mysterious. He was a fantastic person for us to meet at this point in our lives because he knew all about psychic energies and parallel dimensions. Of course, the first thing we told him about was our little possession experience.

"I know a lot of people won't believe me, but it was definitely real," Morgana informed him, referring to the time a wayward demon that may have been Beelzebub had entered our bedroom and tried to destroy us.

"I definitely believe you," he replied, smiling enigmatically. He told her all about his own, similar experiences, and gave her advice regarding specific crystals, mantras and meditative techniques that would add to her arsenal of unearthly self-defence by helping her attune with certain altruistic higher powers. He also put "protection spells" up all over the house, thereby becoming our saviour and new best friend. For the remainder of the summer, as the rest of the household slept through the early hours of the morning, we would stay up in his room making dreadful art while he played his computer games, both of us smoking weed and talking bullshit about the universe.

During the afternoons we always sat next to each other in the living room. Since he moved in, Honeysuckle had felt far less miserable about the other housemates always having their boyfriends round. Her latest creative venture was a collage sketchbook all about herself and her tragic pain. Some of the pages included a written conversation between her and the magician, both of whom had rudely ignored the rest of the room on one occasion as they each scribbled their introspective drivel to the only one who could identify with their inner torment. The sketchbook now has the abbreviated title of

"Ashes", but was previously named "Ashes Cover my Face, my Hair, my Existence and my Pretty Hands". It was gorgeously pathetic, the front cover being all painted tendril shapes, clumsy cuttings and grim poetry.

"Sit in the cold and the darkness and wait patiently for the sun to rise," scrawled a lonely Honeysuckle.

Little did she realise, she was sitting right next to a thermostat and a light switch.

It is now difficult to read much of the written conversation between herself and the magician because it has been mostly obscured by childlike doodles and pasted scraps of demented photography, but part of the exchange begins with Honeysuckle asking, "I can't imagine ever being happy. Can you?"

Various things that have been known to improve emotional wellbeing include healthy eating, regular exercise, fresh air, sunshine and avoiding chemicals that have a depressant effect on the brain. At no point were we ever advised to sit every day in our dingy living room with the curtains closed, watching cartoons, chain smoking spliffs and discussing alternate worlds with someone who had read too many hackneyed, pedestrian fantasy novels and had started believing they were real. Choosing this lifestyle to help alleviate your depression is a bit like trying to cure foot ache by chopping your legs off.

"I can't imagine ever being happy. Can you?" Honeysuckle wrote.

"Wow, straight in with the deep questions. I honestly don't know..." his reply began.

Yes, that certainly was a "deep" question. Groundbreaking, in fact. Honeysuckle was clearly up there with the great thinkers of her time. The only trouble was, this supposedly "deep" question was basically two sentences, the first being a self-pitying, self-defeating statement of woe, while the second was a half-hearted attempt at showing an interest in the feelings of another human being by giving them the brief opportunity to talk about their problems as well, thereby justifying the questioner's declaration of misery. You would only tell a girl like Honeysuckle that she was "deep" if you were trying to flatter her into trusting you, if you were being sarcastic, or if you were the kind of person who would describe yourself as "deep" and were smugly pleased to have found someone who understood the desolate pain of your existence.

"Wow, straight in with the deep questions. I honestly don't know. I usually feel really down 24/7 but I pretend to be happy sometimes, just for other people's sake. My daughter always makes me smile and feel warm inside but the darkness is always there so I can't call it being happy. So most of the time I think I'll never be happy but then I go and meet people like you and have wonderful conversations, explorations of each other's mind..."

The rest is obscured. In retrospect, it is really difficult to interpret those last five words in a way that isn't at least a little bit creepy. Oblivious, our girl continued to whinge about her own harrowing existence.

"See, somebody wanted a child with you! Nobody's ever liked me that much. Once an ugly girl, always an ugly girl. I'm so jealous of everybody. Everyone knows what love is except me. I only know hate. You must be a better person than me to have somebody like you in that way. There must be something horribly wrong with me."

She eventually got an assessment with a new consultant psychiatrist, who figured out what was "horribly wrong" with her, ascribing the diagnosis of borderline personality disorder, which we later discovered was a disabling clinical condition with a ten per cent mortality rate from suicide. This same psychiatrist then declared there was very little that could be done to help her, as she struck him as someone who would be uncooperative and unresponsive to therapy. He prescribed a new course of anti-depressants that killed her appetite, enhanced her delirium and made her hair fall out in clumps. This was fantastic, because what a girl really needs when she has a personality that's fundamentally incompatible with human society is to lose all the shine and volume from her hairstyle.

One symptom of her malady was evidently a tendency to idealise others and form unhealthy attachments. The magician had been so kind to her, assigning her enough importance to stop her from feeling dead inside, that she had sadly failed to observe a number of warning signs regarding his character. She had confided in him about Alicia. He could empathise with her pain, because he apparently had an alternate personality of his own who had once raped somebody. He reassured her that there was nothing to worry about now though because he had this renegade component under control. It didn't occur to us until months later that we should maybe have been avoiding this person. It is astounding what you can overlook when you're completely self-absorbed.

He went away one weekend, and we shattered into pieces due to a feeling of abandonment. Honeysuckle pined for him. She totally preferred the company of a pseudo-pagan psychopath to being left alone. It's not fair that insane rapists have to go on holiday. Katie woke up and externalised on a pale, damp morning, and was really tearful and afraid when she saw that her left arm was dripping with a sickly, scarlet confusion. Perhaps the director of Honeysuckle's life story had yelled "Cut!" at the conclusion of a completed scene, and she had taken the instruction far too literally. Serena tried explaining to Katie that she shared her body with a troubled, adolescent alter who had a psychosocial complex that made her prone to impulsive, self-destructive patterns of behaviour. Katie didn't understand and felt frightened. She wandered towards the living room, following the sounds of daytime television and grown-up voices.

"What have you done?" one of the housemates asked her.

"I feel dizzy," she said, prompting the helpful student to bring her some orange squash. They ended up phoning for a taxi to the hospital because some of the cuts looked as though they needed stitches. Little valleys of ruptured flesh welled up with a crimson bemusement.

At the hospital, Katie sat in the reception area and rocked back and forth while she waited for somebody to help her. The other children in the room were kept far away from her by wary parents.

"It's too late to stitch those now, as they've already started to heal," the nurse told her, "but we'll keep you in overnight for observation and somebody from the psychiatry team will speak to you tomorrow."

She spent the evening huddled beneath starched sheets on a ward that beeped and groaned with the sufferings of people with real problems. The next day, everybody from psychiatry was busy, and the obligation of our psychiatric interview was allocated to a reluctant ward doctor. There were no suitable rooms available, so we had to sit on plastic chairs in a walk-in stock cupboard.

"So why have you done this?" the doctor asked her, gesturing impatiently towards her cleaned-up arm that now sported Honeysuckle's latest range of cherry slices.

"A bad man touched Katie," replied Katie, speaking of herself in third person. This is a habit we all have, due to difficulties in thinking in the first person singular.

She had never mentioned this experience previously, and with a jolt of shocked discovery that almost caused her to feel something, Serena began frantically checking her memory files to ascertain which incident Katie was referring to.

Our resident recollection expert had never noticed the gaps before. She'd thought she had been so thorough with her strategic gathering of information.

The doctor began writing Katie's response down on his clipboard. Suddenly, his pager started beeping. He stood up quickly after a brief glance at it and started heading out of the room.

"I'll return shortly," he informed her.

Katie wanted soft furnishings to curl up on and a teddy bear to hug, but all she could see were plain walls and brown storage boxes. The nearest box to her was open, and contained long strips of syringe needles in plastic wrapping that glinted up at her in the dull, electric light. At least sitting alone in a storage room full of needles was a vague improvement on one of her earlier memories of shitting alone in a car filled with hippy clothes. Her situation was still miserable, but at least this time everything was clean and nobody had to stink of patchouli or faeces.

Honeysuckle wrenched control of the vessel to grab a needle, rip it out of its packaging and shove it into the vein in the crook of her elbow as hard as possible. When she pulled it out again, a strawberry stream dripped steady drops onto the sterile floor.

The doctor returned, looking flustered, and glared at her arm in undisguised disgust.

"What were you saying?" he asked her, re-opening his clipboard.

"Please don't leave me again," begged a tearful Honeysuckle.

"I have to work here," he snapped, "as a *doctor*."

Mental health care.

You're doing it wrong.

After taking some brief notes, he offered to make a referral to a therapist who might be able to help her. He then informed her that she was free to leave. She shuffled slowly out of the hospital, hoping all the while that somebody would stop her, tell her there had been a mistake, and that she was supposed to stay so they could help her. Her heart sank as she reached the door and the hopelessness of the outside world. She dragged herself home with heavy feet, soaking blood into the inner sleeve of her jacket. The sky was an empty slate and strange voices whispered from the hollow eyes of grey buildings.

We returned to Home #4 and our stoner family to find that the magician was back. He now sat, brooding, with the other housemates in the living room, which was lit by a pale sliver of sunlight through a crack in the curtains and the glare from an inane television show aimed at children and delinquents. Everything glowed through the fog of earthy, delusional smoke in the warm, stale air.

"Spliff?" offered one of our housemates, clipping the word short in an effort to breathe out as little as possible, still retaining the cloud in her lungs.

"Thank you," we responded, graciously accepting our reward for a hard day's nothing, gliding over to sit peacefully by our magical friend.

The other housemates both had their boyfriends round. It had previously tormented Honeysuckle, to be surrounded by couples, their togetherness serving as a stark reminder of the loneliness that tortured her as though it was an actual reason for psychological trauma. She never was renowned for her sense of perspective. Her mood vastly improved when the magician was home, mainly because he showed enough interest in us to make her feel alive. He had a particular affinity with Morgana, who had now begun externalising more frequently. They could smugly indulge in exceedingly intense conversations because they had both lived through things that were beyond most people's experience.

Morgana was a white witch. She felt a soul connection with the energies inherent within nature, and was able to draw upon the powers of the elements in her ceaseless war against evil. We were born under a curse that marked us as the eternal victim of malevolent occult forces, but she was psychically aligned with powers of supreme goodness that would shine a path through the shadows. She was going to save us all.

Her twin, Estella, wanted to save us in a different way. She believed that she had the power to survive amongst the diabolical spirits and learn their ways, using the nefarious secrets they taught her on the ethereal plane to thrive in the world of mortal humans.

Serena thought they were both full of shit, but she found these two moonstruck ladies even harder to control and contain than the disturbed children or the wayward teenagers, and could only observe in despair as they floated around on clouds of ignorant, superstitious lunacy.

On one occasion, when lightning licked reality skies and the house shuddered with thunder, the magician asked Morgana to visit the park with him, to connect with the energy of the storm out in a place of nature. The logical response would have been to tell him to fuck right off because we didn't fancy getting muddy, wet or electrocuted. However, logic was sadly beyond us during those hallucinogenic days. Morgana acquiesced with her usual superior feeling of blessed enlightenment.

This is how we ended up in a deserted park on a weekday afternoon, lying on the ground beneath a storm, staring up at the violet swirls and stuttering flashes while a mystic nutcase walked around us in circles, chanting something in an arcane language. You know how there are times in your life when you ask yourself, "What the fuck am I doing?" Well, unfortunately for us, this was not one of them. Otherworldly forces were at work, the veil between this world and a parallel universe was being lifted, the ambiguous shapes of a tumultuous sky were morphing into unfathomable creatures, and Morgana was very much caught up in this spiritual moment.

Also, Honeysuckle was loving all the attention.

"Next time some stormy dickhead mutters gibberish at us in the rain, can I stab him?" asks the Alicia of today, as we play back this farcical memory on the internal home cinema system in our brain.

She makes us laugh now, but the angry one was a very different girl back then, one who took her delusions of murderous revenge far too seriously as she lurked in the recesses of the mindscape, biding her time before breaking through as a whirlwind of destruction.

As the tempest abated, Morgana and her magician drifted home, believing themselves to be more in tune than ever with the energies of the unseen realm.

"Spliff?" offered a friendly housemate, still glued to the television, the sofa and the ashtray.

"Thank you," beamed a euphoric Morgana, arranging herself elegantly on an armchair.

"How was the park?" they asked.

"It was amazing, I really connected with the energy of the storm," declared Morgana, before taking a drag from the spliff. She wasn't removed from reality enough and clearly needed to inhale a psychedelic, psychoactive substance at this point.

"Didn't you get soaked out there?" they asked.

That's when Morgana and the magician both noticed that everything they were wearing was completely dry.

"I protected us from the rain with a psychic energy force field," the magician explained.

Sometimes, weird shit happens.

There were no stopping the hallucinations from here on. It was as though our mind had spent its life on a train to crazy town, and now we were past the point of no return. Our bedroom came alive at night with pixies, fairies, intricate winged insects with wondrous eyes, and streams of butterflies that formed tendril shapes as they poured out of gaps in the walls. They protected us from the demons, and sometimes we twirled around the room with them.

Sadly, no supernatural awakening or inter-dimensional mind trip could make Honeysuckle feel better about the fact that nobody wanted to date her. Her self-injury continued unabated. The desperate girl's self-destructive tendencies eventually combined with Alicia's continuing fire fixation to make her add candles to the list of objects that she could potentially ruin her arms with. In a tenacious test of tolerance, she once held her wrist against a shimmering flame for half an hour, staring numbly at the peachy glow of fire against skin. Why just be Barbie, when you can also be barbeque? It was only a pity we weren't getting paid for thinking up these increasingly inventive forms of self-mutilation, because we had run out of money again.

Job #8 was a warehouse assignment for a security firm that looked after money for the major banks. The low ceiling of our workroom was cluttered with cameras, like one of our psychotic delusions brought to life, but the work was easy and we only needed to manage a couple of days a week to supplement our student loan because we lived cheaply. After savouring her breakfast spliff one dreamy morning, Morgana made her way serenely upstairs to say goodbye to her magical best friend before heading off to work for the day.

The blood was a surprise.

She really hadn't been expecting to find his door locked or the doorframe covered in scabs, with rusty smears and russet fingerprints making a Morse code mockery of the magnolia paintwork. We knew he was mad, but surely there were less dramatic ways of crying for help, such as waving semaphore flags, writing a letter to your MP, wearing freakishly uncoordinated footwear or going to see your doctor. However, we couldn't really criticise, having recently made a blister the size of a golf ball on the skin of our long-besieged arms, and owning a sketchbook that contained the word "help" written repeatedly in blood.

Still though, this whole locked door, bloody doorframe malarkey can be a slightly disturbing sight when you have just had your first spliff of the day and you're about to get the bus to work. She knocked on the door and called his name. There was no response. We then became Honeysuckle, who burst into tears because her best friend was ignoring her. The rejected girl stropped downstairs to visit one of the other housemates.

"He's ignoring me, and his bedroom door's covered in blood," she cried, nicely getting her priorities in the correct order.

Our housemate rushed upstairs, banged on the door and yelled at him to open up. Honeysuckle heard shuffled footsteps, the door creaking open and muffled voices.

"Oh sure, he'll open up for her," she huffed, marching back to her room and slamming her door.

We were supposed to be setting off for work, but somebody thought it would be a far more productive use of our time to sit rocking back and forth while staring out of the window. Our housemate knocked hurriedly on our door before swiftly bursting in with the latest domestic headlines.

"He's cut his throat and taken an overdose," she said. "I've called an ambulance and it's on its way."

We just sat there, rocking.

"It's a good job you went up when you did," she said, kindly.

We phoned in sick for work, then recommenced rocking while she went back to look after him.

"You've got a goddamn daughter, you thoughtless bastard!" yelled Alicia, as he shuffled past her bedroom door on his way to the ambulance. Our housemate accompanied him to the hospital.

We spent the day switching between levels of consciousness, rocking, waiting for news, scribbling bizarre nonsense in our sketchbook, and occasionally ranting hysterically at nobody. You know, the usual productive tasks. Our unholy house creaked as its walls and ceilings enclosed us, gloating obscenely at the vulnerable souls it had ensnared. Nobody thought they would get out alive. We couldn't even think of anything funny to write on the Magna Doodle in the landing. It was a silent, shaken group of damaged people who huddled by the television that evening, still sporadically rolling spliffs in numb resignation when the mother of our stoner family arrived home.

"Well, they're doing everything they can for him," she sighed, looking haunted and exhausted. "They've got him hooked up to a drip with the antidote, but it's too soon to say what will happen. They said it's a good job I got him to the hospital when I did, or he'd definitely have died."

We passed her a constructed cigarette containing her favourite low-classification drug and asked her if she was ok.

"I'll be ok," she replied, taking a toke with narrowed eyes and shaking hands.

"I know you don't like us being coupley, but I really need hugs from my boyfriend," she said.

"That's fine," replied Morgana, ashamed by the selfish behaviour she sometimes observed herself exhibiting on occasions when she was staring out in horror from a place at the back of her skull. It really was a comment on our occasionally obnoxious temperament that our housemate felt the need for permission to curl up with her boyfriend for reassurance after somebody almost died.

Honeysuckle externalised in a battered armchair, writing heartbreaking poetry in a tattered sketchbook as her remaining housemates sat either side, snuggled with their partners.

"It's alright for them," she thought. "They have their boyfriends. The person who hugs me when I'm depressed isn't here."

A voice in the back of her head told her to shut the fuck up, and if she dared to vocalise that thought, we would cut her tongue off. She stayed quiet, and clumsily cut out pictures from a magazine to make a collage of a fractured face.

The following day, Morgana went straight to the hospital as soon as she was awake and dressed. Her best friend had turned a slightly amber shade as he festered between starched sheets, either sleeping or just plain unconscious; she sat down in the chair by his bed to read her book while she waited for him to wake up. He surfaced after an hour or so, seemed to vaguely recognise her, and requested a specific chocolate bar as though she was the hospital waitress. By the time she returned with the confectionary, he was passed out again, so she placed it by his bed and sat back down to read her book.

A few days passed in this tortured inertia. Every day, she visited for as long as she could, and each time, he seemed to get more animated but increasingly jaundiced. His mother informed us that the doctors were not sure of his recovery. The tests were yet to confirm whether the antidote was working, and there was still a chance we might lose him. The weather had the audacity to become sublime, and dazzling sunlight shone thoughtlessly down upon our potential forthcoming bereavement. Silver beds and snowy walls gleamed with a mocking radiance.

This is when some of us realised that we couldn't live without him. Nobody had understood Morgana the way he did, nobody had ever paid Honeysuckle so much attention, and Alicia had finally felt as though she could trust someone. That girl usually despises and mistrusts everybody. It's actually better that way, seeing as when she likes somebody she's prone to becoming a pathologically jealous little stalker. It tears her apart. In this respect, it would be better if she was more like the way Honeysuckle is now: self-absorbed, fickle and easily distracted by bright lights and shiny things. As she hunched by the magician's bedside, she was horrifically obsessed, and the object of her fixation was possibly about to die. He was soaking into hospital sheets, yellow and poisoned, like a long streak of piss. There is no accounting for taste, is there? If we had known that this was what she was into, we would have started making random hospital visits years ago.

While he was dying, a fifth housemate moved into the bedroom opposite his. This one had wisely avoided a summer of hazy, herbal, housebound paranoia by staying at her parents' place for the holidays. Second year was about to begin, and she arrived at the giant ashtray that was our house, pulling up in a car with her possessions and her wholesome smile. She was like a princess. Blond and perfectly curved, she was more attractive than Honeysuckle, as kind as Morgana but without her ludicrous belief systems, and as self-assured as Estella but without her contempt for humanity.

"I'll go with you when you visit him tomorrow," she informed us, smiling beautifully.

"That would be nice," said Morgana to the princess.

Morgana got burnt on the walk there, the sun being too harsh on her delicate skin, and none of us owning sufficient grasp on reality to remember the necessity of applying sun block. Another thing we had forgotten was our doctor's appointment. Morgana found the appointment card in her handbag when she went to retrieve the chocolate bar she had brought for her best friend.

"I'd completely forgotten about this," she gasped, stressed and flustered, losing her composure as the pressure of her own illness, combined with the magician's uncertain future, began to overwhelm her easily bewildered mind.

"You go to your appointment," said the princess to the witch.

"I can visit him by myself," she said.

"It will be nice to get to know him," she said.

With a smile, a hug, and the sweetly worded reassurance that she would pass on our love to him, she left us in the hospital corridor.

Morgana never saw the magician again.

The doctor increased her medication because her therapy assessment was yet to come through and she was still so despondent. She arrived back at the stoner house with a collection of chemical crutches in a paper bag, and placed herself vacantly before a screen that showed the latest unremarkable music videos on a repetitive loop, occasionally making vague conversation with our sombre co-inhabitants.

The princess eventually arrived home, looking breathless and radiant. "He's getting better," she beamed to the room. "The doctors say he's going to be ok."

So why did it feel as though the ground beneath us was caving in?

"They said he needs to make some changes to his life when he comes home, though," she continued, glancing nervously at Morgana. "They said he needs to spend less time with Carlie, because he feels like he has to look after her and this makes his depression worse."

Everyone understood.

Everybody agreed that he was clearly so horribly unwell that he needed to concentrate purely on getting himself better, and didn't need any further drain on his emotional energy.

Nobody could look Morgana in the eye.

He was discharged from hospital a few days later even though he was dead. Morgana had watched him die, praying by his bedside every day for his safe return as he slowly turned the colour of death, before he disappeared, never giving her the chance to say goodbye. It was a cold, reserved magician with a secret laughter in his eyes who paraded around with the princess on his arm, ignoring us. Morgana didn't recognise him at all. The only one of us who really knew this person was Alicia. She had seen those eyes before, within the smiling face of everyone who had ever burned her.

Honeysuckle could be a bit slow on the uptake sometimes. Unable to sleep one evening, she wandered upstairs to visit her former best friend, hoping she could talk, draw and smoke with him the way she used to. Outside his door, she heard the voice of the princess, feminine tones that giggled and flirted and were better than her.

There was a switch and a hellish adrenaline rush.

"I hope you both burn in hell," wrote Alicia on the

Magna Doodle in the landing before returning to her room to break stuff and draw pictures of death.

The following day, the princess's parents phoned the landlord regarding their daughter's safety in the house, and we were swiftly made homeless again. Our world crumbled. The housemates had been like a surrogate family to us, and we had lost them over a stupid note on a Magna Doodle.

"You should see what I can do with an Etch-A-Sketch," comments Alicia, as she looks back upon a memory she now finds hilarious. "And woe betide the next person who gives me alphabet letters to decorate the fridge. I'll give them a well sinister kitchen."

Some people just shouldn't be allowed to write things.

Needing a place to go, we answered an advertisement on a student forum and found a room in a home with strangers. We deliberately chose people with whom we had nothing in common, a group of lads from a completely different subculture, to remove the urge to make friends with those we lived with and construct a family unit that might one day disown us.

Unfortunately, there were no protection spells in this residence to defend us from the demon when he returned to claim us. The evenings saw us fighting for our lives once more as something hideous, terrifying and immortal crawled out of a gap in the wall, with eyes full of a ghastly, mocking malevolence, to throttle and crush us until sunrise.

As we fought to hold on to our miserable, friendless existence, we couldn't help but remember Morgana's smug little mantra from the beginning of summer.

"Trust in life."

CHAPTER 14

(Eternal Sufferings Smile Alone)

Morgana's spiritualised lunacy was evidently infectious, because Alicia was now also a fanatical believer. It became clear to her that she was an angel of destruction, a holy warrior of vengeance, on a mission from God to cleanse the Earth of the vile spirits of the impure. The heathen magician and his whore princess would be the first to taste the almighty's wrath. Their petrol-soaked, roasting flesh would serve as a stark reminder to those whose souls were rotten and corrupt, instructing them to repent before their final hour of judgement.

There is no exaggeration here; she really was this much of a liability. We couldn't take her anywhere.

"I need somebody to help me. I'm scared I might kill somebody," Honeysuckle cried at the hospital as they dressed her arm in yet another set of bandages. The poor girl couldn't bear the thought of prison, where she would have limited make-up supplies and most people would be ugly. She had spent her life wanting to be a beautiful princess, but some jagged reflection that lay beyond her control or comprehension had turned her into the wicked witch, banished and friendless.

"Have you thought about how you might do it?" they asked.

"I've somehow stolen a key to their house and bought a container of paraffin," she sniffed, wringing a nasty bit of tear stained tissue in her immaculately manicured hands.

"What's stopped you from doing it so far?" they asked.

"I don't want to kill people!" she wailed. The stench of burnt skin might never wash out of her hair or clothing, and she might reek of hideous murder for the rest of her days. "It's Alicia who wants to kill people. She just takes over and I can't control her. She's a psycho. I hate her."

"Do you ever lose time?" they asked.

"No, I remember it all," she sighed. She wished she didn't. She always found herself back in the vessel eventually, plagued by the awful knowledge of the atrocities committed by the furious girl who wore a distorted version of her face. Even "drinking to forget" no longer worked as an amnesic strategy, because her brain's memory would stay active long after its self-control had vanished.

"Are you on any kind of medication?" they asked.

"I've been prescribed major tranquilisers, but they're not working. There're still always demons in my room at night and I still hear her voice saying she's going to burn people," she told them, desperate for them to help her, to save her from the petrol and the bonfire so she could be a normal girl who got dates and went out dancing.

They increased the dosage of her medication and sent her home. Nobody set fire to anybody that evening, because we were all far too tired.

We were, in fact, severely fatigued from here onwards, bloating out while shutting down and waddling through life in our new chemical straightjacket. Alicia still wanted to burn her enemies, but lacked the motivation to fulfil God's mission, and was unable to prevent Honeysuckle from returning the pilfered keys to our previous housemates in an effort to make them like her again. It was a pointless exercise, because even when we weren't trying to set fire to people, we still weren't particularly likeable, being too slow from those bothersome tablets to keep up with even the most basic conversation.

Alicia still dreamed of murder. In her fantasy world she was strong and lethal, like heroin or a gun, destroying all in her path with no fear of the consequences. Unable to bear our reality of being a friendless nonentity on the margins of society with no power, money or future, she sank further into her delusions of fire, terrifying us with her sociopathic ambitions, but lacking the energy to fulfil her terrible plans.

"I still don't think the anti-psychotics are working. The angry girl in my head still wants to commit murder," Morgana confided to the consultant psychiatrist at our next appointment. Our benevolent believer felt the unacknowledged grief of a secret widow, and had been seriously struggling to connect with the positive energy of the universe. In the mindscape, she lay crippled on the ground by an unconscious Estella, since they had both been knocked from their clouds by the recent shock of abandonment. Alicia's barely contained rage had ignited nearly everything around them, and Morgana's tears were the only thing soothing her blisters. In reality, she was surrounding herself with healing crystals to ward off the encroaching satanic forces, but nothing seemed to work. An eternal curse within us would always draw them back like a magnet.

"I think perhaps you also need a mood stabiliser," said the psychiatrist, writing us a prescription for anti-epilepsy drugs, making us a test subject for their effectiveness in alleviating homicidal impulses. All those tablets did was make us twitch violently. Why just be crazy, when you can be crazy and hysterically twitchy like a frog in a washing machine?

The new medication destroyed all visual imagination, and our attempts to make art merely saw us staring at the blank page of our sketchbook. Our last job had slipped away from us while we'd watched our best friend die, so we spent the days walking around the city centre, handing out résumés to places that might hire us, trying to hide the hopeless desperation in our eyes. The evenings saw us alone with the diabolical imp that climbed through the walls to crush and strangle us.

Honeysuckle was devastated, having yearned for the romantic but ended up with the necromantic. One lonely, friendless, dateless night, isolated and unable to endure another evening with just her malevolent hallucinations for company, she took all of her medication at once. Unable to swallow any more disillusionment, she swallowed a stash of potential suicide.

At the hospital, they were inundated with patients who were genuinely unwell, and Honeysuckle felt like time-wasting scum. The twitch from the overdose was excruciating, her nerves screaming with a tortured itch that made her wince and judder on starched white sheets as the chemicals did damage to her central nervous system that was destined to never fully heal. Barely conscious, she was made to strip from the waist upwards so they could attach a heart monitor.

"Stop pulling that blanket back up, we can't see if the electrodes are still attached properly if you do that," the doctor said, folding the blanket back down again.

Even Honeysuckle didn't like being topless in that horrible room. The other two beds were empty, but the janitor kept coming in to sweep the floor, and was particularly interested in the area of floor around Honeysuckle's bed. After a while, he stopped even pretending to do his job, and merely stood there, staring at her chest.

"What are you in here for?" he asked her breasts.

"I took an overdose, and it's made me ill," her mouth replied.

"You shouldn't have done that, should you?" he responded without shifting his gaze, in a creepily condescending voice that suggested he was talking to a naughty child.

With muscles weak from poisoned convulsing, our pitiful girl used her uncoordinated, shaking hands to manoeuvre the bed sheet up to at least cover her nipples.

"You're not supposed to do that, are you?" he asked the covered place where her breasts used to be, before shuffling disappointedly away with his broom.

When the doctor came back, he testily pulled the sheet back down, saying, "I told you about this, didn't I? We need to make sure the electrodes are attached properly so we can monitor your heart rate."

Exposed once more, it wasn't long before Honeysuckle was being stared at by the janitor again. There was something about his presence that was worse than any hidden camera, but she soon lost consciousness from the sedative side effect of everything she had taken, making it no longer matter.

She awoke the following morning under a blanket on a busy ward. Feeling suitably chastised for her vile, self-absorbed behaviour, she vowed never to take another overdose. All she needed was some regular talking therapy and a few friends, and she was sure she could be a normal girl, without a care in the world other than which hand cream was best for her cuticles or which cleanser was most suited to her combination skin type. The sun made a half-hearted attempt at illuminating a ward full of coughing geriatrics as she waited patiently for her psychiatric assessment.

It turned out that everyone in psychiatry was busy that day, but their secretary was able to take some notes about her condition before telling her she was free to leave.

"Is somebody going to help me?" asked Honeysuckle.

"I've taken these notes, and your case will be discussed by the team next time they have a meeting. They'll decide what to do then, and we'll write to you," the administrator said.

We went home to wait for our letter. One day, at one of those team meetings, somebody would agree to take us on as a case for long term therapy; they would teach us how to control Alicia, we would learn how to be sanguine rather than suicidal, and they would show us how to permanently banish the demons. Unfortunately, this day was a long time coming. We had already been allocated a consultant psychiatrist, so the incident was merely referred back to him, and he wished to do nothing more than continue his monthly reviews while steadily increasing our medication, because he didn't think that therapy would help us.

The brand name for the drug he prescribed was written all over his office on a selection of complementary stationary items. His facial expression was a benignly patronising smile as he wrote yet another prescription, while his favourite pharmaceutical company's motto stared at us from a branded box of tissues.

"Compliance is the key," it said, in innocuous, pastel blue writing.

The sedative effect of the tablets, combined with our continuous and un-diminishing battle with the nocturnal ghouls, meant that we were soon going days on end without washing or eating. Honeysuckle decided that if nobody came to save us before the end of this miserable winter, she was going to kill herself on Valentine's Day. Alicia was determined that our death would be a blaze of righteous glory, and we would take as many people with us as possible on our final descent to hell. Morgana became terrified of the future and what we might become, and prayed to God every day for rescue.

"Thank you for everything you've already done for me," she would begin, ever fearful of sounding ungrateful. "Please let me find love before Valentine's Day."

Those two sentences were repeated as a desperate mantra as the days counted down towards a looming massacre. Serena, looking for practical solutions based in reality, realised that it wasn't safe for us to stay in that lonely house where malicious phantoms crawled out of the walls, and arranged for us to move back to the family home.

"I'll look after you," said Mother. She always was very loving.

However, Father #2 wasn't quite so pleased to see us, and the house was in a constant state of verbal warfare. Alicia began making plans to kill Father #2 in his sleep.

"There's a petrol station just round the corner," she thought. "It would be so easy. Mum often sleeps away from him, so I wouldn't need to burn her, I could just burn him. It would make everything ok again. Like it was before he came along and started hitting me all the time. That'll teach him to destroy my childhood. He'll look so much better on fire."

Serena got the impression that she really meant it this time and realised she had made a mistake in bringing Alicia back home. We needed to return to the city. From the social network we had built up in first year, there were only four people left who still spoke to us. One friend said that we couldn't stay with her because her possessive fiancé wouldn't allow it. Another told us that she had to work three jobs to pay for repairs to her girlfriend's gravestone, so she didn't have time for guests. We later found out that she was lying, there was no dead girlfriend, and she had just wanted her own space so she could sleep with lots of men. It's good to have hobbies. Another contact said we couldn't stay with him because he was quitting university to move back to his mother's. That only left one option, Jane's former best friend, the evil boy who had hurt Katie on the vessel's twentieth birthday, who Honeysuckle had recently decided to start speaking to again. He said we could stay in the spare room of his house.

"I know where the nearest petrol station to here is as well," grinned Alicia, as she lay drunkenly awake on a filthy mattress in his home, staring at a cracked ceiling and picturing the neighbouring bedroom on fire.

It clearly wasn't safe there either. We desperately needed a peaceful home with no ghosts, a place to heal our mangled mind and learn how to function as a capable human being. We could find no respite from the dreams of burning in any of the places we turned to for shelter, and every abode increasingly resembled a potential slaughterhouse.

"Thank you for everything you've already done for me," prayed Morgana. "Please let me find love before Valentine's Day."

This was when a member of the evil boy's social group started showing a special interest in Honeysuckle. She didn't like him at all, because he was ugly and smelt of rotting garbage, but Morgana thought that our attracting somebody so soon after her prayer was surely a sign that we weren't supposed to set fire to anybody or jump off the multi-storey car park, so he became Boyfriend #3. The fact that we were supposed to be a lesbian had become pretty much irrelevant by this point.

The next few months were a blur of alcohol, self-loathing and depressive music, but we managed not to douse anyone in petrol or plummet to our demise from the nearest tall building, so that was good. Having someone to share a bed with meant that our nocturnal hours were less likely to be wracked by morbid hallucinations or waking satanic nightmares. Sometimes we even went out dancing.

Summer eventually stumbled back into town, which meant a new wave of housing contracts for the academic nomads. Our friend with the imaginary dead girlfriend came through for us by organising a shared house that she promised we wouldn't get kicked out of. We had just about scraped through our second year of university. Since our anti-psychotic prescription had been swapped for a brand with fewer side effects, we had managed to finish the collage book that we'd begun in the stoner house, presenting it to the class with a padlock holding it closed and merely showing people photographs that may or may not have depicted the inside pages. It was Schrödinger's emo art.

Home #6 was another typical student dwelling, with plates that gathered mould in the kitchen and a backyard full of rats. Kathy constantly got stressed about the filth in the communal areas, but she managed to make our room presentable, in as much as a room with deranged collages of death on the walls could be considered "presentable". She learned to work with what she had.

Boyfriend #3 eventually left the city to take a job somewhere else, and Honeysuckle ended up feeling suicidal again because she was alone. This was around the time we found out that our friend with the possessive fiancé was being cheated on, and the majority of her friends knew about it but were refusing to tell her because she was mentally ill.

"Well, I'm mentally ill, but I sure as hell would want to know if I was being cheated on," fumed Alicia, who in this person's place would be driven more berserk by the deceit of her supposed friends than by her twattish partner's duplicity. However, it is possible to be too honest sometimes. Alicia is eternally tactless, being so pathologically obsessed with the truth that she would put liars in the same bracket as rapists and murderers on her hierarchy of people deserving to be burned.

Our friend ended up leaving the city to move back with her family before Alicia could bless her with the truth. She wanted to tell her over the internet instead, but was held back from doing so by an internal restraint that she couldn't quite fathom. Morgana was worried about our deceived friend, and arranged to visit her, to assess whether she really was as unstable as people claimed, before deciding whether telling her the truth would be the right thing to do. We visited her family home, and the whole time we hung out with her, she never once mentioned demons, multi-storey car parks or setting anyone on fire.

"She's saner than I am," thought Alicia. "Not that it's a goddamn competition or anything."

"If I had a friend who knew that I was being cheated on but never told me because they were worried about what I'd do, I would want to stab the dishonest, patronising twat in the face," she thought.

Morgana took the responsibility of telling our friend herself, because she wanted to do the right thing and knew she had a tactful kindness that her livid alter ego sadly lacked. We presented her with the truth in her mother's living room, where we both sat on comfy chairs, eating colourful sweets.

"I need to tell my mum," our friend said, rushing out of the room, leaving us to stare at the vivid confectionary packet with a queasy sense of foreboding.

We never saw her again. She stayed upstairs while her mother came down to deliver a verdict on our behaviour. "My daughter will probably kill herself now, and it's all your fault," the matriarch told us, before expelling us from the residence.

Drenched in guilt and unable to handle being kicked out of yet another house or blamed for another friend's suicide, Honeysuckle slit her wrists on the train home. This was her first occasion of going down the road rather than across the street. The sight of a properly slit wrist looks freakishly peculiar, with the cut being no bigger than a regular emotional slice but the blood pouring out of it like a tap. All she could think of was how surreal it looked, with that red ribbon of oxygenised haemoglobin unravelling onto the dirty train floor at an alarming rate, to fall upon the worn out carpet with its trodden-down patches of discarded bubble gum. She could only stare at the scarlet vitality unfurling from her wrists as she got chillier, sleepier, but oddly contented.

Close your eyes like a good girl.

Before she could slip away, a nearby passenger noticed what she had done. They stopped the train, halted the flow from the incision and sent her off to the nearest hospital. The usual notes were taken by a tired employee with a clipboard before she was sent home with her rejection and her bandages.

Our former friend never did kill herself, but called us a liar instead, which made Alicia add her to the Petrol List.

The next day, we nearly missed a job interview on account of being weak from blood loss, but we dragged ourselves there just in time, with long sleeves over our bandages, and Serena managed to externalise throughout the whole affair and secure the position. On occasions when Serena was able to speak to people, we usually gave the impression of being clever. Her ability to take control at this point was very fortunate, because if Alicia had gone instead, she might have threatened to set fire to the interviewer's face, if we had sent Honeysuckle, she might have cried on them before humping their leg, and if Jane had turned up, she might have cried on them, humped their leg, and then vomited into the filing cabinet.

Job #9 was a cash office job in a large high street store. We worked there every weekday afternoon while we completed the final year of our degree, and the flashes of extreme volatility sometimes exhibited by the children and teenagers were overlooked on account of the adult alters being extremely skilled at the work.

Alicia's behaviour was fairly manageable during the

day, but by evening her temper would get stupidly out of hand. Her adrenaline surges made her fiendishly strong. There was a table in the living room that the rest of us had once struggled to move whilst tidying, on account of our feeble arms. Alicia would sometimes throw this table across the room in a livid frenzy, hitting the wall, spraying ashtrays and beer cans everywhere in a haze of alcohol, ash and dementia.

One of her worst outbursts happened after a housemate supposedly betrayed her by not coming out for her birthday. Alicia painted "Fuck You" on the hallway wall in massive, black letters, and tried to smash a wine bottle into the upstairs bathtub for our housemate to cut her feet on, but the bottle turned out to be more resilient than the bathtub, so she smashed the bathtub instead. The next day, Morgana felt excruciatingly guilty. She re-painted the hall, used filler on the cracked tub, and painted a picture of a fairy for our housemate to put on her bedroom wall. We were forgiven.

Morgana's behaviour was an embarrassment to Alicia, who didn't want anybody apologising for her. She didn't give a flying table what any of them thought. Her rages were becoming so irrational that we couldn't take her anywhere, because at any given moment she could threaten to set fire to something ridiculous, like an irritating side table or some judgemental potted chrysanthemums.

"I hate that plant!" she might scream, dousing its accusatory leaves in stolen petrol.

"What the fuck are you doing to my houseplants?" the host may well demand to know.

"That planty bastard was looking at me funny. It was like, 'you come around here, not being a plant. I'm trying to be a plant over here. I judge you with your non-planty ways.'"

Her eyes would narrow to dangerous, glinting slits as she'd give that green bastard one last stare before throwing the match. "Don't ever judge me, you planty fuck," would be her final words to the burning mess before her. This is how convinced she was that the whole world continually judged her for things that were never her fault. It was the genuine possibility of this kind of chlorophyll-related catastrophe that meant we had to keep her away from decent people and any household objects she might take exception to.

Alicia eventually got diagnosed with Anti-Social Personality Disorder and referred to anger management classes. These were part of a support group called STOP, which stood for "Start Treating Others Positively", not to be confused with wildlife liberation movement, "Stop Torturing Otters Politically". Nobody likes those guys. They are the kind of organisation that might attract some hippy douche who would sanctimoniously beat up his mentally ill girlfriend for wearing a hat that once looked at a mongoose.

There was a notice on the wall, informing us that "anger" was just one letter away from "danger". That was useful. It's also one letter away from "banger", "ganger", "manger" and "ranger". Also, "rage" is only two letters away from "forage", "fury" is just three letters from "fubbery", and "the bad hatred" is a mere fifteen letters away from "theological badgers chattered". You learn something new every day.

In our final year of university we specialised in conceptual film making. Disability services gave us a free computer on account of us being insane, so we could avoid scaring our classmates by working from home, staying in our room, and merely scaring ourselves instead. First, the footage from the multi-storey car park that we had spent two years being obsessed with was made into a time-based digital collage about suicide. It was very moving, and must have been really pleasant for our peers to watch at the end-of-term review. Our second film then depicted over one hundred and fifty paracetamol tablets being pushed out of blister packs, intercut with erratic domestic footage, weird art shots, news clips, documentary material about depression, obligatory drug references, and a layered soundtrack of gloomy music and grim documentary sound bites. We clearly weren't getting any more cheerful.

Honeysuckle cried herself to sleep most nights, because for some bizarre reason, nobody wanted to date her. She eventually got herself a girlfriend, but lost her within a few weeks after a series of vitriolic outbursts from Alicia drove poor Girlfriend #1 into the arms of someone who resembled a truck driver.

CHAPTER 15

(The Sickness Breeds a New Infection)

The first incarnation of our autobiography began with Honeysuckle regaining consciousness in her vomit-soaked bed after ingesting over one hundred and fifty paracetamol tablets. There was more than a hint of gothic melodrama as it described her alternative fashion aesthetic in great detail, as though her physical appearance was even remotely important when she was potentially about to expire from major organ failure.

"Hey! My liver's fucked to the point where I'm probably going to die, but my exquisitely blended dark eye make-up looks fantastic!"

We are no longer writing a pity-me novel, so we will spare you the finer descriptions of how painful it felt to be single again and dying alone. There were only two decent lines in that whole first chapter.

"She needed someone to call her beautiful."

"She needed someone to call her an ambulance."

Awesome.

She's a goddamn beautiful ambulance. She's also an attractive police van and a weirdly sexualised fire engine, as well as being an attention-seeking imbecile who nearly got us all killed.

We had wanted to use this slightly over-medicated incident as the prologue to our book because it was supposed to mark a vital turning point in our lives.

The whole abomination was divided into three parts.

The first part was named "Sad Girl with Dreams", and was basically several poetically bleak chapters about our tragic childhood. It mentioned domestic violence, drug abuse, molestation, mental illness, selective muteness, bullying, self-harm and anorexia, all without a single punch line or even a passing nod to the potential hilarity of these topics. There's nothing quite like feeling sorry for yourself is there?

The second part was called "Mad Girls with Nightmares", and described the heartbreaking events that began with us having to drop out of school, afraid for our lives, and led to us waking up covered in sick in our sad, student bedroom, possibly about to die a slow suicide. It described us all in pathetic detail, while constantly making excuses for our behaviour and neglecting to mention the fact that we're all twats.

The third part was called "The Long Wake Up".

Do you see what we did there?

Dreams... of a happier, less self-absorbed tomorrow.

Nightmares... of realising you actually are the main character in a book about a loser who has wasted her life.

Waking up... because, bacon.

The final section was going to detail our miraculous recovery from traumatised suicide survivor to productive member of society. We were going to break out from the toxic trap of our own poisonous dreams, destroying all delusions, to take our place in the real world with the ordinary, sane people.

"Do you realise, Honey, that all your dreams are dead?" Alicia would ask her twin as we all faded away from our life of creative madness.

Honeysuckle was going to smile as she replied, staring out across the scarred landscape before her, where things had begun to grow again and the sun was rising.

"That means I can finally wake up."

We never got around to writing that final section, and the three hundred page, hand-written draft of the first two sections ended up in the trash. Besides, it's not as though that girl ever actually wants to wake up. She lives for the fantasy, the oblivion, the perpetual delusion sequence; if she ever truly woke up, she just wouldn't be her.

When she regained her own special version of consciousness on that fateful morning of her early twenties, it was New Year's Day. Refrigerated sunlight threw accusatory beams through a gap in the indigo curtains, the house was silent apart from the faint background ringing of empty noise, and the chemical vomit on the floor and bed sheets smelt acrid and inhuman, all blood-flecked bile and strips of stomach lining that were limp like soggy leaves.

There are various ways of dealing with your girlfriend leaving you for someone resembling a truck driver. Get a new girlfriend. Go straight, and shag one of the dick-ridden Neanderthals that letch on you in grimy nightclubs. Get a HGV licence. It was unfortunate that none of these perfectly valid options were considered suitable by Honeysuckle, who decided that she would much rather kill herself.

Even before being treated for our dissociative condition, we had been telling therapists about Alicia for years, but we had never mentioned Honeysuckle, despite being aware for some time that she existed. There were two main reasons for this.

Firstly, it was only Alicia whom we viewed as being trouble. She would sporadically surface to wreak havoc, and we did not find her aggressive behaviour or abrasive disposition the least bit acceptable. Honeysuckle, however, had begun her existence as something we believed we were supposed to be, the typical teen of the magazines, with her dumb obsessions with beauty and romance. Something real had grown behind that facade, a genuine dream, tragic and poetic, yet despite her hungry delirium and ceaseless mission for self-obliteration, we had never seen her as being part of the problem. Having considerably more charm than Alicia, she had manipulated us into thinking she was "the nice one", even though she was less honest and far more self-serving than her furious twin.

There is clearly something about not threatening to set fire to people that can make a girl more likeable.

Honeysuckle convinced us that she was totally sane, and it was merely the rest of the world who were at fault for not loving her. This is why we had complained endlessly to therapists about the horror of lethal Alicia, but never sought their help for dealing with her suicidal sister, despite the number of times she had nearly killed us all.

The main reason, however that we had never complained about her in the therapist's office, is because that was when we were most likely to *be* her. Sometimes, we would turn up as Serena and get told what remarkable progress we were making, other times, we would be Alicia and our discussions would get confrontational, but mostly, we would be Honeysuckle, and the rest of us would remain stuck back in the mindscape while our hopeless girl sought assistance with the endless problem that was her life. She would tell them about how her vicious alter ego kept ruining everything, but would fail to accept any suggestion that her own self-absorbed neediness and noxious insecurities were equally destructive.

Unable to stop retching, she telephoned for the ambulance that she so desperately needed, not because she had changed her mind about dying, but because she suddenly recalled everything she'd ever heard about how paracetamol overdose brought a slow, painful, ugly death. This was not the beautifully tragic demise she had envisioned.

Suicide.

You're doing it wrong.

On her way to the hospital, she threw up in a series of cardboard hats while answering questions regarding her personal circumstances in the gasping breaths between stomach heaves. At the hospital, they hooked her straight up to a drip containing an antidote to the lethal by-product of paracetamol. They then took a blood test and gave her an injection that slowed her vomiting sessions down to once an hour. She passed out on a gurney in the corridor.

We woke up as Kathy, who was frantic that her bedroom back home was dirty. "When can I go home?" she asked the nurse who came to replace her sick-filled cardboard container with a clean one.

"As soon as that drip's finished," the nurse replied, pointing to the plastic sack full of life-saving fluid that hung by the bed.

"How long will it take?" Kathy pestered her, aware that the stress of her filthy room would be driving her to hysteria right now if she were not so horribly tired. She desperately needed to launder her disgusting bed sheets and scrub that soiled carpet with an anti-bacterial cleaning spray and boiling water.

"It will take at least another six hours," said the nurse,

patiently.

Kathy drifted off into a fitful slumber, knowing that the stench of chemically corrupted bodily fluids was presently seeping into her bedroom's soft furnishings. To make matters worse, we had recently gotten some pizza grease onto our jeans that hadn't come out in the wash, and the matter of how to remove those unsightly blotches from the thigh was still unresolved. She shouldn't be falling asleep when there was so much that needed cleaning.

When we woke up, we were Honeysuckle again, and the first thing she noticed was that her immaculately straightened hair had begun to wave and amplify in an attempt to return to its natural, frizzy state. She was desperate to return home to her straightening irons.

"We're taking you to a ward now, there's a bed available," they said, wheeling us down the corridor, as Serena attempted to pull us all together.

We didn't understand why there was any need for us to have a bed on the ward when our drip was nearly finished. Kathy had a bedroom to tidy, Honeysuckle had a damaged hairstyle to rescue, and Morgana didn't want to take up any more of their time.

"It's just until your blood tests come through," they explained.

In our hospital bed, we watched the bag slowly run out of antidote until it was almost deflated. To our dismay, it was then promptly switched with a replacement twice its size, bringing us even further away from the presentable appearance and clean bedroom that would make everything better again. This was all incredibly inconvenient.

A lady in a lab coat came to see us.

"Carlie Martece?" she asked, observing us with a bizarrely formal mixture of shock and pity.

"Yes," we replied.

"I'm from the toxicology unit," she informed us. "I've just been analysing your results, and I've never seen anything quite like it. We've got a graph that tells us how much antidote is required for cases like this, with the concentration level of paracetamol in the bloodstream on one axis and the recommended amount of antidote on the other. These are the first results I've ever seen that have been *off the graph*. If you wanted to kill yourself, you've done a pretty good job."

We always had excelled at tests, being such an over-achiever. We had been top of the class at English, maths and science, and now we were getting top results on liver poisoning too. Hopefully, they have since put together a new graph for hardcore suicidal twats like us. It probably wouldn't take too long to throw one together with an Excel spreadsheet, or whatever they use.

"Am I going to die?" we asked her.

"Hopefully not," she said, "but there's no way of knowing yet. We'll keep administering the antidote and taking blood tests, and if there's no improvement in a couple of days, we'll transfer you to another hospital that has a specialist unit for liver damage."

Having delivered the news that we might die soon, she briskly walked off to leave us to our remorse.

Honeysuckle didn't regret the people she had done, she only regretted the people she hadn't done. The future paraded its potential experiences before her on a taunting conveyor belt of dreams, in the game show style of "here's what you could have won", and it occurred to her that she was possibly missing out on more than a fancy dinner set and a brand new washing machine.

Estella and Alicia merely regretted our lack of revenge upon the world and all our enemies left unburnt. Serena lamented over everything that we had yet to learn or achieve, all that potential so carelessly discarded during a night of alcohol-fuelled oblivion. The one with the most remorse, however, was Morgana, who was wracked with devastating guilt at the hurt that our death would bring to those who cared about us. She did a great deal of praying that evening, in the hope that God would save her. Some people believe in that sort of thing.

The only other patient in the room who wasn't depressingly ancient was the blond girl at the other end of our ward. She noticed Honeysuckle looking at her in the midst of our regretful reverie, and wandered over with an oddly curious look in her abnormally wide eyes.

"What are you in here for?" she asked us, after briefly introducing herself with a name we can't remember.

"I took some tablets after my girlfriend dumped me," replied Honeysuckle.

"Are you a lesbian?" the girl enquired, her eyes expanding wider, until they almost filled an entire face that would have been cute if it wasn't slightly freakish.

"Yes," said Honeysuckle, demurely.

"I'm a lesbian sometimes," the staring girl informed us.

"Really?" asked Honeysuckle.

"Yes," she said, "I have a boyfriend now, but before that, I had a girlfriend. She was really pretty."

"Why are you in here?" asked Honeysuckle.

"I'm in here because they need to give me this medicine," she replied, gesturing to the drip in her arm that went up to a bag on a metal pole on wheels, just like ours. It's nice to have things in common.

"It's difficult to keep taking this medicine though, because of Grandma," she said.

"Because of your Grandma?"

"Yes. My Grandma doesn't like me taking this medicine. Whenever she visits, she tries to rip this thing out of my arm. I'm like, 'Don't do that, Grandma,' and she's like, 'That's nasty medicine, you don't need it.'"

"Really?"

"Yes, but the thing is," she said, "my Grandma's been dead for nearly seven years."

Our blond acquaintance stared vacantly towards us, smiling weirdly, before saying, "I think I might be in here for some time."

"You don't say," we replied. It made a refreshing change to not be the most mental person in the room for once.

Another person giving us a run for our money in the crazy stakes was the elderly lady on the bed opposite, who loudly yelled, "Who's this man?" when her daughter and son-in-law visited, and then repeatedly demanded in a shrill, birdlike voice, "What am I doing in this box?" when the curtains were drawn around her bed.

Fortunately, we soon left behind the Ghost of Christmas Past and this chilling glimpse of the future, because they moved us to another ward. Our new bed was in a quiet place with no haunted stories or dementia trips, and we soon fell asleep after they administered our anti-psychotic medication.

The next day, we were interviewed by someone from psychiatry.

"I'm scared that if I get sent home, I'll just do something else to kill myself," said Honeysuckle, having lost all faith in her ability to control her own behaviour, desperate for the long term therapy that might teach her how not to be a train wreck.

"I shall discuss your case with my team, and we'll try to get you some help," said the man with the clipboard.

The day floated past in a shell-shocked haze. We were visited by our housemate, who brought us a puzzle book, and our mother, who brought us a magazine. Kathy asked Mother for advice on removing fast food grease stains from clothing, and she was recommended a specific brand of stain remover. The doctors moved us to a different ward that was excessively lit and inadequately heated, everything cold and glaring like an open fridge. All the other patients were elderly and crippled, withering their way through years that we might never reach. We were lucky enough to have remembered our massive, black, fluffy coat before stumbling into the ambulance. The children clutched it like a comfort blanket during the day, and at night it served as an extra layer, resting over our body and head to preserve our heat and block out the light. In the middle of the night, a bemused doctor asked a pile of ebony fluff to wake up for another round of tests. A pale, scrawny arm stuck itself out of the heap, and then became limp from chemical sedation, its owner managing to return to sleep as the needle was sliding into her skin.

"We'll need your other arm please, because we need to change your IV," called a muffled voice through the fog of sedative sleep. We can vaguely recall presenting our opposite limb to the chill of the night air, before sliding back into nothingness while the IV was being changed.

It wasn't until early the next afternoon that we had

toxicology results come back clear and found out for definite that we weren't going to die. Kathy couldn't wait to get home and stop her bedroom from being dirty, but she made us go into the city centre first, to buy the stain remover for our jeans that Mother had recommended.

A few days after the overdose, we were still on a waiting list for therapy and the teenagers remained infatuated with the former Girlfriend #1, with Honeysuckle pining for her, all lonely and tragic, and Alicia still wielding a fiery eyed fixation. Somebody recorded a vocal death threat in the bathtub of Home #6, and this spoken word track eventually became the main audio of the Fail Trilogy. It was about our ex girlfriend, it was about the magician, it was about everyone who ever abandoned us. There are certain states of mind in which people can become interchangeable.

The object of our then-current obsession invited us out for a drink when she heard that we had been discharged from hospital. Unfortunately, she took us to a nightclub where we didn't know anyone before disappearing into a cubicle with her truck driver friend. We still didn't have that HGV licence. Alicia screamed through the cubicle door that she would kill them both, and then took Honeysuckle home to slice her face open. There was a certain clarity of thought and purity of vision as she stared at the girl in the mirror whom she barely recognised, blood dripping down to her chin from three horizontal slivers of lacerated skin across the cheekbone, her eyes smouldering with a sullen venom. She had never felt more alive.

We had a camcorder on loan from the university library and she used this to document the experience, capturing frames of crimson-smeared breakage, empowering herself by being in control of the camera as well as in front of its prying lens. This time, she could edit the footage. This time, she would be King.

We're not entirely sure what she meant by that. Perhaps she thought that being King of the Misunderstood Emo Teenagers was something to aspire to.

She looked ridiculous.

Luckily for us, some people, for some inexplicable reason, are majorly attracted to self-absorbed insanity. The lights had been jarring and the music had been irritating when the lesbian who was to become Girlfriend #2 first approached us in a crowded nightclub.

"Would you like to dance?" she asked the haunted looking girl with the mild facial scarring who was hunched at the edge of the dance floor with her vodka and her bitterness.

"I would, but I actually hate this song," replied Alicia. The DJ had found the audacity to play something corporate and cheerful, and it jangled her nerves something dreadful, with each saccharine note hammering at a fault line in her skull.

After the gothic lesbian walked off, we switched and became Honeysuckle, who was devastated that we had just sent someone away who might have loved her. Luckily, our admirer soon returned.

"How about this one?" she asked.

"It's my favourite," beamed Honeysuckle.

She had no idea what it was. She was just overjoyed at the opportunity to dance and have kisses. Somebody was paying her attention, somebody wanted her, the world was a wonderful place and her existence was validated.

Over the next few months, the relationship built into something sweet, quaintly schizophrenic and masochistically co-dependent. Girlfriend #2 was a submissive and a self-confessed alcoholic. Drunk, in a crowded pub, she once lifted up her T-shirt to proudly show off the faded bruises we had given her. A friend asked us whether we had coloured in our girlfriend with a yellow highlighter.

"Is that what you people do?" he asked.

Lesbianism's clearly all about the luminous ink.

Honeysuckle now enjoyed the company of someone who was as perverse and frequently wasted as she was, and Alicia liked having her occasionally violent tendencies not only accepted, but also weirdly appreciated. She had found a way of releasing her anger whilst also making somebody strangely ecstatic. How romantic.

The remainder of our time at university spun by in a frenetic whirl of jealous strops, drunken bondage and emotional, conceptual video projects. Our most impressive creation was called Constructed Sanity. It began with a disembodied doll's head being returned to her body, where her empty eye socket could bleed, and then her arm was hacked off with a razor blade while a spider scuttled across her pretty dress. Her dismembered arm and one of her eyeballs were placed in an envelope, a crucifix was drawn in place of an address, a stamp was affixed, and this delightful parcel was placed in a post box while cars passed by on their daily mediocre journeys.

A reply envelope with a heart for an address came through our letter box and fell onto the hallway carpet. We opened it up and the world was inside. We gave the world to the devil as we stole his lipstick. Honeysuckle applied the plum purple shade in a dusty mirror by candlelight, before stealing the candle. The candle was then placed at the edge of a pentagram made from pastel blue ribbon, on which a ragdoll lay, oblivious.

A delicate hand took the ragdoll and drowned her in the sink, using a child's spade from the seaside to baptise her in the Godless tap water. That same spade then dug in the dirt to the sound of birdsong until a silver key was retrieved from the soil. The key unlocked the padlock on a sketchbook. This sketchbook was our collaged monstrosity, complete with magazine cuttings, photographs of toys and a written conversation with a magician, and now it held a knife between its pages. We put the knife in a vase, exchanging it for a flower. We approached a hooded figure in a deserted alleyway and tried to give her a bunch of flowers. After turning away from us three times, the stranger took our offering and presented us with a box wrapped in ribbon and shiny paper.

Honeysuckle in a white dress picked up the box while a spider scuttled across the wall. Alicia in a red dress merely observed the box, unimpressed, as the telephone rang. Honeysuckle in a white dress stood to answer the telephone, her uneven hemlines swirling over the fishnet lattice of her exposed legs. Alicia in a red dress walked out of the room. Honeysuckle was back on her shadowed bedroom floor, opening her present, while the printer spat out reams of the same question, the one we so desperately needed to hear. She eventually got the box unwrapped and inside was a disembodied china doll's head. You could see she was missing one glass eye as our hand pulled her out through a hole in the cardboard, clutching her matted hair to the sound of insects scuttling.

We could never forget those five, final, famous words that seemed to magically type themselves across the screen.

"Constructed sanity falls to nothing."

CHAPTER 16

(Our Skulls beneath a Jagged Stone)

After graduating from university with second class honours in artistic bullshit, we moved with Girlfriend #2 into Home #7, left Job #9 for Job #10, and finally found somebody who wished to take us on for long term psychiatric treatment, Therapist #4. The therapy was supposed to save our co-dependent lesbian relationship, but ended up destroying it.

It still remains a mystery why Girlfriend #2 wanted us to get a place together, seeing as Alicia kept pushing her tolerance to its limits with her jealous tantrums and Honeysuckle was always hysterically crying at her over fear of abandonment. Some people will tolerate possessive craziness out of a misplaced notion of responsibility or an inherent sense of masochism. You could call this love.

Home #7 was a pleasant, suburban house rather than a shared, student cesspit, but it would never be tidy enough for Kathy to breathe properly. Girlfriend #2 was a naturally untidy person, and the sheer amount of clutter that she insisted on surrounding herself with made it impossible for the snug little abode to resemble anything other than a junkyard.

The reason that Job #9 had to go was because we could no longer justify part-time employment with our student days behind us, and we were trying to wilfully ignore our lack of compatibility with the real world. Job #10 was a full time administration position that we took because we didn't know what else to do. We had spent the past few years expecting to be dead, in jail or locked up in a psychiatric ward at some point in the near future, so nobody had made much of a long-term career plan. Serena could cope with the work at first because she was convincing at talking to her co-workers in their ludicrous bureaucratic language as well as being an efficient and accurate typist. However, each day was a battle to restrain the more tempestuous elements of her character within the confines of the office environment. She had no idea how most people managed this. Alicia's anger was stored until the evening, when it would burst out into a domestic fury, turning our cluttered home into a warzone.

One evening, Alicia became convinced that Girlfriend #2 was going to split up with her, and decided to cut her up with a razor. She loomed over the bed where her partner slept, clutching a blade in her clenched fist, breathing heavily. "She'll never be able to leave me if she's dead," she thought.

Fortunately, there was a presence at the back of her brain that could still sometimes control her, and it forced her to step away from her partner's sleeping form and lock herself in the bathroom until the urge to commit murder subsided.

The bathroom was full of colourful, plastic bottles and infuriating, intrusive cameras. Pinned down by a tormenting spotlight, Alicia realised that the only way the urge to kill was exiting her body was via the drain, so she hitched up her long, black skirt and carved the inside of her thighs open with a furious force, shredding her skin up to create a scarlet disaster.

"That bitch should see what she made me do," thought a defiant Alicia, unlocking the door and stomping her injured body back into the bedroom. It was with a venomous, lunatic grin that she smeared handfuls of blood off her legs and onto the walls, the floor and her lover's sleeping face. The untidy bedroom now resembled a murder scene. Alicia completed the picture by writing her girlfriend's name in sticky blood on the shiny floorboards.

Fake murder scene... because actually killing people is too much like a hard day's work.

Other ways to impress your partner include a fake arson scene, where you cover everything in soot and turn the central heating up ridiculously high, or a fake burglary, where you sell all her possessions on the internet, and smash a window.

Honeysuckle eventually externalised within a blood-soaked reality and burst into tears. She went down to the living room to continue crying because nobody would ever love her, and was sat scabbing over in her desolate misery when there was a knock at the door. It was her girlfriend's work colleague and one of her friends. They had both been at the pub earlier, before the homicidal wrath had taken over, and one of them had recently received a worrying text from Alicia.

"Is everything ok?" they asked.

Honeysuckle mumbled a tearful response before shuffling back to the living room to slump dejectedly onto the sofa, leaving the front door open. She was never going to win any prizes for Hostess of the Year. They came in. One of the visitors spoke to her kindly, trying to ascertain what had happened, while the other, worried about her colleague, went to check upstairs, where she found what appeared to be a murder scene.

Girlfriend #2 told us afterwards that her colleague

had initially thought she was dead, until she had stirred after hearing her name called. When she had woken up in a room full of blood, she had initially thought that it was us who'd died, and had taken a long time to calm down from the overwhelming response of panic and horror. She presumably realised eventually that she didn't have a dead girlfriend, just one who behaved like a violent, abusive nutcase. The only plausible defence of our actions is that we had been trying to get psychiatric help for years, and had been continually rejected by the system. Admittedly, this isn't great, so far as excuses go.

With regards to the ongoing saga of our quest for a sympathetic therapist, we had now moved to a different area of the city, and a new postcode meant a new doctors' surgery, which in turn meant a referral to a new consultant psychiatrist. When our appointment finally came through, this one seemed to show an interest in Honeysuckle's complaints about a continuously demented Alicia.

"Do you ever lose time?" she asked us.

"No," Honeysuckle replied, as usual. It was difficult to describe that sense of otherness while admitting to a lack of the expected, accompanying amnesia.

"I remember all her rage attacks but I have no control over them, it's like being someone else. When I look back on Alicia's memories, it's like I wasn't actually there. I can remember everything she does, but it's not ever anything that I would choose to do. I can even remember everything she was thinking at the time, but it's completely different to the way I think. I hate her. She's an absolute psycho, she drives everyone away and she ruins everything."

"Does this ever happen when you're sober, or just

when you drink alcohol?"

"It does get worse when I drink," Honeysuckle confessed. "But it happens when I'm sober too," she hastened to add. She could remember feeling suicidal when she was four years old, and majorly resented it when professionals blamed all her psychiatric difficulties on her adult alcoholism.

"How many units of alcohol do you consume each week?" the psychiatrist asked.

Honeysuckle admitted to drinking every evening. She resided with an alcoholic, and was easily influenced by the addiction of an accomplice.

"I may know someone who can help you deal with the problems you're having, but I'm afraid she won't be able to do anything for you unless you cut down on your drinking," the psychiatrist warned.

Honeysuckle relayed this advice to her girlfriend when later discussing her recent appointment. "We need to stop drinking every evening because it's making me worse," she told her.

"Well, you can stop drinking if you like, but I'm not going to," said Girlfriend #2, pouring herself another glass of wine.

"You know I can't stay sober when someone else is drinking," said Honeysuckle, pouring another glass of wine for herself. Addiction loves company.

"You knew I was an alcoholic when you met me," said Girlfriend #2, who had bizarrely agreed to continue our uncivil partnership despite everything Alicia had done, presumably for the same self-despising reasons that she continued to drink.

After a few weeks, a letter came through the post, offering us an appointment with the lady who was to become Therapist #4. Nobody was expecting much, because we had been accused several times of being deliberately uncooperative and unresponsive to therapy by professionals who didn't wish to work with us, and we were beginning to consider ourselves a lost cause. Therapist #4 was an approved social worker who specialised in treating an illness called dissociative identity disorder, which none of us had ever heard of. Apparently, it was previously called multiple personality disorder. People with an already unstable sense of identity could possibly do without the name of their affliction being changed, but the previous name had been somewhat misleading, as none of the patients actually had more than one personality. They merely had a single personality that had been dismantled into component parts, with each fraction thinking that it was a separate person on account of a dissociative barrier between itself and the other aspects.

"Well, that explains Alicia," remarked Honeysuckle.

"You may actually find that you have other alters besides Alicia," said Therapist #4.

This didn't seem likely to Honeysuckle, but she smiled and nodded nonetheless. "The thing is though, if I do have this dissociative identity thing, that doesn't explain why most of the time I'm convinced there are cameras watching me. Apparently, that's not normal," mused our little starlet, checking the corners of the room for signs of obvious surveillance and hoping they were getting her best angle.

This is when Therapist #4 said the most curious thing.

"Usually, when my clients are convinced they're being watched, it's because at some point in their childhood, somebody *was* watching."

The vague suggestions of this odd statement provoked the most unsettling feelings, a memory of being trapped beneath a voyeuristic gaze, of being small and humiliated.

"I don't know what you're talking about," said Honeysuckle.

"But maybe somebody does," said Therapist #4, looking at us, meaningfully.

Our mind suddenly became full of hideously unglamorous flashbacks that we really did not need. Honeysuckle felt nauseated.

"I don't know what you mean," she insisted.

We were given a homework assignment of drawing a "personality map", naming the different facets of our psyche and jotting down their accompanying character traits. Our therapist was sure there was more to our madness than just the dreaded Alicia. This is how a certain young lady ended up sat on her lunch hour writing down the names of her alters in a battered notebook. It was as though a piercing light was flooding her usually clouded mind, and she was blinking confusedly in the glare, suddenly recognising the strangers who had always lived in the mirror. There was a calm, intelligent woman called Serena, whose measured diligence was the only reason we ever achieved anything. There was a hyper child called Clairey, who irritated everybody. This little girl had a twin with a timid and terrified demeanour, named Katie.

"I've got four alternate personalities, not just one," thought Honeysuckle, astounded by her own complexity. However, despite the wonder of these revelations, she still could not shake the feeling that she was missing something. This was when, staring out through the weird electric light of an evolving mindscape, she caught herself reflected for one fleeting instant in a hallucinatory looking glass, wide eyed with selfish dreams and toxic aspirations. She suddenly realised that she was Honeysuckle, a twisted, teenage entity, just as vile as that awful Alicia, but with better hair.

"You were right, there were more alters than just Alicia," she later told her therapist, proudly handing over her personality map, with a flourish.

The therapist studied our little psychological self-portrait. Honeysuckle had written her own name in pink, surrounded by cartoon hearts, accompanied by a brief list of her traits: shallow, manipulative, obsessed with finding love, uses people. Alicia was to the right of her, with her hostility and hatred. Manic Clairey was beneath Honeysuckle, frightened little Katie was under Alicia, and Serena was at the top, in the centre, so placed due to her being superior in intelligence to her deranged siblings.

"You need to be careful you don't imagine aspects of yourself during this process," Therapist #4 warned her.

"What do you mean?" asked Honeysuckle.

"I'm not sure Honeysuckle's real," said the therapist.

"Why not?" asked Honeysuckle.

"She seems a bit like something that an insecure girl would pretend to be, a kind of 'femme fatale' delusion, perhaps more of a performance than a real aspect of the self."

"But she feels so much emotion..." argued Honeysuckle.

"Yet this list of qualities doesn't seem like the way a genuine human being would describe herself," explained the therapist. "She's more like a character from a film.

Perhaps if you combined her with Alicia..."

"Combine her with Alicia?" asked our little actress, horrified at the very idea of merging with someone whom she saw as being a malicious sociopath.

"Yes," said the therapist, "if you put them together they make a typical teenager, don't they? The girl who wants to be popular and adored, but keeps having these angry strops and destructive moments of self-sabotage. Together, they're your teenage self."

"I can't imagine how they could ever become the same person... Alicia's such a psycho," declared Honeysuckle.

"Maybe she's not a 'psycho' at all. Perhaps she just behaves that way because she's frightened," suggested the therapist.

"Maybe..." sighed Honeysuckle, thinking. There was a great deal for her to take on board, with the recent revelations from Katie about our molested past, the possibility of Alicia acting out of fear rather than spite, and the startling notion that she herself might not be real.

"So, do I definitely have this dissociative identity disorder?" she asked.

"I believe the best diagnosis would be dissociative disorder not otherwise specified, which is a mild form of D.I.D.," explained the therapist. "You clearly have different selves and need to learn how to function as a whole person, but you don't have the amnesia that accompanies the full condition."

"So how can I learn to be one person?"

"Your mental health problems are basically the result of bad parenting. What you need to do if you want to recover, is re-parent yourself, learn how to look after yourself the way a competent parent would do: reward yourself for good behaviour, but also take responsibility for your self-destructive actions."

This was the best advice we could have been given, but it proved difficult to adhere to. Everything we believed about reality began to crumble as further monstrous memories fluttered to the surface of our consciousness, and it was only the release of our creative output that kept Alicia from stabbing her girlfriend then turning up at the office with petrol and a match and burning the place to the ground. She had yet to see the humour in her situation. To be fair, not everyone sees the humour in child abuse, but luckily for us, it's now one of Alicia's favourite punch lines.

"Why did the chicken cross the road?"

"Child abuse."

None of us understand this joke except Alicia, who falls around laughing whenever she tells it. When we ask her to explain, she suggests that maybe there is an infant on the other side of the road, and the chicken is a paedophile.

"Knock knock."

"Who's there?"

"Child."

"Child who?"

"Child abuse."

She says she's allowed to joke about it, because she has been through it. She claims she is merely "taking it back".

Her present attitude is actually a relief to us, because there were times when we thought she would never see the funny side, times of shattered glass, exploding mirrors and serrated bitterness. It's great that she can laugh about it now, even if it means having a juvenile sense of humour that gets us into trouble in certain social contexts. Hatred is always better with hilarity. We honestly never believed that our life could ever be so funny. At the time of our initial revelations, there was only a shell-shocked feeling that the world was ending, and an eager need to communicate our inner trauma through tragic, childhood imagery. One fairy smiled obliviously amongst the flowers while a spider crept up behind her. Another mystical creature lay bleeding in a lonely spotlight, real flecks of haemoglobin on her wounded back, while ripped off and discarded on the ground behind her lay her bloody wings.

Bloody wings... like a mutilated fairy, or an inadequate feminine hygiene product.

She should have worn white shorts and gone roller skating.

CHAPTER 17

(Delirious Thoughts of Vicious Powers)

The mindscape was changing rapidly. We had all previously believed ourselves to be the "real" Carlie Martece and had thought that every other aspect was merely a delusion. Now, we began to notice what one-dimensional caricatures we all were. With a dissociative condition, each alter is a fragment of the whole unit, but doesn't initially realise this. This lack of awareness can give it the unfortunate tendency to walk around thinking that it's an entire personality in its own right. Like a deluded member of a manufactured pop group.

Following on from the awareness of our affliction came the desire to learn how to work together and function as one stable entity. We needed a leader. The children needed a parent to look after them, and the teenagers needed an internal authority figure to teach them responsibility.

There were three candidates.

An obvious choice was Serena, whose impressive memory skills were the reason we had rarely exhibited signs of amnesia. A girl who can quite easily recite the first hundred digits of pi is hardly likely to forget threatening to set fire to someone, even if she was not in control of her actions at the time. She had certain powers within the mindscape. Environmental factors such as the lack of sunshine, the monsters in the shadows and the sporadic fall of acidic rain were beyond her jurisdiction, and a great deal of the behaviour of her alters was beyond her comprehension or restraint, but she could build various constructions to improve our situation. Her latest creation was a set of floodlights. Harsh, artificial lighting now illuminated the centre of a wasteland that was once a wonderland. In the ruthless glare, we could see our battered surroundings, view each other's demented faces and begin to gain a hideous new self-awareness.

"Well, aren't we a heterogeneous bunch of delightful girls..." drawled the arrogant Estella. Our swaggering narcissist had finally regained consciousness since her fall from the dizzying highs of the magician's pseudo-pagan mindfuck and was keen to exercise authority over the teenage elements.

"Oh, I'm not straight," Honeysuckle swiftly informed her.

Some of us lacked Serena's obsession with knowledge and the truth, and actually preferred it in the dark.

"Great, now I can see your ugly, whore *face*," snapped Alicia at Honeysuckle. She had been trying for years to ward off the vultures with her aura of hostility, so it was not particularly helpful to share an identity with a girl who portrayed herself as a vulnerable baby doll.

"Now I can see the girl who's been driving everyone away and ruining my life," moaned Honeysuckle. She had been desperately attempting to find someone who would cherish her forever, and it had been an ugly inconvenience to share an identity with a malignant sociopath.

"Please stop bickering, children," sighed Estella, somehow managing to seriously look down upon them even though she was only slightly taller.

Not responding to authority particularly well, Alicia's first reaction was to stomp over to Estella in order to punch her in the face. However, she only managed two steps in her direction before the arrogant one lazily swiped a hand towards her and she was thrown to the ground by an invisible force. The sound of vicious laughter accompanied the sight of Alicia flying backwards to land in the dirt.

Estella was another candidate for leadership.

"Idiotic little thugs like you eventually end up in prison, my dear," she informed Alicia. "While your indignant fury at the world is completely understandable, you need to find more intelligent ways to express it."

Alicia picked herself up, brushed the dust off her heavy clothing, and glared uselessly at this infuriating ego. As if this one's condescension was not enough, Morgana, our third candidate for leadership, was now gliding over on her cloud of judgement.

"All the bitterness and hatred that cuts you up inside could disappear completely, if you simply learn how to forgive," the kind one informed her, smiling benignly, with the glow from her aura still softly visible under the floodlit glare.

This piece of wisdom prompted Estella to pull an ironic, straight expression for approximately two seconds before bursting into her most hysterically venomous fit of laughter yet, pointing at her hippy twin and clutching her aching sides.

Alicia was also unconvinced. "Yes, thank you, *Jesus*," she responded, glaring at Morgana before giving Estella a grudging smile.

Morgana and Estella then began a debate over whether we should walk patiently down the path of forgiveness or drive a war machine down the road of revenge, while the teenagers just stared at them, feeling confused.

Even though Estella came from Alicia's hate and Morgana came from Honeysuckle's love, like when a fallen woman sees the light and puts her promiscuous days behind her, in many ways, they both had more in common with their opposite teen. Both Honeysuckle and Estella were endothermic, self-absorbed and self-serving, although Honeysuckle's selfishness came from insecurity and a constant hollow hunger, whereas Estella's came instead from a fabulously emancipated egotism. Morgana and Alicia were both exothermic, eternally radiating outwards, and each high on her own particular brand of morality. However, Alicia's anger came from an injured notion of injustice, while Morgana's kindness and decency towards others came from empathy and a calm sense of ethical obligation.

The arguing continued unabated while the children, Clairey and Katie, played in the bloody dirt at their feet. Katie had some grim memories to share with us all, but nobody had any time to listen. Clairey built a morbid sandcastle out of muck and fragments of bone.

"Hooray!" she yelled, having completed another turret. Her eyes were clouded over, which meant she was probably skipping around somewhere in reality, annoying everybody nearby.

Serena was doing some building of her own. Her underlings had wandered lost and deranged in a wilderness for far too long, and it was time to create some suitable accommodation for us all, so she used her thoughts to morph the barren materials around her into a construction we could reside in. If she was going to spend so much time trapped inside the mindscape, she may as well make it a pleasant place to live. In the new home in our head, every wall would have a television that could play the Reality Show, and we would all have our own bedroom. Serena, Estella and Morgana would get the fancy suites on the highest floor.

When the three candidates for leadership first made their presence felt to the subordinates, they existed almost entirely as cognitive entities, living within the brain and struggling to connect to the physical vessel. This was the main difference between themselves and the teenagers, who could exist very much within the body and often had difficulty in thinking clearly due to the physicality of their nature.

Honeysuckle was all hormones and nerve endings, all sensation rather than strength. The heightened sensory experience of her amplified nervous system could certainly make life interesting, but also made her vulnerable, needy and weak, and too much of a liability to be allowed out of the house unsupervised.

Alicia existed on the physical level as her twin's polar opposite, all of the strength and none of the sensation, less of a slow melt and more of an unhinged explosion. Struggling to contain her resentment, she seethed with an adrenaline surge that raged like a bad amphetamine trip, tensing the muscles, numbing the skin and corroding all reason.

Neither of the teenagers was actually stupid, but they both behaved as though they were mentally deficient, due to an unfortunate lack of self-control. They did get away with a great deal though, because while a grown woman who behaves like a teenager can be a tedious train wreck, she may merely appear insecure and immature rather than downright insane. The child alters, however, were a completely different problem. Clairey and Katie were still only four years old, and expressed themselves accordingly in terms of voice, mannerisms and conversational content, making them a weird embarrassment on social occasions and at the office.

Maintaining full time employment became increasingly difficult. We attended fortnightly therapy sessions where Katie recalled a childhood spent riding a tricycle of shame through a playground of disaster. It was all very moving. We had to change the time of these sessions so they occurred after work rather than during our lunch breaks, after Honeysuckle started to cut herself in the workplace following some particularly repugnant flashbacks. Kathy was horrified on one occasion to find herself in a toilet cubicle with her arm sliced open and the word "Daddy" written on the floor in blood. She had a great deal of cleaning up to do. This ridiculous blood-writing really was the dumbest method of communication. Maybe for our next trick we could write "Aunty Gladys" on the wall in our own tears, or "Uncle Cedric" in vomit on the ceiling.

"Most of my clients are signed off work while they go through this process," said Therapist #4 when we told her about our difficulties in employment. We had been hired to type letters and arrange business trips, not to bleed everywhere like a damaged teen cliché. It was not as though we had included self-injury on our résumé. So far, we had managed to be relatively secretive about this ludicrous behaviour, but the mask was slipping and our instability was beginning to show. The three adult personalities found it nearly impossible to control their subordinates while simultaneously carrying out their administrative duties.

Our therapist helped us to fill in the forms, and we

ended up on benefits for the first time. Girlfriend #2 was unimpressed, as she had been a child abuse victim herself and yet she had always worked hard, so she did not think there was any excuse for our laziness. She started spending all her free time with her work colleague, the one who had previously found her lying in the pseudo-murder scene. This was fair enough. Our recent behaviour had been less like Girlfriend of the Year and more like Attention Seeking Psycho of the Year. She eventually terminated our relationship on account of us being completely self-absorbed. "I do everything for you," she said, "but you never think of anybody other than yourself."

Honeysuckle turned to her sisters in the mindscape. "Are we really that self-absorbed?" she asked us.

"I don't know, lets discuss it amongst ourselves until we figure it out, shall we?" replied Estella.

Not registering the sarcasm, Honeysuckle spent some time considering the matter. Unable to reach a conclusion, she asked her therapist about it at her next appointment.

Her response was sympathetic but interesting.

"Child abuse victims often do grow up to be incredibly self-absorbed. When you're a child, adults are so much bigger and more powerful than you, and you get accused of controlling their behaviour. 'This is your fault.' 'You're making me do this.' To be told that you have that kind of power, to make someone so much bigger than yourself do something, it's hard not to grow up thinking that the world revolves around you."

Reassured that our fixation was perfectly acceptable, we moved our fascinating selves into Home #8, while Girlfriend #2 replaced us with her work colleague.

Home #8 was a hostel for young homeless people. We had tried to get into this kind of supported accommodation before, when we were semi-vagrant after the magician had destroyed us, but it was only available to people on benefits and we had not wanted to quit our degree, our education being the only thing that sustained us. Now, it felt like we had nothing left to lose.

Everyone there was allocated their own room, there was a rota to get everyone involved with housework, and they did activities with us, such as teaching us how to cook for ourselves so we might one day function as independent adults. It was fantastic that such an establishment existed to help young people rebuild their lives.

"Do you want to come round our mate's house and smoke some crack?" one of our new co-inhabitants inquired.

This was Morgana's fault for wanting us to make friends there. She had insisted on not being prejudiced towards the other residents just because they wore sportswear and gold jewellery, and on talking to them the exact same way in which she had spoken to her peers at university. To her condescending surprise, they were mostly friendly and capable of intelligent conversation, so she had been right not to disregard them. To be fair though, they had been genuinely shocked to discover that people who dressed the way she did and listened to her sort of music did not worship Satan, and they had initially thought she was joking when she told them that such practice was actually incredibly rare within her subculture, so they had clearly held a few false assumptions of their own. It was sweet of them to make her feel included by inviting her to hang out with them at the crack den.

However, she had other plans.

Our previous housemates from Home #6 were, bizarrely, still speaking to us. Perhaps there was something vaguely likeable about us when we weren't being a suicidal whirlwind of booze-drenched destruction. Having heard about our recent break-up, they invited us out to a club night, followed by an after-party at our previous abode. They had become part of the Scene. By this, we are referring to a real life social network of people who dress alike, have amazing parties and go to clubs where they all know everybody. The group came complete with its own obese pill dealer and cross-dressing coke dealer.

A door now opened for Honeysuckle into a world she had always wanted to be part of: a land of cool hedonism and drug fuelled popularity. We really should have waited until we were fully integrated and living as a productive member of society before allowing her to partake in this lifestyle, but the girl was impatient and looking for a temporary solution to the misery of flashbacks and a quick fix for her depressive issues.

Some people get into recreational drug use and then lose everything.

"I lost my job, then my wife, then my home, all due to drugs," some unkempt failure might whinge on a bleak documentary.

Well, we had already lost our job, our wife and our home, so we thought, "what the hell!" If your life's going to fall apart until you end up in a home for drug addled delinquents, then you may as well have some fun and take some stimulants while you're there. You've done the time, so do the crime. It appeared to Honeysuckle that two life paths lay before her... speed with Goths or crack with chavs. She thought the Goths had better outfits, so she went with them.

Not knowing about our recent move to the party lifestyle, our therapist believed it was an appropriate time for us to gradually reduce the dosage of our anti-psychotic medication, with a view to becoming completely free from it within a couple of months. Those tablets were interfering with therapeutic work, making us overweight, and failing to make the cameras go away.

"You don't have a psychotic illness. Those nocturnal hallucinations you experience are the result of repressed memories coming to the surface, and your constant sense of being watched is probably also a result of the abuse," she explained.

There is a certain feeling of humiliated powerlessness that can come from having your privacy severely violated. If you experience that feeling at a very young age, it may never leave you, and could remain with you every waking moment for the rest of your life. There are various ways of learning to deal with this. Some of them include being an exhibitionist, turning to spiritual belief systems, becoming a purely analytical entity that's emotionally dead, being absorbed by narcissism, or wanting to set fire to everything.

The chemicals helped us deal with the cameras by turning our weekends into a movie... a delirious, narcotic comedy with a pounding techno soundtrack.

Never wishing to be idle before our viewers, we spent our weekdays playing the role of misunderstood writer and visual artist, painting a witch burning at stake and a fairy with no mouth, and writing our misery memoirs. The flashbacks would no longer hurt us once we had turned them into a story. The awful revelations of those terrifying days were going to be the main focus of our true life survival tale. They would be our redemption and they would excuse all behaviour that later followed by highlighting the pain we were suffering deep inside.

We were to later change our minds about all this, after realising that this particular book had already been written several times before, often by people who had suffered a great deal more than us. Also, we lost the urge to defend our behaviour when we stopped caring what people thought. If people ever thought we were a self-absorbed, drug addled loser, it's probably because that's what we were. We'll explain how we got to this point in our lives because people always ask us about the influences behind our work and this leads to a more complicated tale than a few sentences that mutter fraudulent crap about society, but nobody is trying to defend themselves here.

Seriously, we're a big box of bastards.

CHAPTER 18

(Acidic Smiling Hides My Fears)

Here began a toxic era of doing ourselves zero favours and turning our life into a continuous exercise in foot-shooting. It was simultaneously both the best time and the worst time of our foolish existence so far. In many ways this synthetic mode of survival was just what we had always wanted, which wasn't necessarily a positive thing, seeing as some of us were known to hopelessly crave our own annihilation. Throughout these dizzying days, Honeysuckle was on a constant mission to turn the mindscape into a noxious discotheque, dancing around with the monsters and sprinkling glitter onto open wounds.

We hooked up with the abrasive speed freak who was Girlfriend #3 because she was the first woman to show an interest in us since the break-up. Honeysuckle thought we had spent far too long being obsessed with finding "the one" and not enough time having fun, and to begin with, she was the only one of us who really took part in that particular "relationship".

"I do care about Honeysuckle's new girlfriend, but I don't think we're compatible enough to have a future together," explained Morgana.

"We think she's scary, the way she gets so angry with people," said the children, who were disturbed by her frequent, aggressive outbursts.

"She doesn't interest me at all," said Serena.

Girlfriend #3 was frequently offended by the intellectual snobbishness that she perceived within

Serena.

"I often feel like you look down on me," she complained.

It was all we could do to stop Estella from replying, with a smirk, "Well, what do you expect when you're five foot two?"

Honeysuckle decided to override the snooty condescension of her boring elders and externalise as much as possible to savour her new life of self-medicated lesbianism. She decided that our wretched past had made us repressed and miserable for far too long, and now we should move on by doing whatever we wanted with our lives and not letting childhood trauma hold us back. Basically, she wanted to lose herself within the role of shallow whore. The best thing was, Girlfriend #3 was interested in making a film with her, and this made her ecstatic.

"So you were abused as a child?" a snide Alicia asked her twin. "Tell me more about how taking drugs and making amateur pornography is an intelligent way to deal with that."

Honeysuckle snorted up another powdered line in exasperation because her defensive sister would never understand her. "You're too quick to blame my behaviour on madness and abuse sometimes," she said. "Childhood's over, and I wasn't even around when it happened. I should be allowed to do what I want as an adult, and maybe I want to have fun. Is that so bad? Some girls are just like me anyway, and they're not even 'disturbed', they behave like this because they want to. Some people actually enjoy life, you know."

Unconvinced by her bravado, Morgana could not help but worry about her fragile subordinate. She would never despise Honeysuckle the way Alicia did, because she was not capable of such negative sentiment, but she was concerned that our eager starlet only behaved in such an uninhibited way due to an underlying lack of self-regard. "I don't think you'd still want to act like this if you truly respected yourself," she told her.

"Morgana doesn't approve of me being a whore," remarked Honeysuckle. "She's one of those emotional types who believe in *making love*."

Alicia laughed. If there was anyone she detested more than her sluttish twin, it was Morgana, for being a damn hippy. "*Making love?*" she asked, in mock confusion. "What's that? Shagging, but with slow music and candles?? It sounds shit."

Over the next two weeks, our wannabe porn star and her delightfully degenerate companion staggered around being publicly affectionate, poisoned and poisonous. "Aw, look at you two," a friend of ours commented on one occasion as the ludicrous lovers curled up in each other's scarred arms in the middle of a narcotic house party. "You look just like a fairy tale."

Honeysuckle giggled flirtatiously. "A fairy tale about lesbians on speed?" she smilingly inquired.

The gathered crowd joined in with her laughter, impressed by one of her few additions to the general conversation. Considering she was supposed to be a social entity, she was often disappointingly withdrawn when it came to speaking, habitually spending most of her time talking to the other presences in her skull without realising.

"Our life *is* a bit like a tragic fairy tale," she said in her head, "we're so exquisitely broken into crystalline pieces."

"Yeah," replied Alicia, "like a cross between Cinderella and Humpty fucking Dumpty."

Alicia's occasionally acerbic humour may have appealed to our new social group more than her twin's subdued, coquettish drivel, but we remained in the habit of holding her back. At this stage in her development, she was still more likely to make a death threat than say a decent one-liner, and girls who threaten to set fire to people are often better off restrained.

Unfortunately, our attempts at holding back the now infuriatingly hyper Clairey were proving almost impossible. It seemed that every other word we came out with was, "hooraaay!!" She had spent about four years randomly yelling, "Yaaayy!!" before upgrading her choice of irritating catchphrase to this slightly longer utterance. She still sounded ridiculous, but perhaps she was making some progress by adding that extra syllable, and maybe her exclamatory evolution would continue in this direction, with her joyous outbursts lengthening in gradual increments.

"Yaaayy!"

"Hooraay!"

"Chardonnaaay!"

"Ash Wednesdaaay!"

"Memorial Daaay!"

"It's my way, or the sociopathic crackwhore waaay!"

To be honest, we yearned for a day when she would either a) become mentally older than four years old; or b) fuck off. The good news was, the teenagers' newfound awareness of each other was helping them to slightly grow up. Honeysuckle had now reached the age of consent, which was just as well. She still wasn't an acceptable age to be making pornography, but that didn't matter, because our physical vessel was plenty old enough, and getting more haggard with each wasted weekend.

It was just a typical after-party that we brought our camcorder to. We were trying to amplify our lifestyle, which meant that Alicia was exploding like a song, Honeysuckle was bleeding like a poem and Serena was recording everything but playing nothing back. We were surrounded by people with undercuts, dread falls, corsets and giant boots. Our poverty prevented us from having the best hairstyle or the correct waist-constricting garments, but we had managed the oversized footwear and a suitable lack of sobriety. Any unlucky fashion choices we had made would be irrelevant in our film anyway, because we would be naked.

"Shall we get some footage now?" Honeysuckle asked her girlfriend.

"Yeah, come on then," the uninhibited girl replied, before sniffing loudly, a habit she had acquired due to a constant need to unclog powder-filled sinuses.

You have already had the film described to you in painful detail, so you don't need much further information about what happened next; if you are unsure, just re-read the third chapter. The precocious actress of our fractured system will never be on page three of a tabloid newspaper, but we have devoted chapter three of our supposed work of literature to some of her sexual antics, and this should keep her vaguely satisfied until she gets her next fix of drug, orgasm, pain or attention.

The only things we have not already mentioned are the out-takes. Pornographic out-takes can be acutely embarrassing, mostly because of the nudity. For example, try picturing the following two scenarios...

In scenario one, somebody is walking down the street, they trip over something and fall flat on their face. This is mildly amusing, providing they don't crack their head open and die or anything, in which case it would be fucking hilarious. Anyway, the point we're making is, now imagine that exact same pedestrian accident, only this time, the person who falls over is stark bollock naked. It's loads funnier isn't it? And presumably a great deal more embarrassing for the person involved. It seriously sucks to be them.

One of the Honeysuckle Blue out-takes involved Girlfriend #3 getting carried away while writhing from an orgasm and nearly falling out of the tub, arms flailing in a comedy manner. Another out-take happened right at the beginning, when we first switched the shower on and could not get the correct temperature, doing a daft little leap out of the way when the water scolded.

"We'll edit this bit out," said Honeysuckle, gravely.

What we clearly needed at this point was for the plumber to arrive. He would have a dodgy looking moustache and say something like, "Hey ladies, I've come to fix the shower," before proceeding to check out our internal plumbing. Classy times.

Being far too wrecked to competently operate something so complicated as a shower, it was a shamefully long time before we managed to obtain any footage worth keeping. Not that any of it in the end was particularly worth keeping. Afterwards, we felt a bit stupid and couldn't work out what we were supposed to have achieved with this pointless exhibitionism.

Two girls, one existential crisis.

To say we had an unstable sense of identity would be

an understatement. For a while, there was a great deal of disagreement between Honeysuckle and Estella in particular, regarding who Carlie Martece was supposed to be, and how she should behave and present herself to others. Honeysuckle never quite understood Estella. They were both completely self-absorbed, but while Honeysuckle always needed approval in the same way that most people need oxygen, Estella preferred to hold herself aloof, disdainful and untouchable.

"You get a lot of women like that," remarked Honeysuckle. "They like to do that whole 'unattainable' thing. What I don't understand is, why be unattainable all the time, when getting attained is such fun? After a while a girl just needs a damn good attaining. I'm sure we can let Estella flounce around being 'unattainable' for a while, but soon, I'm gonna be like, 'I'm bored, attain me.'"

Estella rolled her eyes.

"Yes, thank you for that, Honeysuckle."

Honeysuckle grinned.

"You're welcome."

As our fortnightly therapy sessions continued, despite the constant battering that her psychological power was taking, Serena still managed to construct some rather impressive accommodation for us all in the mindscape. She'd had her own library for years. It had now been seriously expanded and surrounded by a variety of bedrooms and living areas, all under one mentally fabricated roof. Who cares if you live in a hostel for delinquent failures in real life, when the house in your head is fabulously decorated and lit up by the power of a glorious imagination? Serena was working hard at gathering us all together. Unfortunately, this task was often hindered by the fact that we all despised each other.

Honeysuckle was especially disliked, for bringing shame upon us all. "I always step forward to deal with those ubiquitous hidden cameras so that you never have to," she berated us, "and now you complain that I adore attention. Slightly hypocritical, don't you think?"

Estella laughed derisively. "I just can't help but notice that you've gone from being what the women's magazines told you to be, to being what the lads' magazines think you should be," she observed. "I wonder if you're actually attracted to anyone at all, or if you just want to be wanted. Will you still be gay when it's no longer 'fashionable'? When the cameras are on but nobody's watching?"

"We'll just have to see, won't we?" replied Honeysuckle.

"Yes, my dear," said Estella, "we'll all see, before we change the channel."

Honeysuckle merely rolled her eyes and started reapplying her lip gloss.

"My twin has a spectacularly weak grip on reality," explained Alicia.

"Reality is for people who can't handle their delusions," retorted Honeysuckle.

Estella watched the precocious one's preening as though it was some sort of circus act. "How very 'deep'," she commented, with an ironic smile.

Serena was hoping to eventually bring about fusion on the adult level, with Estella, Morgana and herself gradually merging into one higher-functioning entity. One of the main problems with this was the morality divide between her grandiloquent sisters, with Morgana being smugly moral and Estella being coldly immoral, while she herself was amoral and purely logical. Also, the raging ego of Estella meant that she soon declared herself to be the spokeswoman for the attempted hybrid.

"I am a tri-partite being," she said, "like God."

Although the teenagers behaved like a tempestuous mess, they were in many ways saner than the weird women above them. Perhaps the lunatics had taken over the asylum. Even Alicia thought that Estella was completely mental, which was admittedly quite hypocritical coming from a girl who dreamt of paraffin-fuelled revenge upon the world. "Estella doesn't half talk out of her arse sometimes," she commented, apparently referring to her regal sister's delusions of grandeur.

"Well," said Honeysuckle, "I guess, if people didn't keep kissing it, it wouldn't think it was a mouth."

She then smiled prettily and snorted up another line of white powder. With Honeysuckle and Alicia, everything got demoted to the lowest common denominators, sex, drugs and violence, unlike our three leaders, who considered themselves far more cerebral, being uncommonly detached from most physical impulses.

"I'm like a brain in a jar," explained Estella. "What can I say?" she asked, looking down upon our well-presented physical vessel. "It's a nice jar."

This is when Honeysuckle whispered in Alicia's ear, "I want to make a joke now about someone putting their fingers in the jar, but I'm not sure she'd appreciate it."

It was a shame the teenagers never learnt to work together sooner. Maybe they could have combined their interests by making a sex tape with somebody who was on fire.

Our blue romance with Girlfriend #3 fell apart extremely quickly, to absolutely nobody's surprise. We could have blamed our lack of personal compatibility, the fact that all we had in common were psychiatric issues and a vague interest in making digitally filmed lesbianism, or the fact that we were constantly consuming a corrosive, white powder that filled us both with animosity. Instead, we blamed Satan.

Vulnerable young women have been enduring demonic possession experiences for centuries. We're not special. We had come to realise that we were not exactly his first victim, and so it didn't surprise us to meet someone else who had spent terrifying nights battling for her soul. What did surprise us was what a whiny bitch she was about the whole thing.

We were in her home, which was a typical student dwelling that she shared with trendy young people who took cocaine and studied things like events management and media studies. She wasn't a student herself. Like us, she was generally bewildered and had ended up somewhere she didn't understand, by accident. In common with most houses in this particular postcode, the residence had once been a large family home, until it had fallen into disrepair and was turned into overpriced and under-maintained rental accommodation for people who didn't have proper employment. These places generally came with mouldy bathrooms, faulty boilers and metal grills on the window so that nobody could steal your stereo. This particular abode also came with added Antichrist.

"He's crushing me! He's crushing me!" our partner cried, woken up in the early hours of the morning by his suffocating advances.

Morgana reached over to hold her safely in her arms. "You need to align yourself with forces that are stronger than him, and then he can't destroy you," she told her.

"She can't fight him, because she's weak," laughed Estella in our head, disgusted by the girl's desperation to be helped.

"I can't breathe..." our besieged girlfriend moaned.

Morgana surrounded the bed with a positive energy force field, preventing the abominable spirit from doing anything but hover above us in the damp air. All that the hysterical girl beside us needed to do was have faith in the benevolence of creation, and his power would be diminished, but she refused to even attempt any spiritual resistance to the horror of his presence. Our good witch spent all evening battling against his malicious psychic energy, while simultaneously comforting our wounded partner. It was incredibly draining.

When morning finally arrived, Girlfriend #3 was shaken from her ordeal, but determined to better defend herself in future. "These sacred energy crystals will stop him coming back," she informed us, placing the semi-precious stones at five strategic points around the room and then drawing a pentagram on the floor in salt.

Other ways to fight the sinister occult include wrapping the furniture in tinfoil and painting a crucifix on the floor in chutney, or wrapping your body in clingfilm and painting a Star of David on your forehead in jam.

That'll show Satan.

After this incident, we didn't want to stay at her place anymore. However, after about a week, Honeysuckle was bored, wanted to have sex again, and thought it might be worth putting up with Lucifer to get laid.

"Can I come over?" she asked her girlfriend via text message.

"Yeah. I'm not well though," was the unenthusiastic reply.

"I'll cheer you up," replied Honeysuckle.

She walked all the way across town due to our ongoing fear of public transport, only to get there and find Girlfriend #3 collapsed on the bed with the words, "help me", written in blood on the mirror beside her. This was not the easy lay she was looking for. If Honeysuckle had cut herself right then, she would have bled disappointment.

"This is not a turn on," thought Honeysuckle.

"This is basically *us* last year," thought Alicia.

"The poor girl," thought Morgana, gently helping her up. She cleaned her wounds, brought her a soft drink, listened to her woes and then stayed the night in order to assist her in fighting that pesky demonic entity.

After a couple of weeks, the only thing stopping us from leaving her was Morgana's compassion. This was spectacularly pushed past its limits when our troubled partner turned up at the pub one evening and mumbled something incoherent before staggering off, leaving a folded piece of paper on the table that turned out to be a suicide note. It said that she had taken an overdose and she was sorry. The group's transvestite coke dealer ran after her to take her to the hospital. She didn't die, but she had blown everything with Morgana, who couldn't cope with being a suicide widow again after what happened with the magician, and decided to end things with her as tactfully as possible once she was out of hospital. There was very little fallout to the break-up other than some thrown furniture.

Single again, Honeysuckle continued the party lifestyle, but also returned to her previous hobby of writing poetry about her feelings. "Hate is the fuel in your veins. Love is the gun to your head. Hands reach out for redemption. Eyes devour the room. Brains are rearranged in a deranged mockery," she said to herself. Sometimes these things were accidently said out loud. How embarrassing.

"What did you just say?" one of the gang asked her.

"Hooraaay!" replied Clairey.

Everyone repeated Clairey's catchphrase sarcastically, while laughing at her. Honeysuckle retreated to continue her poetic dementia within the safety of her skull.

"The smiling face of suicide. A worthlessness that's advertised. A conscience drenched in cyanide. Join me to be crucified."

We were still very much an outsider within our social group, but thanks to the occasional charm exhibited by Honeysuckle and the sporadic wit displayed by Alicia on occasions when neither of them was being overly emotional, there was usually somebody paying us attention. At one party, a lady whose corseted breasts had been made into a fleshy shelf invited us to lean back against her while she gave us a shoulder massage. This is when two socially inept boys who didn't talk to many women decided to each massage one of our feet.

Honeysuckle leant back and relaxed.

"Are you alright there, Carlie?" a friend asked her.

"Well," replied Honeysuckle, "I've got three people massaging me, I've got my head between some tits, and I'm on ecstasy... Do you know what..? I'm OK."

CHAPTER 19

(A Corpse amongst the Poison Flowers)

That stinging splash of reality rarely had the decency to wait until Tuesday afternoon, preferring to greet us like a knife to the throat midway through Sunday morning. A choking gloom descended until nothing was bright and shiny any more. We had escaped into a chemical mediocrity, wiring our lives away for fleeting moments of bandaged delusion, trying to pretend that we would never die.

The fact is, however, that we are all mortal, and no frequently repeated in-joke, no nihilistic subversion, no hilarious photo sequence, no meticulously-orchestrated chemical holiday, no snide one-liner and no alternative designer club wear ensemble was ever going to make things otherwise. The toxic aftermath usually saw us trapped in the mindscape, being spectacularly mean to each other and throwing vicious home truths into each other's loathsome faces.

Clairey was an irritating abomination, and Alicia had taken to hitting her on the head both in and out of reality whenever she yelled her annoying catchphrase.

Katie kept crying over abuse that happened over twenty years ago, as if there had not been plenty of time to move on, and as if anybody actually cared.

Alicia was just a frightened little girl. The belief that she was a super villain, psycho-killer, mass-murdering megabitch was no closer to reality than Clairey's infant, intergalactic adventure, and Honeysuckle wouldn't recognise reality if it clawed her face off. She was not a porn star, she was a fucked up, deluded mess. We edited her footage into a montage of depressive insanity, because it suddenly seemed important to portray her the way she actually is, rather than how she thinks she is. If we didn't tear down her delusions then somebody else would, and it would sound better coming from us.

We knocked Estella down from her illusory throne because her ego was an embarrassment when she had so little to be egotistical about. She possessed the kind of arrogant swagger that might look cool to the impressionable teenagers, but there was a good chance that everyone else just thought she was a dick.

Morgana was a spineless hippy. If she was so keen to live in harmony with nature, then why did she choose to artificially alter her brain chemistry with substances made in a laboratory, and why did she spend so much time in front of the damn computer? You are never going to save the world playing FreeCell on a comedown and wishing you were a tree.

Most of these observations came from Serena, who in the name of fairness asked the rest of us what we honestly thought of her. We thought she was a joke. All those fantastic grades at school, all that impressive memory work, all that power within the mindscape, and yet, in reality, she lived in a hostel for delinquent failures, could not hold down a job, and rarely stepped forward to share her supposed intelligence with the world, preferring to let a drugged up teenager or a disturbed four year old speak on her behalf. It was clearly easier to be an obvious moron than an attempted genius. It didn't matter that her life was an utter mess so long as no one expected anything from her, so she hid dumbly behind her more ludicrous aspects, refusing to take control and save us.

Our ability to concentrate had become so weak that we could no longer read, but Honeysuckle was more upset about losing her looks. During our first three months on the Scene, we lost all the weight that we'd previously gained from being on anti-psychotics, the Class A drugs reducing our appetite so severely that we lost three stone in as many months. Our breasts almost completely disappeared from taking too much ecstasy. We had quite literally pilled our tits off.

As we began to look like a haggard little girl, we started to increasingly talk, dress and behave like one. Clairey started carrying Tyler everywhere, a stuffed monkey that also functioned as a novelty rucksack. We'd owned him since we were five, which made him eighteen now and old enough to come out clubbing. We were pretty sure they let some people into the local nightclubs who were younger than him.

One time, at the pub, a drunken student was seeking attention by running around with a strap-on over his jeans. We had sat Tyler on a bar stool, where he could survey the room. Just for a laugh, the boy decided it would be fun to pretend to rape him. This was a bad move. That monkey was a great source of comfort to Katie, and Alicia had started being occasionally protective of the little ones. Serena took control of our right hand just in time, when the pint glass was a mere inch from the foolish boy's horrified face, halted mid-swing from its potentially maiming trajectory while its contents drenched his skin, his hair and his fashionable T-shirt.

Never try to dildo-rape a crazy girl's favourite stuffed monkey.

That, right there, is a rule for life.

Back at the hostel, the staff decided to fast-track us on

to independent accommodation, seeing as we were failing marginally less at life than the other inhabitants. Home #9 was the first place we'd had to ourselves, and we were initially concerned that the loneliness would drive us all insane, until we remembered that we were pretty much already crazy. Most of the time, we were actually less lonely in our flat, where we had our creative projects to keep us occupied, than we were at nightclubs and parties, where most people ignored us.

Honeysuckle was concerned about being a social outsider, but Alicia could not give a fuck. "Some people may remember the experience of being the weird kid who stood alone at the school disco because nobody understood them," she observed. "Looking around certain dingy nightclubs, it appears as though they've taken all the strange children from all the corners of all the tragic discos and put them in one room together. The grim irony is, some people end up trying their hardest to emulate the popular people they used to despise."

Alicia had once seen the alternative subculture as a place where she could belong, but now she decided to hate it as much as she hated the mainstream, and was embarrassed by her twin's eagerness to win approval.

"It's wonderful when people attempt to show how unusual they are by being completely like everyone else around them," she continued to rant, oblivious to whether anybody was listening. "There are so many women within mainstream culture who paint their faces orange, bleach their hair blond, get crushes on footballers and only wear bland, pastel coloured clothing. They parade in floral prints like botanical clones around shops and offices, indistinguishable from each other as they discuss soap operas and swap diet tips. Luckily, there's also the so-called 'alternative' option of painting your face white, dying your hair midnight ebony, getting a crush on a rock star and only wearing black, for those misunderstood creatures who need to show the world they're *different*."

Honeysuckle despaired of her insufferable sister.

"Thank you for your 'insight'," she eventually replied, "and I'm so sorry for trying to fit in. Perhaps I should be more like you, with your bitter, cynical misanthropy, which makes you oh-so unique in this subculture."

The bitch had a point.

CHAPTER 20

(Their Ancient Misery Draws My Tears)

We brought Alicia to a gothic festival, but she was far too full of hatred to appreciate it. "There doesn't seem to be much point to this festival," she sniped. "That is, unless you relish spending hundreds of pounds on an eccentric outfit just so you can stand there ignoring bands you don't care about, being bored and superior, in which case, I suppose it must be the place to be seen." Eternally disgusted with reality, she disappeared into a lurid fantasy world where it was more acceptable to stab people.

At least Tyler seemed to be enjoying himself, the hairy elitist. He was being passed around by corseted ladies, who found it hilarious to take turns getting photos of him squished against their cleavage. When not living vicariously through a stuffed monkey, Honeysuckle was fond of drinking, dancing and meeting new people. Unfortunately, the drinks were expensive, there was not much to dance to, and with her cheap outfit and insecure smile, Honeysuckle found most people unapproachable. Unnoticed by the crowd, she disappeared into the mindscape, to dance among her delusions. She was replaced in reality by Clairey, whose hyperactive friendliness sought to mask the fact that some of us were unable to breathe.

"Does anyone fancy coming for a walk?" the group's coke dealer was asking people. Most people were ignoring him because they found him creepy and his skirt clashed horribly with his T-shirt.

"I'll come for a walk," offered Clairey, with naive enthusiasm.

He gathered one more recruit while Clairey dragged Tyler away from a voluptuous embrace, then they all went outside to walk through the town. In the crisp, night air, away from sources of social anxiety, our rising panic began to subside. Clairey stared at the old buildings and costumed socialites in childlike wonder as she drifted past, walking slightly behind her friends, who were having a conversation she could not quite understand. They eventually approached a waterfront, where a mock pirate ship was decked out as a tourist attraction.

"I've always wanted to be a pirate," said the coke dealer, "I think I might steal that ship."

He then proceeded to climb over the railings, step across the gap and board the ship, while Clairey gazed on in rapt confusion.

"Aarg!" he cried, running around on the deck.

Eventually, the police came to investigate, and he was literally arrested for piracy. The only way this could have been better is if he had brought a laptop on board with a mobile internet connection, and had sat there defiantly making illegal downloads.

We switched and became Katie. These days were full of switches, and inconsistency was our only constant. Immediately before leaving our holiday accommodation, we had been Honeysuckle, hurriedly preparing for a wasted evening and trying to quickly get her stuff together because everybody was heading out to the pub and nobody wanted to wait for her. Half of her things were in a battered, old rucksack and the rest were in Tyler. The drugs were in Tyler. She had wanted some speed for the evening because she was always tired, but people had been about to leave and she didn't have time to separate an evening's supply from her stash for the week, so she had left the lot in Tyler's back and brought him out with her. It was decisions like this that made people think she was possibly less intelligent than her stuffed monkey. It was no wonder he was getting more action.

"We'll need to have a look in that bag of yours, love," the police officer said.

The drugs were in a red purse that had "Diva" written on it in sequins. The girl who was sometimes possessed by demons was now to be arrested for possession.

Katie vomited in the back of the police car. She spent the whole journey to the station telling the police officers her story; she was only four, she could not grow up because she held too many disturbing memories, there were big girls whom she did not understand because they were clever, there was Alicia, who was scary, and there was Honeysuckle, who the drugs belonged to.

"So, you're saying the drugs aren't for yourself?"

"No, I don't take drugs because I'm only four. Clairey takes them sometimes but that's because she's a magical creature. They're mostly for Honeysuckle though... she takes them all the time because she's bad."

When they arrived at the station, Katie had to fill in some forms. Wishing for official confirmation to back up her declaration of mental incompetence, they asked for her therapist's name and telephone number. Katie was too scared to divulge this information because it might get her into trouble with Therapist #4. They asked her if she wanted to call someone, but she couldn't think of anybody. They made her take out her piercing jewellery then they took Tyler away. Much to her distress, he was placed in a large, plastic evidence bag, which they proceeded to seal up in front of her.

"He can't breathe!" screamed Katie.

Slowly smiling and nodding, the police officer unzipped the bag and walked away calmly, holding the bag open until out of sight, making no sudden movements. Katie was taken to a cell where she had to strip so they could make sure her charity shop T-shirt wasn't stuffed with heroin and there was no crack cocaine in her cheap, black underwear. She was to be kept in the station overnight, pending psychiatric assessment, which would determine whether she was to be treated as a criminal or a nutcase. She was given a dress to wear that was constructed from some kind of sponge-like material that was too flimsy for a person to hang themselves with.

The next morning, Honeysuckle woke up naked under a rough woollen blanket, lying on disintegrated pieces of a sponge dress on a bench in a police cell.

This had been bound to happen eventually.

"Would you like to talk to me about drug counselling?" a nice lady asked her, peering around the half open door.

"Yes please," said Honeysuckle.

She always did like to talk about her feelings.

She told the nice lady all about it. She told her how worthless she felt, about how she was getting daily flashbacks about being sexually abused, about the domestic violence, the bullying, the homelessness, and how she turned to drugs as a temporary relief from her hideous memories. It was great to talk to such a sympathetic listener. She should have gotten arrested years ago. The counsellor left her with a kind smile and some magazines to read. She was allowed all her clothes back once it was ascertained that she would not use her purple and black stripy socks to strangle herself.

She floated contentedly out of reality, and her eyes in the mindscape became clear again while Katie's misted over.

Katie found herself back in that strange, cold cell and was petrified.

"I'll sing Katie a song to make her happy!" exclaimed Clairey in the mindscape, as she looked outside through a chunky, pastel pink television and became concerned about her long-suffering twin's agitation. Clairey liked to look after Katie now, because Clairey was good.

"That's a nice thing to do, Clairey," said Morgana with a smile.

Estella was in her room, asleep. She wanted no part in this situation, because jail was simply not convenient. Serena had retreated to her library to formulate some sort of plan. As was typical at times of turmoil, the teenagers had gone missing and could possibly be anywhere in this hallucinatory land. Honeysuckle was most likely lying drunk in a ditch somewhere waiting for her chance to externalise again so she could finish reading that magazine, and Alicia was probably off setting fire to things. Her final comments before she disappeared had been a rant about the criminal justice system.

"Great, so we get abused, grow up mental, turn to drugs to deal with it all, and this makes us criminals. I bet loads of child abuse victims end up in jail. Thanks to antiquated drug laws, they probably incarcerate more abuse victims than abusers, because of course it is far more important that we penalise those who are a danger to themselves than those who are a danger to others."

Luckily, we were not all being so negative. Morgana sat in our imaginary abode with the children on her lap, trusting in the universe to save her. Clairey sang enthusiastically to a Katie with colourless eyes. For no reason at all, there was a switch, and Clairey's eyes clouded over in the mindscape as the physical vessel burst into song in the echoing police cell.

"I have no idea how to control this situation," said Serena to herself, as she sat at her desk, staring at a glowing monitor with her head in her hands. Less control over the external environment equalled less control within her imaginary kingdom. In her present position as captured criminal, she was powerless until further notice.

She assessed the situation, and decided that nobody would be caught carrying that amount of drugs unless they were stupid, crazy, or an actual dealer. If the authorities chose the latter interpretation, it meant prison, where recovery would be next to impossible. On the other hand, they might decide that we were just a user, albeit one who was fairly brainless. This would not necessarily mean prison, but it would still be a possibility. She figured, however, that our biggest chance of avoiding incarceration lay in being found insane.

"We wouldn't even need to fake being mad," she thought. "All we would need to do is stop pretending to be sane."

An ancient misery made this place so precariously fragile that all it took was for Serena to lose psychic focus for our sanity to crumble.

Her mind made up, she backed up all files, shut down all programs, switched off her computer, took a gun out of a drawer in her desk, stared calmly out of the window and then shot herself in the head. Splattered blood and brains dripped down a nearby bookshelf while her lifeless body slumped back into the swivel chair. As plaster flaked from the ceiling to the sound of thunder, Morgana grabbed the children and ran to escape from a house that was collapsing around her. Still sleeping, Estella was crushed within the rubble as the structure disintegrated.

Standing outside the remains of her home, failing to hold onto a now freakishly hyperactive Clairey, Morgana burst into tears as one by one the floodlights were extinguished. The bloodcurdling screams of a renegade Alicia were carried to her across the wasteland by a biting wind that hacked its way over serrated rocks.

It was difficult to tell what was happening in reality because nearly all the screens had shattered. Morgana saw a flickering glow beneath fallen timbers and climbed towards it with Katie in her arms. She needed to assess the external situation and make sure Clairey was not in danger, since the manic one just ran off into the darkness with her eyes still clouded.

In the stuttering light from the rusty television, she observed the view of a small, concrete courtyard, all grey walls and jagged wire, with a slab of blue sky in the upper peripheral. The view careened around rapidly to the sound of "la la la la la", and then there was a flicker of static noise. As a clear image emerged from the electric miasma, we saw the same courtyard view, but this time it was blurred and moving painfully slowly as though seen through the eyes of one devoid of energy and will.

In the bitter chill of the cemented enclosure, Katherine hobbled in listless circles, holding her coat closed with folded arms and weeping.

"It's time to come in now," the officer at the door informed her.

She was escorted back to her cell, where as soon as the door was closed, her right hand took on a life of its own and began gouging swollen welts into the skin of her left arm.

The officer who brought her lunch was unimpressed. "What have you done that for?" he gruffly enquired.

"I didn't do it," she cried in response.

After he had walked away, shaking his head, she sat meekly on the comfortless bench, eating microwaved food from a plastic dish, with cardboard cutlery.

Switch.

Alicia screamed and threw the dish across the room. It hit the wall and bounced off, splattering gravy everywhere.

They came to investigate the noise and found Honeysuckle rocking back and forth, with hideous grazes on her arm, gravy in her hair and a look in her eyes of tortured lunacy.

"You were happy and singing earlier, why are you behaving like this now?" they asked, suspiciously.

"I need someone to help me. I can't stand being trapped in here with her. She's evil. You've got to help me," she pleaded.

"Well, you were fine earlier, weren't you? If you're not well, then we'll need the number for your therapist."

Honeysuckle agreed to provide contact details for Therapist #4. They brought her mobile phone and watched carefully as she retrieved the number, then they went to make the call. They had a more sympathetic tone when they returned.

"Your therapist told us you're not well," said the police officer. "We'll be interviewing you this afternoon. Do you want a social worker there as well as a lawyer?"

"Yes please," replied Honeysuckle.

She was eventually put on the phone to the free lawyer they were providing, who convinced her that unless there was something she had not told him, it was highly unlikely that she would go to prison, seeing as it was her first offence. He asked her not to say anything else to the police until he arrived.

In our internal headspace, the scrambled remains of Serena's bullet-stricken brain began to slowly regenerate. Our wounded leader surveyed the wreckage of all she had constructed as she hobbled over to Morgana and Katie, joining them in front of the television. Behind them, encroaching monsters could view the screen's rancid light glimmering through the shrinking hole in her head.

"What have you done?" cried Morgana, protectively clutching a now cloudy eyed Katie. She appeared exhausted, with her hair in disarray, dirt on her face, and her arms covered in claw marks.

Their view of external existence showed the inside of the police cell once more, and the physical vessel's knees under a woollen blanket. Yellow, electric radiance bathed the dull scene with sickly fear. The cell door opened and we were called to our interview.

"I wanted them to believe we were mentally unsound," explained Serena, impassively watching the screen as the predators crept closer. "I knew that without me here to house and instruct you, there was a good chance you would all go insane."

"Well," said Morgana, "the monsters nearly took Katie away, I've lost Clairey, and Estella won't wake up to help me because she thinks this entire situation is beneath her. Also, the teenagers still haven't returned.

Alicia has lashed out in reality, gouging our physical arm and throwing a plate, which is why we now have gravy in our hair. She's clearly been on a mission to wreak internal damage as well. I heard some explosions a minute ago, coming from over there."

Morgana pointed to a splintered horizon, where the orange glow of a fuelled combustion smiled through the smog of a starless nightscape. The nefarious creatures that haunted Katie had crept up so close by this point that Serena could feel their breath on the back of her blood-drenched neck. She breathed in slowly, blinked her eyes, and an artificial floodlight materialised above her to illuminate the scene, bouncing harsh rays off the ruined walls and driving the fiends back into the distant gloom.

In reality, Katie had been rocking, whispering "Demons, there's demons", as she waited to be interviewed with her lawyer and the social worker.

"It will be ok," said the lawyer.

The social worker merely glared at her, saying, "Well I was supposed to go home an hour ago, but I had to come here instead."

A voice in Katie's ear told her to tell the lady she was sorry, so she did. The police officer arrived to conduct the interview, and the voice in Katie's ear told her how to explain what happened. She told them about how she was not well, she had made a mistake and she wanted help to get better. After taking fingerprints and a DNA swab for their records, they eventually let Katie go with a referral to drug counselling. Tyler was released from his plastic wallet and returned to her. We became a cheerful Clairey, who wasn't sure which was better, regaining her freedom, or the return of her stuffed monkey.

The following evening we were taken to the ruins of

the abbey, a place where it's traditional for Goths to stand around under the moonlight wearing dark trench coats. Many of the assembled crowd had steel toe capped boots and contact lenses to give them the eyes of monsters. People like this are fazed by almost nothing. Tell them you just killed your own sister and ate her brains, they merely laugh condescendingly, because that whole sororicidal zombie trend is so last season, darling. However, if you skip around them in circles wearing a dolly dress and singing the Haribo theme tune, you just might disturb the shit out of them.

"Kids and grown-ups love it so, the happy world of Haribo," sang a hyper Clairey, who we had yet to regain control over. She was so delighted to be reunited with her best friend that she skipped around merrily, introducing him to everyone.

"This is my monkey, Tyler," she grinned. "He is eighteen years old and I'm his mummy. He used to carry drugs for me all the time, but he can't any more, since he got into some trouble with the police. He was caught with a week's supply of pills and speed. He had to go away in a police car, and I went with him. They made him spend sixteen hours in a plastic bag! Poor Tyler! I think they thought he was a dealer. I had to wait for him overnight in the cells. In the end, they let him go because they felt sorry for him because his mummy was mad."

One dark coated spectre turned to their ghostly friend and said, "Do you know, I get the horrible feeling that the story she just told is completely true."

"Of course it's true!" exclaimed Clairey. "People think I make things up because I'm mad, but what they don't realise is, all my stories are true."

CHAPTER 21

(Such Painful Harmony Comes To Something)

It was Jane who met him first, the guy who accidently became Boyfriend #4 despite a lack of even basic compatibility or mutual attraction. She was out with friends and everyone was on ecstasy even though it was the middle of the week. We all decided to head from the local pub to a busier one in town, just as the drugs were kicking in, making everything faster, shinier and more worth talking to. As soon as we arrived at the new venue, the girl with whom we'd been chatting on the walk there went running up to some guy who was stood at the bar.

"Oh my god, I can't believe it's him!" she exclaimed, before abandoning our conversation to dash off in his direction.

From her superlatively enthusiastic reaction, we thought perhaps he might be some sort of local celebrity, although he didn't look like one, he looked more like a homeless person. Straggly hair fell around the ruins of what might once have been a presentable face, and his clothes had disintegrated from having that deliberately ripped look to giving the impression he had spent the night in a hedge. Despite all this, our friend had been oddly impressed by his presence. Jane merely bought herself a drink and then began a conversation with a different acquaintance, one who was presumably less excitable when it came to vagrants.

Our friend soon came back. "That was my ex-boyfriend," she said. "I'd heard he was gay."

At least that sounded like what she was saying. The

music was gratingly loud, and it turned out that we'd totally misheard her.

Her actual words were, "I'd heard he was dead."

There was some confusion when Jane looked across the pub with her wide, druggy eyes at the strange guy stood at the bar with his friends, and asked, with a tone of genuine curiosity, "So is he?"

Oh, the hilarity. A brand new scar on our headfuck reality.

Not being dead, he was able to come back to the after-party with us later on. We saw our friend there chatting with him on the sofa. "Is he gay then?" asked Jane, drunkenly laughing.

"I'm bisexual actually," he informed us in a tone that suggested we would actually care. Jane got distracted and stumbled off as her friend regaled him with the vaguely humorous anecdote of our previous misunderstanding.

Despite this unlikely beginning, we somehow ended up going out with him. Alicia was still pretty much a lesbian at this point, so she was not particularly interested, and Honeysuckle prefers men who make an effort with their appearance, so he wasn't really her type either. However, like all expert manipulators, he pandered to our insecurities, telling Honeysuckle how pretty she was, telling Alicia how strong she was, noticing Morgana's kindness and Serena's intelligence, and worshipping Estella.

Nobody had seemed remotely attracted to us since our little piratey escapade, and Honeysuckle was feeling lonely and desperate for approval. We were besieged by daily flashbacks of sexual abuse, giving Alicia a loathsome feeling of helpless vulnerability, so it felt comforting to have someone praise her feisty strength, particularly when all the rest of us could do was resent her for all the damage she'd done in the past. Estella's dizzying ego highs, rather than being embraced and integrated within the system to balance out our insecurities, were instead an embarrassment to us all, and she needed external reassurance to help her stay up on the pedestal we kept knocking her down from. Serena was so shy that until he came along, nobody seemed to notice she was there. His main target, though, was Morgana. All she ever wanted was to be a nice person, but she was continuously plagued by guilt over the egocentricity of her twin, the depravity of Honeysuckle and the bloodlust of Alicia.

"It's amazing how after everything you've been through, you're still such a lovely person," he enthused during our first conversation together.

This was spectacularly reassuring veneration for a girl so tormented by her demons. He kept luring us into private conversations away from the banter of our social group, and so the manipulation began in secret, and his hooks were already in our head before anyone could warn us what sort of person we were dealing with.

We thought he'd told us everything.

"I've been away for a while, getting my head together," he explained, "because I didn't used to be a very nice person. I've really changed though, and I'm hoping people will give me another chance."

We figured that after everything Alicia had done, who were we to judge him? Being in a similar position of trying to sort out our messed up lives, gain control over our behaviour and find a place for ourselves on the Scene despite a spectacularly atrocious first impression, we believed there was a mutual understanding.

Lunatic plus lunatic equals romance.

What was the worst that could happen?

The change occurred gradually, with compliments turning to criticism by progressive increments as promises became threats.

He blamed his continued alienation from the popular clique for his ongoing misery. He had big plans for making a social comeback, but he first needed to change his image to a more alternative aesthetic. "I suppose I need to dye my hair black," he mused as we sat writing.

Honeysuckle started playfully pretending to pigment his hair with her ballpoint pen, saying, "I'll make you into a pretty Goth boy."

"Carlie, pen doesn't stick," he frowned, condescendingly, in a tone that suggested he was explaining something for the thousandth time, to a moron.

"That depends where you put it," responded Honeysuckle with a smile as she continued to make a nuisance of herself.

He looked at her as though he was in love.

We had decided to hold back on letting Honeysuckle sleep with him until we were sure we could trust him. This was achieved by never leaving her unsupervised in his company, a difficult feat under the effect of alcohol and narcotics, but not impossible. He kept asking us to stay over at his house. "I don't expect anything from you, I just don't like being apart from you," he lied.

"I don't know," we replied, "I get really bad insomnia. It gets worse when I'm away from home, and I won't have any of my creative projects with me to keep me occupied. I don't really like staying away from home, to be honest."

Our insomnia had genuinely been dreadful ever since

we'd stopped taking anti-psychotics at bedtime. The evenings usually saw us staying up to draw curious dreamscapes or work on the tragic autobiography that we had yet to abandon, our "true life tale of courage and survival". We were still writing down all our sad little stories of abuse and neglect so that one day everyone would know how brave we were.

"I'll stay up and talk to you," he promised.

"No you won't," we replied, laughing. "You're totally gonna pass out drunk, and I won't be able to wake you. I'll get bored."

"Look, if I fall asleep, just hit me," he said. "Seriously, just hit me until I wake up. I won't mind. I'd rather be awake and talking to you."

Honeysuckle agreed to stay over, because the attention he paid her made her feel alive. Going to his house meant taking a horribly long bus journey to one of those insular villages where the residents all vote for fascist political parties and everyone has the same face. He was staying with his mother while he saved up for a place in the city. His room was a dilapidated mess, with a broken mattress on the bed, stacks of video cassettes on the shelves, and photos of ex-girlfriends on the walls.

"I can't wait to get out of here," he said. "This place is driving me to drink."

A few seconds later, he asked, "Can I get you a beer or anything?"

She sat with him until the early hours, drinking cans of lager and making plans for the future. He had saved all the money needed for a deposit, and was soon going to sign for a place near the park, sharing with a couple of friends. The house would be our clique's new premier party location, and the gang would begin to accept him because of his crucial role as party host.

She was able to talk to him about the abuse, and he had nothing but admiration for how resilient she had been to all that life had thrown at her. Rarely breaking eye contact, he would launch upon hypnotic monologues that tapped into her brain and made her sense a unique connection, a feeling that she'd always known him. He told her that she wasn't alone anymore and he'd always be there for her.

Then he passed out.

His head was near her feet, so Honeysuckle decided to cheekily tap on his head with her toes, saying "Wake up, silly." She wanted him to be awake so he could say nice things to her again.

He suddenly sat bolt upright, flashing the burning eyes of a potential murderer from a face contorted with fury.

"If you do that one more time, I'LL CUT YOUR FUCKING FOOT OFF."

The world went cold.

"But you told me to wake you if you fell asleep," pleaded Honeysuckle, stunned. "You said I could hit you to wake you up."

"Yeah, but I didn't say KICK ME... DID I?" he roared, with the countenance of a carnivore before it goes for the jugular.

"I thought... you said you wanted to stay awake with me... you said..." Honeysuckle tried to explain as she tried not to cry, her hands shaking and her spirit breaking.

"I DIDN'T... say KICK ME... DID I???" he hollered, lurching towards her.

Honeysuckle leapt up like prey springing from a trap, dashed to the bathroom, turned the lock and cowered in a ball with her back against the door, retreating into the mindscape while tears made bitter tracks down her devastated face.

"Good call, Honeysuckle, bringing us round to the house of some psycho," seethed Alicia, completely overlooking the fact that she had also been sucked in by his supposed adulation.

It's astonishing what you can sometimes see on projected movies that fill the skies of your mind; a dream of empathy and compassion burns to the ground, a child hits her head on the table as she's knocked to the floor, a lost girl holds a knife to her throat, a muddy boot collides with a tiny stomach and mirrors break into tortured fragments.

In reality, the shell of a fractured disaster was propped with its back to the bathroom door, staring at nothing, while the mindscape was in turmoil. In the rubble of her ruined home, Serena was frantically sifting through reams of notes that had scattered on the wind, trying to ascertain the most logical way of responding to this unprecedented situation.

"We can't afford a taxi home. By my calculations it will cost approximately twenty pounds from this distance, and we only have four pounds fifty. We don't have a car. There's nobody we can call. The last bus was at half past eleven, it's now a quarter to twelve. It's too far to walk, and besides, it wouldn't be safe at this hour. We don't know anybody in this village so there's nowhere nearby that we can go," she muttered.

Her eyes raced nervously across one sheet of paper after another as she ran through all possible responses to this present crisis. There was nothing in her notes to help her. Boyfriend #4 had become Father #2, had become the demon, had become Alicia. Our Estella controls our

Alicia, but his Estella aspect clearly had no control over his Alicia aspect, and our Estella had been knocked from her pedestal, hitting her head as she fell, and was unconscious again. We could have fought fire with fire and sent our Alicia to retaliate, but we weren't sure how well she would hold up against a man who was a foot taller than her and had an equally livid ferocity burning in his eyes.

For the moment, Alicia was blaming Honeysuckle rather than him, and her hands were wrapped around her tearful twin's throat. "So you wanted a goddamn boyfriend, did you? You've done this to us. It's always been your fault. You probably wanted the abuse to happen. Didn't you?! Didn't you?!" she screamed, shaking her sister violently.

Serena paced around them in circles, smoothing out crumpled instructions written in neat handwriting, and mumbling to herself. "We can't send Honeysuckle back in there, he'll annihilate her. We can't go home, so we're stuck here in this house."

"I'll go to him," said Morgana. "He's only like that because he's upset, just like Alicia lashes out when she's upset. I forgive him."

Having volunteered to be his benevolent nurse maid, our internal mother returned to him and managed to calm him down by being caring and apologetic, so we stayed in our hideous new partnership. The awful days went past, in which she cared about his problems enough to listen sympathetically to his eternal self-pity, but unfortunately did not care enough about herself or her fellow alters to leave him. Serena wanted to get us away from him, but he had made allusions to the fact that he might kill us if that happened, and at this time she lacked the clarity of vision to see any escape route. After a while, he stopped even pretending to be a decent human being. He was always drunk, always obnoxious and always threatening, but luckily, he was not always conscious. When he passed out in his room, we would find a pen and paper and sit there writing down our personal tragedy, taking utmost care not to disturb him. These were seriously depressing times.

It was much funnier when he passed out at parties. We were with him and the party crew one time when he passed out on a plastic chair in the host's back garden. He had managed to fall asleep sitting up, just hunched over slightly, with dishevelled hair falling over his oblivious face. The gang saw the chance to have some fun with him. The thing with Boyfriend #4 was that he was trying to manipulate his way back onto the Scene, but nobody really liked him because he was an arrogant, abusive alcoholic. He would have gotten away with being an arrogant, abusive alcoholic if he had been incredibly funny, but he took his booze-drenched ego far too seriously, and so people were forced to laugh at him rather than with him. On that hazy, scorching afternoon, he had certainly picked the wrong place to pass out.

First, they tied him to his chair.

He failed to wake up and threaten to cut anyone's foot off. In fact, he failed to wake up at all, even after he was repeatedly poked with a wooden broom. This broom was eventually propped between his folded arms, with the handle resting on the grass and the bristly end near his listless hands, which kept distractedly stroking it as though he had made a new friend. Everyone was in hysterics. Just when we thought the situation could not get any funnier, some neighbouring children from the council estate walked past, and randomly started throwing vegetables at him. At one point he had cauliflower ear. By this, we mean that he had pieces of cauliflower in his ear. Our coke dealer decided that this was not good enough because he didn't have matching cauliflower pockets, and promptly set about rectifying this situation.

While all this was happening, we were mostly Jane, the shadow of Honeysuckle who lives for the chemical insanity, wandering in and out of the house, full of nervous energy and unable to find a location in which she didn't feel restless and insecure.

Jane suddenly remembered that her drugs were in her boyfriend's pocket. She never carried anything herself since she'd had all that trouble when her stuffed monkey got busted.

The crew groaned when she stumbled over to him, with everyone thinking she was going to untie him out of girlfriend loyalty.

"Erm, what is she doing?" they asked each other, when instead of untying him she reached her scrawny hand into his jeans pocket.

She pulled out bits of cauliflower, a bus ticket and a few coins before she found what she was looking for. Grinning, she triumphantly waved her prize in the air, a plastic baggy full of ecstasy, and everyone laughed as she staggered back indoors.

When he eventually woke up, she was terrified of retaliation, and hid from him for the rest of the day. Luckily all he did was glare at her like he wanted to stab her, but he managed to restrain himself as he brooded before passing out again in the downstairs bathroom. By the time he woke up again, he seemed to have forgotten his earlier experience of regaining consciousness in the garden, tied to a chair, clutching a wooden broom, and merely wanted to buy more drugs.

The next time we socialised with him was not quite so amusing. Katie decided that a party full of loud music and illegal substances would be the ideal place to unleash one of her memories about the abhorrent things that were once done to her in the bath. She had a way with timing. At least this explained why there had always been more cameras in bathrooms than anywhere else. This is when we realised that Katie was a four year old alternate personality locked inside the body of a grown woman, due to a childhood lost.

She had somehow misplaced her infancy.

How careless of her.

She should possibly try looking behind the sofa, checking all her pockets, or taking out an advertisement in the local newspaper... "Have you seen this childhood? Please call 0800 NOBODY CARES."

It will probably be in the last place she looks. It's always the way.

None of the other guests wanted to know why Katie was rocking back and forth, but Boyfriend #4 took her upstairs to a spare room and told her to stay there until she was feeling better, and not to answer the door to anyone except him because nobody else cared about her. He then returned to join the party. She kept trying to have a little nap, but every time she managed to get to sleep, he would come in to wake her up by shaking her and telling her what an awful person she was.

We spent most of the party being the tortured infant, huddled under a blanket, being frequently shaken in our sleep by something malicious. Seeing as we already spent nights like this alone in our flat, without the need to drug ourselves up or put together a co-ordinated outfit for the occasion, it might have been a better idea to have stayed at home.

Morgana dutifully returned to the village with him that evening, where he immediately wanted to take his dog for a walk. Some of us were terrified of dogs. They made Katie curl up in horror, they made Terra even more petrified than usual, and they drove Alicia into a self-protective rage. Honeysuckle disliked them because they were filthy and made her feel physically sick.

Morgana accompanied him through the dim twilight of sullen streets, listening to him patiently while he ranted about all the people who had done him wrong.

We were about to turn a corner when his dog started whimpering as though it didn't want to go that way. "We'll have to go this way instead," declared Boyfriend #4, turning to walk in a different direction.

"I heard you were supposed to be strict with them when they don't do what they're told. You could try using an authoritative tone of voice," Morgana hesitantly suggested.

He turned to her in disgust, staring down like she was the most enraging piece of dirt. "I'm not going to scare my dog!" he yelled, looming angrily over her like the shadow of a nightmare.

How foolish of her. Of course he wouldn't. Dogs are innocent, living creatures that must be protected… unlike vulnerable, mentally ill girlfriends who are more like masochistic robots and are only there to be yelled at.

Not particularly renowned for her high self-esteem, Honeysuckle was usually the main focus of his verbal abuse. It was as though he could look into her head and always knew the perfect insult to make her despise herself further. The problem was that Morgana had trustingly told him about all of us, because she was deluded enough to believe she saw some good in him and wanted him to understand us, to make an emotional connection. He now knew that Honeysuckle was supposed to be the promiscuous one. This meant that she was the one he was most furious with for the continued lack of sexual intercourse within the relationship, rather than blaming himself for behaving like an aggressive, alcoholic sociopath. He had implied on a few occasions that if she would only give him what he wanted then he wouldn't get so angry with her all the time. Of course, it's every girl's dream to be seduced by the ongoing fear of getting her head kicked in.

Alicia's anger should have been defending us, but it was pitifully misdirected. Before she became a liberal misanthrope who despised everyone equally, she used to be very much the jealous type, and he had managed to divert her hostile attention away from himself and towards his most recent ex-girlfriend, an attractive posh girl who some of us were previously attracted to, by making constant unflattering comparisons.

"That's a cheap version of the perfume she used to wear," he told her, making her embarrassed by her poverty. He also told her that this privileged young lady was still a close friend of his, and she seriously disapproved of his present choice of partner because she thought he could do much better. Easily manipulated, Alicia could not close her eyes without imagining her supposed rival on fire. Her jealousy was in fact aimed at completely the wrong target, as we later found out that he was cheating on us with a homeless seventeen year old instead.

In the penultimate fortnight of our time together, before everything crashed to its predictably horrific conclusion, he got the knife out.

"I'm gonna kill that fucking bitch!" he yelled, with eyes of murderous fury, referring to his disabled mother who was downstairs and had selfishly refused to lend him any more money.

Katie cowered on his bed, making herself as small as possible. She would have lent him money herself to calm him down, but he had already bullied eighty pounds out of her wallet in terrifying increments and she had nothing on her today.

"First, she says I owe her forty thousand from my credit card bills, when it's actually only thirty thousand, and now *this*," he fumed.

Women.

You can't live with them.

You can't even threaten them with violence for financial gain without feminists and the liberal press making a big deal about it.

Next, the damn things will be wanting to vote.

"I'm gonna teach that bitch a lesson," he declared, taking a large kitchen knife down from its illogical place on the bedroom bookshelf before storming downstairs, blazing with indignant rage at being denied any more pocket money.

Katie hunched herself up, face against her knees, frozen useless by terror. She tried to focus on her rapid breathing and the vermillion patterns behind her eyelids, to block out the scary shouts from the angry grown-ups downstairs.

She looked up with frightened eyes when he

eventually marched back into the room with a clean knife, looking very proud of himself, and drank an entire can of beer in one prolonged gulp before passing out on the bed. Katie reached for her puzzle book to keep herself occupied before bedtime because she was not yet sleepy. She soon heard a noise coming from the sleeping ogre beside her that sounded like a tap running, an incongruous bathroom sound in this messy bedroom. Turning towards his unconscious form, she stared in wide eyed horror as the damp patch on the front of his jeans spread outwards in a stinky puddle. Katie didn't like it.

"You need to wake up and have a little wash," she told him, her voice barely more than a petrified whisper. He was very smelly.

His eyes snapped open with threats of death.

"I should smack you for looking at me like that," he shouted, as he lay there covered in urine.

Seriously. How is one supposed to observe a partner who has just pissed themselves? What is the correct etiquette for this situation? Do they teach the required facial expression in finishing school? Regardless, Katie had clearly made an embarrassing faux pas in her inappropriate reaction to his accidental soilage.

Honeysuckle was just exceedingly disappointed that her life had come to this. She had wanted to be Sleeping Beauty, but had ended up being The Princess and the Pee. This was not quite the fairy tale she had in mind.

He got cleaned up and calmed down, and explained how the people he had killed when he was a drug runner came back to haunt him in his dreams. How thoughtless of them. We spent the next two weeks planning how to get away from him without him carrying out his implied threat of destroying us.

The next weekend, Honeysuckle told him that she didn't feel well enough to see anybody, so she didn't want him to come over.

"I'm coming to see you anyway," he said.

Luckily, she wasn't at home at the time.

"Why won't you answer your door?" he demanded, via a series of increasingly irate text messages.

It was also fortunate that he guessed the wrong location when he came to find her, practically kicking down the door of one friend's house while she hid in a different friend's living room.

The flashbacks from childhood became increasingly frequent. It would have been nice, while dealing with those revolting memories rising to the surface of our conscious mind, to have a sympathetic partner by our side, someone to hold our hand as we made the tempestuous journey from damaged victim to brave survivor. What we had instead was a psychologically abusive boyfriend who insulted us, threatened us with violence, and pissed the bed. Ah well, shit happens.

And evidently, so does piss.

Honeysuckle took a bath during an afternoon of particular horror because she was remembering many disturbing things that made her feel ugly and she wanted to feel clean again.

Switch.

She became Alicia, who decided that those foul memories were all Honeysuckle's fault, and decided to attack her repeatedly with the knife she had started carrying. "It's all your fault, you dumb bitch," she told her, as she stabbed her.

Switch.

Honeysuckle got out of the bath, threw the knife away, and ran to call her therapist to make an emergency appointment. "I think I need to go stay in hospital, it's not safe for me here," she cried.

"Well, I can fit you in tomorrow, and we'll talk about what's happened," said Therapist #4.

The next day was the date on which Boyfriend #4 was finally expecting a pay cheque from his new shop assistant job, which he was supposed to be using to pay back the money he had bullied out of us. The timing was horrendous, but Honeysuckle needed her money so she could buy more clothes and make-up, so when he telephoned she agreed to meet him in a public place before her appointment, so he could pay her back.

She approached his favourite drinking establishment feeling so afraid she thought she would vomit. Her memories were spinning tortured images that were beyond her control, and the sun was so bright it felt like it was trying to set fire to her.

"I'm on my way to an emergency appointment with my therapist to see whether I need to be sectioned," she told him, wishing he would care, wishing that her suffering would magically transform him into the supportive partner she so desperately craved. He responded by marching her to the nearest cash machine to make her lend him more money.

"Please don't make me do this," she begged him.

"I've got no choice," he told her, groping her, while she got the money out.

"What are you doing?" she sobbed.

"Boyfriend's privileges," he replied, with a derisive laugh.

In the therapist's office, Katie divulged yet more

shocking memories from the past, as though childhood wasn't long over and these things still even mattered. She was informed that she couldn't go to hospital because there were no beds available, but she should go home, stay sober, and stop seeing her abusive boyfriend.

We had no idea how to get away from him, but that problem was soon rectified. Having come to the conclusion that he had destroyed Honeysuckle as much as he possibly could, and yet she still had not slept with him, Boyfriend #4 decided to abandon the lost cause that was our supposed relationship. It was a crumbled wreck of a fractured girl that he split up with in his favourite beer garden.

He has since been in prison for mugging his disabled mother.

The logical reaction would have been to rejoice at being free from him, but we were all too much of a mess to celebrate. Alicia was glad he was gone, yet she still managed to divert most of her incendiary hatred towards his ex-girlfriend rather than him, her rivalry issues taking priority over her need to despise an abuser. She cheered herself up by painting a picture of the posh girl being eaten alive by demons, with spiders crawling up her body and her hair burning a merry halo around her beaming visage. Pleased to see Alicia being creative rather than destructive with her animosity, we let her get on with it.

Morgana was quietly relieved that he had gone, and the children felt safer without him in their lives. Serena had been keeping a low profile for weeks, seeming to have given up on being our genius leader and reverted to being a timid secretary. The only truly devastated aspect was Honeysuckle, who occasionally enjoyed revelling in the role of Tragic Victim #1. She still remembered their first week together. Nobody had ever been so nice to her, and she was heartbroken that such things have to end, that you can go from being somebody's obsession to being nothing, so easily. She fell around the mindscape, reciting her usual emotional poetry to anyone who would listen.

"Suffocating sweetly with a sick fallen angel, too tainted to know he torments me. The hideous mockery of a love that decayed, tripped over his pain accidently. He sleeps in his filth, cries in his beer, staggers to work, then crawls home to die, while I pray that he never forgets me," she lamented, sighing despondently.

"That's great, Honeysuckle," responded Alicia, "I'll find out where the nearest homeless shelter is, and we'll find you someone to serenade with that drivel. You might catch AIDS, but at least there'll be free soup."

CHAPTER 22

(Destructive Beauty Paints It Black)

We had always held Alicia back because we didn't want to be a horrible person. There was ever the possibility that if we allowed her to attack one of her enemies, she would be unable to stop until they were dead, breaking their knees and gouging their eyes out, leaving them crippled and blind while she doused them in petrol before laughingly throwing a match. That would just not be polite. We somehow always managed to restrain her from attacking others, directing her anger instead towards our physical vessel or nearby inanimate objects. As a result of this, many people merely saw Alicia as a source of amusement, an open wound surrounded by eggshells, someone you could torment at no risk to yourself. This is why somebody was able to kiss the girl she was on a date with, right in front of her, knowing that she wouldn't do anything in response. Everyone just laughed.

We managed to get Alicia away from the group, walking ourselves off to the ladies' room as the adrenaline rose.

The toilets were ridiculous. The two cubicles were never enough for a club full of wasted women, and they were tiny, making it really difficult to invite anyone in if you wanted to share your drugs. There was a unit opposite the cubicle doors with space to leave your drinks, two dirty sinks that were often blocked and a massive mirror that filled the wall. Alicia detested mirrors. Looking at them was like looking at

Honeysuckle, her least favourite person.

Honeysuckle's most poisonous shadow, Jane, had previously enjoyed some intoxicated times in here. Once, perched up on the sink unit, socialising with friends and clutching her ever present glass of vodka and lemonade, she watched with chemically expanded pupils while a girl she didn't know kissed everyone in the queue before trying to walk past her out of the room.

"Hey! What about me?" she demanded, hating to be left out.

"Oh, I didn't think you'd kiss me," the lesbian said, "you're really pretty."

Jane leaned forward for a conspiratorial whisper.

"I think the other girls can hear you..."

The other women in question all gradually walked off as Jane's new friend proceeded to kiss her and then started trying to have sex with her right there on the sink unit.

"We can't do it here, people will judge me," slurred Jane, suddenly pretending that she had dignity.

"Come in here with me," the lesbian said, opening a graffiti-addled door before trying to enter the nearest cubicle.

That's when Jane suddenly realised how overweight her new acquaintance was. For a few seconds she felt almost sober as she watched the girl try to fit her overfed body through the cubicle doorway, getting stuck halfway. Figuring it might not be the best idea to try and fuck someone in a cubicle they couldn't fit into, Jane jumped down from the sink unit and ran out of the room.

"Where are you going?" asked her gay friend.

"Run away! Run away!" laughed Jane, stumbling down the corridor and then shimmying onto the dance floor, lost in the moment, the melody and the narcotic smile. If you do a spectacular enough impression of the world's shallowest train wreck, then it won't matter that you're about as lovable as cancer.

Alicia felt no association with this memory. So far as she was concerned, she had been a different person then. Now, she was on her own, having just been provoked into a livid frenzy, and the familiar, blinding resentment felt like it wanted to explode out of her.

Her vision was filled by that awful mirror containing Honeysuckle's wretched face. Looking around for something to smash it with, all she could find were half empty plastic glasses and discarded scraps of tissue. She wasn't looking to mess the damn thing up; she wanted to destroy it, indulging the urge to bash something into pieces until the release could make her numb. Something metal would do it. Marching her synthetically shrunken frame into the narrow cubicle, she ripped the metal toilet roll dispenser off the wall, the screws easily tearing out of plaster whose grip was no match for her hate fuelled idiocy.

Smash.

She launched that metal shell into the reflection of Honeysuckle with the force of a sledgehammer. Intricate spiderwebs made an instant barrier between reality and that other world of sinister opposites.

Crash.

Another throw, and the jagged mesh that divided the worlds thickened like a murderous black lightning.

Bash. Flash. Other words that rhyme with hash.

This repeated assault on the reflected universe just wasn't breaking it. The cracks were getting deeper but not enough of the fragments were falling. She could still see too much of her twin's fractured face on the other side. The tissue dispenser was as hollow as a junkie's skull and lacked the mass to wreck a full oblivion.

She then saw the heavy ashtray made from thick, moulded glass, her new crystalline friend.

She'll burn so much brighter when she's covered in ash.

One furious motion, and the splintered slivers of Honeysuckle tumbled to the floor, a kaleidoscope of glinting threats and shattered promises. Alicia completely failed to notice when a falling shard gouged her shin open, dripping a strawberry rivulet down her scrawny ankle.

Her mission complete, she stormed home with hunched shoulders, tortured eyes and a heavy booted stomp on filthy concrete.

She had killed Honeysuckle. We were informed a few days later that we were now banned from the nightclub our entire social group regularly frequented. No more dizzying nights out on the shimmering dance floor. It turned out that venue owners do not approve of clientele who violently vandalise their property. Who knew?

In the mindscape, Honeysuckle lay motionless, not breathing, covered in intricate fracture lines that bled poison.

"My poor girl," sighed Morgana, cradling her head and stroking her tangled hair.

"Stop feeling sorry for yourself," snapped Alicia, "we're better off without her. We're better off without any of those facile club kids as well, we couldn't trust them anyway."

"People have often told me that I'd be better off without you, but I've always forgiven you and stood by you," Morgana responded.

"That's 'cause you're a sap," retorted the angry one.

Morgana turned the other cheek.

"We should bury her," she said. "I don't think she's coming back. She never found the fairy tale she wanted in this world, and now she has nowhere left to dance."

"Put her in a cardboard box and set fire to her," laughed Alicia.

Morgana preferred to place the deceased in a sumptuous casket, which she then lowered into the ground and covered with imaginary roses and handfuls of dusty earth that she'd cried onto. Serena didn't attend the funeral because she was too busy learning to read again. Estella was still collapsed by her crumbled pedestal, breathing but unconscious. Honeysuckle's moonlit funeral was attended by Clairey and Katie, holding Morgana's hands, looking frightened and bewildered, and her twin, Alicia who merely looked bored.

Morgana said a few words.

"This way we can keep her safe from harm, and she will always be beautiful," she sobbed.

Alicia yawned.

"Are you finished?" she asked.

With nothing but tears in response from Morgana, she continued. "Well, that was fun. Now let's go get pizza."

Back in the real world, she soon regretted her flippancy when it was time to take a bath. With cameras everywhere, nobody felt safe within the skin of the physical vessel, and we were soon overwhelmed by a near-crippling self-consciousness. We had forgotten what reality had been like without Honeysuckle's exhibitionist streak taking the edge off the constant feeling of intrusion. Alicia returned to her previous habit of tearing things apart to find those hidden devices that spied on and tormented her.

She need not have gone to the trouble. Ruining her gorgeous manicure by clawing her way up through the soil, our delirious starlet soon managed a tragic, glittering resurrection.

"You weren't supposed to bury me under the dirt," she cried, "I was supposed to have a glass coffin where I could look like a princess and be rescued by somebody who would love me forever."

Alicia seethed with furious annoyance and responded to this melodramatic wailing by punching her twin in the face, knocking her to the ground.

"You put the *suck* in Honeysuckle," she told her.

Ignoring this facetious remark, our failed princess picked herself up briskly, choking back tears, and flounced off to regenerate her broken nose and re-paint her chipped nail varnish.

The good news was, even though our mind had become full of inane, pseudo-romantic drivel once more, at least we could now wash. The bad news was that Honeysuckle had arisen from the dead more obsessed than ever with the notion of finding a partner to alleviate her heartbreaking loneliness. Unfortunately, she had no way of meeting anybody because we rarely got invited out any more, and when we did go anywhere we were such an insecure wreck of a girl.

We needed an ego.

We'd had an ego, a delicious, radiant abomination of an ego, but we had continually berated her arrogance, destroying her from within and making her fragile. Lacking internal support, she had been susceptible to the advances of predators who told her what she needed to hear, and had been prone to crashing unconscious to the ground as soon as their approval was withdrawn. We were a mess without her. When our personality got divided and compartmented, she had taken most of the confidence, surrounding it with a dissociative barrier until it became a swaggering caricature. Without her, we had gone to the other extreme, lacking even basic assertiveness, mired in self-pity and self-contempt. We clearly needed her back. For our continued social existence we would need at least some of her presence, even if it meant putting that bitch back on her pedestal.

A few months of our reality were spent drifting through life, increasingly isolated and miserable, before Alicia decided it was time to wake the arrogant one. Her mind made up, rolling her eyes, she stomped over to the collapsed form of the deranged lady who was once born from her hatred.

"Wake up, dickhead," she said, kicking her.

Estella stirred, eyelids flickering, mumbling something in her sleep about being better than other people.

"I'm going to regret this," muttered Alicia, psyching herself up until she had painfully tense muscles and eyes of fire.

Slam.

She punched Estella, hard, on the chest. There was a crackling flicker of static electricity as the energy of Alicia's rage shot adrenaline through Estella's icicle heart.

Estella's eyes snapped open to mock the world with her glorious power trip. "You should have woken me ages ago, you stupid girl," was all the thanks she gave Alicia.

"You're welcome, bitch," was Alicia's response, as she marched off in disgust.

Rising gracefully, dusting dirt from her expensive clothing, Estella summoned the presence of her soul and her brain, Morgana and Serena.

"I see that things are more of a mess than ever around here," she berated them.

"You," she said, turning to Serena, "are supposed to be the clever one. You should try exercising some authority over this place and stop letting Morgana bleed her heart everywhere while the teenagers behave like imbeciles."

"And you," she smiled, turning her vicious eyes to Morgana, "are an absolute fucking disgrace, draining me dry with your guilt to leave us defenceless, being a gullible doormat to an alcoholic scum boyfriend, failing to contain Alicia's violent tendencies despite all your talk of love and peace, while indulging Honeysuckle's suicidal melodrama with your ridiculous sympathy."

While she was speaking, the rocks behind her were rising into the air, hovering like deadly clouds around the static of her aura.

"I'll give you something to feel sorry about," she laughed.

The rocks flew at Morgana.

Morgana raised her arm in an attempt to defend herself with a force field of positive energy. She need not have bothered. With a split second before impact, Serena blinked her eyes and the world went white.

Estella and Morgana spent a few moments feeling numb and disorientated, before colour drained back into their vision, and they found themselves sat in a plain, functional room with a large screen on the wall. The screen showed a living room window that was repeatedly moving marginally closer and then further away, being transmitted live from the optical nerve in a skull that rocked back and forth. Beneath the glowing pixels of this rectangular view into a worthless reality, the three ladies were seated around a board table, with Serena at the head and her sisters sat motionless on either side. Morgana was frozen in place on Serena's right, while Estella was restrained to her left.

"Here is the authority you requested," she began, impassively regarding Estella. "While you were sleeping though situations supposedly beneath you..."

"And you," she said, turning to Morgana, "were busy indulging our ludicrous teenage aspects and our embarrassing child personas, I have been learning how to read again, gradually reducing our recreational drug intake, rebuilding our home in a more stable location and gathering my strength for the next stage of our evolution.

"We are presently situated in the new residence that I've constructed for us, complete with rooms suitable to most of our requirements. This is the central meeting room, where we shall gather in future, to make group decisions. I shall be in charge.

"Morgana, you're an excellent internal mother and greatly skilled at healing the sorrows of some of our more 'emotional' elements, but you are far too weak in the face of abuse and forgiving towards those who would destroy us. Estella, all we need is to believe in you, and you become a fantastic addition to our character, holding our head high and refusing to accept a second class existence. However, you are also dangerously close to becoming a psychopath. I can see it in your nature, and I don't like it. In order for us to have stable leadership, you two need to be placed equally, where you can debate major life choices between you, and I can make the final decisions with my more rational, balanced nature."

So this is how Serena became our overall leader, charged with keeping the peace between Morgana's wholesome goodness and Estella's egocentric narcissism, keeping us mediocre but stable.

Serena blinked her eyes, unfreezing her underlings.

"What about the teenagers?" asked Estella.

"What about the children?" asked Morgana.

"You can have the children," said Estella to Morgana, "because I, personally, cannot stand those irritating little shits. You look after them, and I'll take command of the teenagers. They would do well under my leadership. I could have far more power over them than you could ever have."

Serena gestured towards two vacant seats, and the teenagers materialised into them, slowly fading into existence, paralysed and confused. Honeysuckle, in heavy make-up and a hopeful dress, appeared in the seat next to Morgana. Alicia, hunched in dark clothing with a face full of fury, was opposite her desperate twin, in the seat by Estella.

"These two have far more physical presence than the children," Serena began, observing them as one might view insects beneath a magnifying glass.

"They have the strongest connection to the vessel that contains us," she explained, "with Honeysuckle experiencing more sensation and Alicia having more energy. The little children cannot comprehend our adult form, are incredibly vulnerable, and need to be kept internalised as much as possible. I cannot kill them off, but I believe I can keep them asleep the majority of the time.

"We understand our adult form, and find it more

fitting to our requirements than our previous, childhood vessel, but the psychology of our aspect is more suited to cerebral operation than physical function. We three lack the raw immediacy of these two. At our level, there will always be a detachment from the body, due to Morgana's supposed spirituality, Estella's imagined superiority and my lack of feeling or emotion. While we are operating within this segregated system, we need to connect to the vessel through the teenage aspects. I shall allocate you each one teenager to control.

"Even I cannot decide who externalises, and when. If I could, then all this would just be the mind of an imaginative young lady with a versatile character, rather than the symptoms of a potentially debilitating mental illness. What I can do, however, is ensure a certain amount of supervision over whoever is representing us in reality.

"Estella, you came from Alicia's hatred, and you are the only one who can effectively wield authority over her. I know that you'd also be competent at monitoring Honeysuckle's behaviour, as she blatantly holds you in high esteem, but I am wary that her neediness and your narcissism may combine to create a self-serving abomination.

"Morgana, I'm going to put you in charge of Honeysuckle. Please encourage her to respect herself, and try to refrain from overly indulging her melodrama."

Having issued her instructions, Serena blinked, and the teenage twins unfroze.

"Why am I still single?" asked Honeysuckle.

"Why are our enemies still not on fire?" asked Alicia.

Serena looked from Morgana to Estella in turn.

"As you can see," she said, "we have a great deal of

work to do."

She wasn't wrong. While a gradual process of restructuring, rebuilding and containment took place within the mindscape, in reality, we threw ourselves into our artwork, choosing the medium of collage as a means of expressing our chaotic, heterogeneous nature. Our work had always been incredibly autobiographical, so it made sense that we enjoyed the process of fitting disparate visual elements together to make one whole composition. It was all about making order out of chaos. Drawings, paintings and photographs from completely separate projects would end up on the canvas, along with toys, make-up, and various random objects that found their way into our life and called out to be immortalised in our latest twisted dreamscape.

For our first major construction, we found some pastel pink and milky white wrapping paper. It depicted a smiling, cartoon baby who held heart shaped balloons in a cutesy pram, tiled in repetition with the words, "Baby Girl", written in soft, round print. Honeysuckle said that the imagery was creepy and it reminded her of death and suffocation. She liked it. We pasted the sheet onto the top half of our canvas and then ripped bits off to leave jagged edges before searching the market and generic gift stores for more objects that resembled childhood detritus. We found a hideous colouring book, miscellaneous buttons, and cheap packets of pencils, pens and children's watercolour paints. Little Katie contributed some Lego from her toy box. Alicia offered us some matches that were left over from her most recent doll combustion, while Honeysuckle provided a handcuff key and some razorblades. The centrepiece was the severed bear's head drawing we had made from obsessive biro dashes three years previously, right after the evil boy stabbed Katie. Now it was in the middle of a fragmented fairy tale that seemed to bleed from the canvas.

We went into a trance as we assembled the composition, gazing through it rather than observing the surface, working instinctively to wrench something dazzling and deranged from our subconscious. The release brought by this visionary outlet must have made us far more resilient, because when Satan returned to possess us, Alicia literally laughed in his face.

It began with us being woken by a knock on the bedroom door. "Come in," mumbled Honeysuckle, still half asleep.

Alicia woke with a sharp jolt of piercing anxiety. Only the barest hint of orange from the streetlights shone through her paralysed eyelids. "Honeysuckle Martece, you crazy bitch," she thought. If your insane twin invites the demon in, doesn't that make you powerless? Or does that just apply to vampires?

It was the thought of vampires that made her realise the absolute ridiculousness of the situation, as though her life was some made-for-television, teenage horror film, as though there really were supernatural beings that could pass through space and time, and they had nothing better to do than pester socially awkward young women with a series of failed murder attempts.

"Oo, look at me, I'm a scary demon. I've risen from a place of fire and torment, up to this nondescript suburb, to give this mortal female a good scare by pulling her greasy hair, crushing her flat chest and throwing her around her cheaply furnished, magnolia bedroom, because that's how I roll," she laughed to herself, as her limbs contorted and her ribcage constricted.

The evil crawled into her ear again, spreading out through nerve endings, killing the sensation in one arm and half of her face, but all she could do was chuckle at the melodramatic idiocy of it all.

"There's no psychosis here, he really has come to claim our soul, we're so special," she giggled, with caustic sarcasm.

She was still laughing as the sun rose.

Our therapist thought we had made remarkable progress. Having a central meeting point within the mindscape in which to gather ourselves helped us present a far more cohesive social front, with whoever was externalising being supervised from within by our logically structured management team. The most frequent surface character was still Honeysuckle, as Alicia was generally too misanthropic for public outings, the children were usually asleep and the adults worked better behind the scenes. We were gaining a small amount of control over the switches, providing we stayed relatively sober. Honeysuckle was still yearning to meet someone who would alleviate her loneliness, but seeing as desperation is not a serious, psychiatric condition, we got discharged from therapy.

CHAPTER 23

(A Needful Hatred Steals My Hurting)

Morgana was asleep when she heard the explosion. We were in Home #10, our own sparse but adequate residence, allocated by a government sponsored, subsidised housing scheme for the economically challenged. Morgana was very liberal. She had decided not to make assumptions about our neighbours based on their clothing or lifestyle choices, because she would not wish to be judged herself. The neighbour who played his generic dance music from midnight until mid-morning on a weekday may just be unwinding after a late shift at work. The children who played with fireworks in the street were just having harmless fun, out enjoying the fresh air rather than being cooped up in front of the television, and they surely didn't mean to aim those explosives at houses, cars or people; not those innocent, laughing children. Yelling vile insults and spitting at passers-by was probably just some quaint form of greeting among people of this culture, and there was no need for us to be judgemental merely because we were unfamiliar with their customs. Our neighbours were our friends.

Alicia was not so convinced. She had always felt the need to be fiercely protective of the oppressed, generally wanting to burn people who indulged in prejudice against women, homosexuals, minority races and the impoverished. However, she did not particularly appreciate having to dodge fireworks to get to her own front door. It is hard to defend people who want to see your face explode.

Having been discharged from supported accommodation and therapy, this was where we had been sent to rebuild our life. We had been determined to make the most of it, putting our time and money into doing enough decorating to make the place habitable, and promising ourselves that as soon as we had finished this task we would look for work straight away. We were actually keen to pay our own rent and work our way towards a more comfortable existence.

Bang.

Morgana heard it as she slept, but she was in such a peaceful place, floating above this drab dimension in a place of light and colour, that she felt no need to let this loud noise alarm her. It was probably just a car backfiring or a door slamming, nothing that she was required to investigate by fully waking up. She then heard a peculiar crackling sound, like something softly rustling or scuttling, creeping into her dreams with a bizarre insistence. It got gradually louder, building to a whispering roar that no amount of meditative slumber could distract her from.

She opened her eyes to see murky fog instead of lilac plaster. All the windows had been open due to a heat wave, and now the ones to the back of the flat had bitter fumes pouring through them. The atmosphere tasted of burnt plastic, the crackle of nearby flame was becoming louder and sharper, and the ebony haze that covered the ceiling was inching ever downwards.

The children woke up, terrified, and the jolt to our system allowed Katie to externalise. "Katie's frightened!" yelled our anxious four-year-old alter, staring in horror at the dusky swirls above her.

Morgana pushed her way back to reality. "I must get them safe," she thought, leaping from the bed to save the physical vessel and its vulnerable inhabitants from danger.

Not wishing to run past flames in a nightdress with her hair loose and end up flailing around on fire like a giant, dancing candle, she allowed herself to quickly put on jeans, trainers and a T-shirt and tie her hair back. She then doused a cloth in cold water and held it over her mouth. The only way out of the building was down the stairway that led to the porch, which was where the smoke was billowing up from. She dashed down the steps as rapidly as possible, her eyes stinging and streaming from cinder particles in the air, and unlocked a front door that leaked smog from its seams.

Pulling open the door, she saw the cause of the problem. The entire porch was on fire. Without pausing to think, she unlocked the metal grill that barred the doorway, while flames flickered overhead. The grill open, she raced outside, running underneath the burning porch roof, feeling its searing heat radiate onto her scalp but emerging from the bonfire unscathed.

The neighbours had gathered round to watch.

"Are you alright?"

"Is anyone else in there?"

"Do you have any pets?"

"Yes... no... no..." replied Morgana, who then became Honeysuckle.

Having gotten dressed in a hurry, there had been no time to ask the fashionable one's opinion regarding the coordination of our outfit before leaving the house. Our T-shirt was most unflattering and really didn't go with the jeans that Morgana had chosen, plus we were wearing no make-up and our hair was in disarray. Honeysuckle burst into tears.

She needed someone to call her beautiful.

She needed someone to call the fire brigade.

Failing to resemble an attractive emergency service, she texted her new boyfriend to tell him what had happened and get some reassurance and support. His response was a text saying, "Bloody hell, how did that happen?" with no enquiry as to her state of mind and no offer to come round and look after her. She cried on the pavement in her uncoordinated clothing, feeling unloved and worthless, while the apartment she had helped decorate filled up with soot and disillusionment. To make matters worse, she had broken another fingernail.

"Don't worry, love, the fire brigade are on their way," one of the neighbours told her, offering her a glass of water. Some of them were obviously decent people. Unfortunately, there was clearly evil among them too, because after the fire fighters had arrived and drenched the flames they said the blaze looked like the work of arsonists. We became Morgana once more, who reported the matter to the local police. She wanted the perpetrators caught so she and those she cared for could live in safety.

"Do you have any idea who did it?" they asked her.

"No, I haven't fallen out with anyone around here," she told them.

"Round here, you don't need to," they said. "You should ask the council to move you somewhere else."

This was not an option. We had waited a year for this place, and nobody was in any fit state to go through the application process again, so we stayed where we were, in our home that shook with the neighbour's music, surrounded by freshly-painted walls that were stained by smoke and paranoia. We never slept. If we had woken straight up when we had first heard that bang, we would have gotten out when the fire was smaller, and there would not have been so many flames to run beneath, scorching our scalp as they licked the porch above our head. For the next few months, every time a firework was set off in the street at night we jolted into an enhanced state of consciousness, heart beating louder than the neighbour's bass lines, sucking breath into gasping lungs.

During this era of lying awake at night in fear of being burned to death, the irony of her situation was not wasted on Alicia. She had spent so long being morbidly preoccupied with fire, fixated by the thought of burning her enemies, unable to see a candle without staring at the flame in a hungry trance, and now the flames had finally found her.

She experienced that awkward moment when you realise that nothing you've ever "been through" justifies you behaving like an absolute twat. If the delinquent piece of scum who had tried to burn her alive turned out to be a mentally ill child abuse victim, it still would not justify their behaviour. Nothing would. This realisation helped her to evolve. She would always picture her enemies on fire, because she was the rage aspect of a compartmented system, and that was in her nature, but she would no longer use her past as an excuse.

"Never try to justify me to anybody," she warned the rest of us. "I don't want you to make excuses for me. If people want to think I'm dreadful and hate me, then let them. I am dreadful. They should hate me. I don't particularly like people anyway, so there's no need to whinge about our childhood in an effort to excuse my misanthropic bitterness. You never know, I could have had a picture perfect upbringing like something from an advert for mass-manufactured confectionery and still turned out to be an absolute dick."

As she aged in her solitary apartment, she finally gained a modicum of self-reflection and self-control. Despite becoming no less furious, she reached a turning point. She thought of all the property she had broken, threats she had made and people she had hurt, and decided that from this point on, she would no longer be an abusive person. It is possible to be overwhelmed with anger, and with a bit of strength of character, not make your hatred everyone else's problem.

This is when Alicia destroyed the first draft of our book. She decided that we could re-write it one day if we ever managed to acquire a less self-pitying perspective. We needed to stop picturing ourselves as such a poor victim, when we were clearly the main villain of our autobiography.

This would have been a time of remarkable personal evolution, if it were not for a certain young lady's new cocaine habit, which nearly ruined everything.

Honeysuckle got hooked on coke because it was available and she was lonely. Boyfriend #5 dumped her fairly soon into the relationship because she cried too frequently for his liking, particularly since the arson attack. Nobody else was interested in her, and unlike Alicia, she needed to be loved. Her social anxiety became almost crippling after her ex-girlfriend's butch mates started threatening her and pushing her around in one of the few nightclubs she wasn't banned from. She tried staying home and reaching out for support over the internet. Of course, nothing awful ever happened to a person who did that. Before long, she was getting abuse on account of being parasitic jobless scum, someone had anonymously sent her a painting of a bleeding girl who looked eerily like her, and there was a parody weblog mockingly impersonating her mental health difficulties in a way that was extremely personal and quite vicious. Clearly, the downside with sending out an online cry for help is that some people may just want to help you kill yourself.

As winter drew in, she just couldn't deal with it all. It was too much for her fragile ego.

Luckily, there was cocaine.

Our friendly local cross-dressing coke dealer started showing a special interest in Honeysuckle and her problems. Before long they were inseparable and everyone thought she was sleeping with him. They frequently went out drinking and dancing in the Scene's newest nightclub, and he gave her plenty of drugs, lots of advice for how to deal with her issues, and sometimes groped her by accident. A few people warned her to stay away from this man due to his reputation for destroying women, but she was very protective of her new best friend. Even after he showed her a bunch of degrading photos he'd taken of a previous girlfriend, she still thought people were lying.

Cocaine has been known to cloud judgement. Just a little bit. It made Honeysuckle the Queen of the Mindscape, flouncing around in her royal robes and battered tiara, thinking she was Estella. On one occasion, her royal highness didn't even bother knocking on Estella's door before she marched into her room of mirrors, brandishing the royal tray.

"Would you like some cocaine?" she offered,

haughtily.

Estella turned slowly away from her reflection, smiling with pity upon her little clone, replying in a languid drawl, "Honey, I *am* cocaine."

Alicia then stomped angrily in, also believing she was Estella. She was seriously backtracking on the road to recovery, seeing only glorious bonfires in the reflective surfaces that surrounded her. Having fallen in hate with the world, she was brandishing a knife to gut her enemies, but her vision was blurred by tears of paraffin as she vacantly stumbled into the nearest looking glass.

Before long, even kind-hearted Morgana began to think she was Estella, drifting blindly into a mirrored room now warped and distorted like a carnival funhouse.

"It's getting ridiculously crowded in here," sighed Estella, who didn't usually welcome guests. Luckily, her thoughts were soon distracted by a complex, cognitive analysis of society, as her mind took a chemical short cut to Serena's level. The reason this was able to happen was because Serena herself had been passed out, unconscious, for some time.

The excess of alcohol and cocaine had disabled our leader, enabling certain other aspects to jump up a level in the chain of command. Honeysuckle and Alicia acquired swaggering Estella-type egos, while the arrogant one herself artificially gained Serena's heightened cerebral powers. The problem was, the teenagers were severely mentally unstable and were not to be trusted with that amount of unrestrained psychic energy. Also, it was unhelpful for Estella to have Serena's speed of thought because she was a self-absorbed, delusional nutcase. Serena was the dependable, logical glue that held us in a state of twisted togetherness and kept us from a life of destitution and solvent abuse.

The disintegrating television screens which we were seriously ignoring depicted a train wreck reality. When Honeysuckle externalised, she didn't know whether to dance or cry. She was wearing a pretty dress, but nobody loved her. He kept paying her so much attention, then suddenly losing interest, and paying other women attention right in front of her. Inconsistent attention was sometimes worse than no attention because her lack of emotional retention meant she needed sustained attention or she would end up in a psychological detention from a lack of attention.

It was all about the attention.

"Can I have your attention please? This house will self-destruct in T minus twenty five minutes," Alicia informed us through a loudspeaker with an insanely sarcastic tone of professional assertiveness. Her eyes then misted over as she externalised to scream and strike at Honeysuckle's so-called best friend in response to his supposedly vicious mind games, before storming home to be replaced by Honeysuckle in her isolated bedroom.

Realising that she would never truly be free from her loneliness, Honeysuckle slit her wrists, pouring her misery onto the floor. She may as well self-destruct, because nobody was ever going to love her.

Realising that she would never escape from Honeysuckle's masochistic idiocy, Alicia burned down our home in the mindscape, combusting the construction that held us all together. She may as well return to the lunacy; it was easier than the vain attempt to build a life she could believe in. Yellow flames devoured our sanity, while in reality, scarlet streams stained the floorboards.

Morgana telephoned for an ambulance, got us to the

hospital, and then proceeded to feel incredibly guilty for wasting their time. Honeysuckle wanted him to bring her coat to the ward so she could go home, but by this time he was busy attending to a cocktail party at his house, where he was handing out booze that she had paid for to a bunch of people who didn't like her. Luckily, a kind friend came to rescue her from the glaring lights and prying questions before Alicia could take over and get us all sectioned.

The following day, when she stumbled to see him with her bandaged arm, weak from blood loss, she heard that he had got himself a new girlfriend and didn't want to see her any more. She dragged herself back home in pieces, to pass out in a sliced up heap on the bed, hoping she would never wake up.

CHAPTER 24

(But Hideous Love Will Bring It Back)

Serena woke up under a wounded sky. Her head hurt, her smart clothes were filthy and she was covered by fallen pieces of scorched rubble from a home gutted by lunatic fire. Honeysuckle wandered past her, tripping over charcoal timbers, dripping blood from her opened veins onto the soot beneath her feet. Just one look at her underling's blotchy complexion and scarlet hands was enough to tell Serena that another attempt had been made to terminate the life of the physical vessel.

To her right, a smashed flat-screen monitor hung from the remains of a wall. Focussing her tired brain, Serena patched it together, using weak psychic energy to fuse loose particles from the atmosphere into something constructive. A weary blink of her eyes, and the screen flickered into life.

All that could be seen of reality was an unchanging view from a window. Rays of sunlight illuminated a patch of grass and a sea of tiled rooftops as gossamer wisps floated across an azure sky. The view never changed perspective, holding steadily in place as the minutes passed by. The physical eyes were obviously unmoving, just staring vacantly, which suggested that one of the elderly ladies was currently externalising.

"Well, at least we're not dead," thought Serena, relieved that the screen showed anything at all and wasn't just running that terminated series in the sky.

Once she had gathered her strength, she glared at the rubble that covered her until it disintegrated, then stood up to survey the internal damage. Our home needed completely rebuilding. Even her central library, which was the sturdiest room in the abode, had been left with no roof and no furniture. Fortunately, the recovery files for her electronic data were secure in their metal safe, so we had not managed to make ourselves into a complete moron just yet, regardless of what our external behaviour may have suggested.

The meeting room was an ebony husk, with just ashes where there had previously been a board table. Morgana's room was empty, dripping with obsidian slime where her flowers used to be. The children lay beneath a layer of ash in the remains of their nursery, clutching at battered dolls whose eyes were missing.

Honeysuckle's room was a mess of burnt clothing, white powder and bloodstained shreds of magazines, where she sat alone, bleeding onto the bottle of vodka she clutched in her shaking hands. Her ancient shadow, Rose, rocked in the corner with her clouded eyes like cataracts.

Alicia's room was devoid of life and still reeked of petrol. She and Morgana had yet to regain consciousness after our latest chemical adventure, and their lightly toasted bodies were still collapsed in Estella's room where they had previously passed out. Estella herself was barely awake, her brain overcooked from short-circuiting her intellectual abilities with a poisonous hotwire. She frowned with disdain at the unconscious wretches before her. "This is what happens when they try to be me," she sighed.

Serena's gaze was impassive as she observed this stilted ego in her ruined room of burnt walls and cracked mirrors. "Maybe you should lead by example, and stop pretending to be me," was her reply.

The toxic heavens broke above them and started leaking a rain that corroded like battery acid. Serena hastily imagined a makeshift rooftop, regenerated her damaged skin and then retreated to what was left of her library to begin reconstruction. Two days passed in reality, in which nobody except Rose externalised. After a couple of merciful sleeps, Serena managed to patch together something resembling temporary accommodation, and finally felt ready to regroup her subordinates. She called a committee meeting of the main five, and they sat at a wonky table in their usual formation, with Serena at the head, Morgana then Honeysuckle on her right, and Estella then Alicia on her left, all perched on cardboard boxes. The minor characters of the teenagers' shadows were silently sprawled around the edges of the room. Morgana had put the children to bed in a rebuilt nursery.

Honeysuckle was still a mess. "I've been replaced again," she cried, "for someone younger than me, with a better figure, who's not as trapped as I am."

"Well, dickhead," snarled Alicia, "this is what's bound to happen when your self-esteem depends on receiving constant attention from a perverted drug pixie. What were you expecting? Did you think we were going to leave you alone with him, and you could go live happily ever after in some dilapidated crack den?"

Alicia moved to strike Honeysuckle, but Serena froze her in place with a glance.

"Being abusive towards each other isn't going to help at this point," she told her. "What we need is a logical plan to move us forward from this present position, break the destructive cycle and prevent further repetitions."

"We need to heal ourselves," said Morgana.

"Yes, quite," replied Serena, with the barest hint of an ironic smile.

"What do you suggest?" asked Estella.

"Well, I have been looking back through the memory files," explained Serena, "in an effort to establish when we were last consistently contented, in control of our behaviour and not mired in self-loathing."

She glanced at the nearest television, and the view from our bedroom window was replaced by the cheerful image of a smiling child. This was Clairey, externalised in reality when we were young, beaming with trust in the universe and pride in her intergalactic mission.

"Shall I fetch Clairey?" beamed Morgana.

"No!" yelled everyone else, simultaneously.

"Leave her sleeping," said Serena. "We do not need to irritate anybody at this point. It's just that I've discovered the last time we were truly glad to be alive, and it was when our conscious energy was mostly divided between me, with my efforts at intellectual development, and Clairey, with her alien delusion. The sad truth is that our existence has been a wreck of anxiety and self-pity ever since Clairey crash landed her space ship at the end of childhood. We needed her illusions. This system clearly wasn't built to handle reality.

"However, pathetic as that sounds, there is possibly a clue here for how to solve the puzzle of our broken brain. That intergalactic fantasy existence could obviously be seen as a symptom of a highly imaginative mind. Without this creative spark, all our artwork, which means the world to us and gives our external life a purpose, might be hollow and uninspired. We all have an above average drawing ability and an eye for composition, but an artist could have these things and still produce mediocre artwork if they were lacking in imagination. Observing the situation this way, the fact that we could create such a complex alternate reality is perhaps a good thing."

"So, you're suggesting we all join Clairey as she gets back into her spaceship?" Estella asked, unimpressed.

"She's telling us to embrace our dreams," smiled Morgana.

"I'm not getting into a fucking spaceship!" snapped Alicia.

"You don't have to," said Serena, "I'm saying that learning to see our disorder as a blessing rather than a curse might stop us from seeing ourselves as a victim and thereby reduce our self-destructive behaviour. You like blessings, don't you, Morgana? And you like not being a victim, don't you, Estella? The fact that we are all figments of somebody's imagination, sat on cardboard boxes around a crooked table, in a shoddy house, at the centre of an imaginary wasteland could suggest that behind all this is a mind that's batshit insane…"

"Who are you calling a goddamn figment? I'm real!" declared Alicia, furious and defiant.

"Of course you are, dear," smirked Estella.

"Real or imaginary, we're hardly the sanest girls in the playground," continued Serena, "and I know it sounds cliché, but I'm suggesting that we try to find some way of being proud of this. It might even stop us all from feeling sorry for ourselves."

In the world of reality, this was the point at which we began seriously trying to sort our life out, determined to reach a new level of social competence, sustained employment and passable sanity. Unfortunately, a combination of ongoing mental health difficulties as well as various practical and sociological factors made this an uphill struggle.

Job #12 saw us working as an assistant in a care home. Morgana genuinely wanted to help people, and she gave so much of herself to the role due to her caring nature, that she truly saw herself having a future there. Her free time was spent creating spiritual artwork of fairies and chakras in an effort to evolve past negativity and heal her severed sisters. The internet abuse we regularly received for being unemployed parasites still continued, even after we had started getting up at six o'clock in the morning to go and clean up shit. We tried to ignore it, and concentrate on the good in our lives. Honeysuckle was fairly happy with Boyfriend #6. Estella was pleased that we might have the beginnings of a career, with the possibility of training as an art therapist once we had gained sufficient care work experience. Alicia was gradually developing a vicious sense of humour and getting plenty of exercise. Our online portfolio was renamed after our extra-terrestrial friend from childhood in an effort to embrace our overactive imagination and see the positive side to our condition. We actually managed a few months of steady psychological improvement that many people around us were impressed by, and our social standing dramatically improved until we no longer felt like an outcast.

It was just a shame that you have to be fairly thick skinned and sound-minded to handle the high-stress atmosphere of the care environment. It was not long before we had another mental breakdown after getting assaulted by a patient, the violence within a domestic setting triggering our issues from the past. Some further failed attempts at employment and one more miserable break-up later, we ended up back on benefits and being referred to a mental health outpatient centre on account of our suicidal thoughts and severe anxiety.

The day hospital was in a comforting building with plenty of soft chairs and no sharp objects. There were timetabled group sessions where you could discuss your woes with other sufferers, and plenty of free time to amuse yourself by reading a book, chatting with the staff, or staring into the air in front of you while rocking backwards and forwards.

Hey, mental health patients, lets rock!

We met a girl who looked like the forgotten dream of a hopeful magazine, whose personality made us think of what Honeysuckle would be like if the rest of us weren't around to control her. Her favourite conversational topics were bulimia and lap dancing. We were always discouraging our shameless alter from pursuing a career involving unedited nudity, as we felt the need to protect her on account of her low self-esteem.

"See, I couldn't do that, on account of my low self-esteem," our precocious teen sighed in response to her new friend's description of a typical working day.

"Oh, you should totally do it. Lap dancing's actually really good for your self-esteem. It gives you so much confidence," she cheerfully informed us.

We did have to wonder what such a self-assured young lady was doing in a day hospital for the mentally ill.

Meanwhile, back in the mindscape...

"Ah yes, lap dancing, that well-known ego boost," remarked Alicia. "Other popular cures for insecurity include prostitution, gold-digging and setting yourself on fire."

"Didn't you set yourself on fire once?" asked Honeysuckle.

"Why the fuck would I set *myself* on fire?" Alicia snapped, looking at the screens in disgust. She glared at the image of the smiling girl sat opposite us, but didn't break through to confront her because there was no point. It would be no different from arguing with herself.

Honeysuckle responded by walking prettily up to the nearest television and putting Alicia's film into the built-in video player. "There you are," she said, pointing to the crazy girl in the dingy student bedroom who was pouring lighter fluid onto her T-shirt.

Alicia laughed and shook her head. "That's you, you dumb bitch," she retorted, as the match on the screen was slowly lowered.

Honeysuckle's face fell in confusion. "If it's me in the Fail Trilogy, then what's with all the death threats? You're the one who wants to kill people," she argued.

"And also, if it's me, why aren't I naked?"

"Firstly," stressed Alicia, with a menacingly deliberate patience, "I wanted to actually do the killing, not just make stupid movies with masochistic imagery and hollow death threats. This psycho-feminine, attention-seeking drivel has your name all over it. Secondly, I would never willingly appear on camera. I hate those damn things even more than I hate hippies. Thirdly, we can't always let you be naked."

"Why not?" asked Honeysuckle.

"Well, you do have a very low self-esteem," replied Alicia. "Also, you're fucking mental."

"Says the girl who wants to burn people?"

"Says the bonfire to the car crash."

CHAPTER 25

(Constructed Sanity Falls to Nothing)

We kept stoically persevering with our little attempts at normality, changing our job and our address almost as often as we changed our personality, constantly striving in a cycle of rebuild and disintegration. We thought that our future might finally hold some long term stability after we landed Job #19, a data-entry assignment for a major bank. Our task for the first three months was to process online application forms for new accounts. We were all adequate at typing and enjoyed doing a repetitive task where we could listen to music and did not need to speak to customers. Conducting ourselves politely and surpassing our productivity targets every day, we were due to obtain an official employment contract after completing our initial probationary period.

Unfortunately, the economy then went wrong. It turned out that the company could not afford to offer us a permanent position while financial losses were being made, but we were welcome to stay on indefinitely as a minimum wage temporary worker.

We were with Boyfriend #7 at this point. His job involved doing something with computers that we didn't understand. We had a vague memory of being clever once, learning new skills and information ridiculously easily and having a promising future. We possibly should have stuck with that, instead of going crazy. Never mind.

Everything began to collapse when they made changes to our routine, and we were required to make phone calls to customers. Hearing a voice without seeing a face reminded Katie of the time she had to keep her head under the pillow while things were done to her. The furious, protective reaction of Alicia towards the younger one's distress led to the return of her death fixation. Needing to keep everyone as numb as possible, Serena began shutting down the energy currents that powered the mindscape, switching off the lights in the latest structure she had built to house us, and starving us of cognitive energy. It seemed like the best way of keeping Alicia away from the nearest petrol station. This method kept us safe, but also made us tired, and it was a daily struggle to stay awake.

The management moved us to a different department where we had fewer friends and the work was even more monotonous. Change made us unstable, so at least the boredom was sporadically shattered by Alicia fighting for control of the physical vessel so she could use it to smash things up. She never won, but it was an increasing drain on Serena's resources to try and contain her.

"Why do you do so much work, Carlie?" one of our colleagues asked us one day, as our shoulder muscles attacked themselves with a crippling hyper-tension while we hunched before the screen, obliterating our productivity targets in lieu of obliterating somebody's face.

"I really need to get a permanent contract soon, so I can afford to eat properly," we replied.

"They're not going to make you permanent, you know. They don't make people permanent anymore," he quietly informed us.

"Well, in that case, I'll seriously need a work reference for when they let me go. I've practically no references because my life's been such a mess. If I work really hard here, at least it will be on my reference that I beat my target every day, so hopefully I'll be able to find another job and won't have to go back on benefits again."

We were forcing ourselves onwards, battling not to slide back into the fractured insanity. The worst thing about being trapped in a mediocre existence was the rise of the motherhood delusion. We were possibly too unhinged to stay in regular work for long, so Morgana thought that she could justify our existence by having a child instead, because when you fail at life, replicating yourself like a virus is clearly the way to go. We were programmed to create, but had given up on our artwork because our brain was too numb, so she wanted to make another goddamn human instead, to fill our psychological void with puke and nappies.

Nobody wanted a child with her.

Morgana's yearning for a family became as desperate as Honeysuckle's hunger for attention, and made her cry herself to sleep at night, but our life was due to fall apart in unexpected ways, to bring her some problems actually worth getting upset about.

"What's up, Carlie?" our boss asked us one day, as we sat in the office, staring through the decrepit computer monitor that flickered just enough to make our forehead feel like it was being jumped on by a deranged moose on crack.

"My Grandma died last night," we replied, in the hollow, ancient voice we get when everything seems pointless: the one that makes us sound stoned even when we're sober.

"I'm sorry," she responded, as we copied and pasted another pre-worded letter to a frustrated customer.

"It's not just that," we explained. "I mean I'm sad that

she's gone, but she was really old and she was so ill towards the end, at least she's not in pain anymore. I just feel guilty that I hadn't been to see her in so long because I don't get on with my dad, and I feel even worse that I can't face the funeral because my dad will be there."

"I just can't face it," said Terra, our panic rising and our vision narrowing as the lights became more jarring.

"Well," our boss smiled kindly, "that's not very fair on your grandma is it? It wasn't her fault that you don't get along with your dad. Maybe you should put aside your problems with him just for the funeral, for her sake."

Alicia smiled a grin that was a cross between a grimace and a death threat, imagining what her boss would look like impaled upon the white picket fence she grew up behind. We kept copying and pasting as the screen continued flickering, the floodgates began crumbling, and our sanity started disintegrating. The hours went past and this was all we did, the same series of useless actions that will soon be more efficiently performed by uncomplaining mechanical constructs as the world evolves towards making hairless monkeys obsolete.

A co-worker behind us had the radio on too loud, and the saccharine, repetitive falsity of another corporate love song was seriously bothering Alicia. What we needed was a quiet, dark place to regroup. What we had was an insufferably bright, provokingly loud, overly air-conditioned office to fracture in.

Alicia's visions in the mindscape were getting stupidly graphic. That pesky radio was getting repeatedly bashed into our colleague's face with the force of a sledgehammer, fragmenting her pretty cheekbones and turning her skull, skin and flesh into a jagged paste.

"That'll teach you to be a radio. Coming around here,

with your radio ways, being all radio. Now look, you're a smashed bit of metal in some bint's skull. What did you learn, hey? What did you learn?" Alicia spluttered insanely.

The children ran for cover behind Morgana's skirts. Honeysuckle twirled around in the shower of blood that emanated from Alicia's imaginary crime scene, laughing coquettishly. The three leaders gathered around the idiot teens and tried to calm the angry one, but their powers were weak from the numb repetition of data entry and the lack of stimulation in their corporate existence. There was the increasingly loud thud of a heartbeat and the rising adrenaline surge of hatred as Alicia tried to break through to reality to do some damage.

"Not again."

Serena took a deep breath and broke through ahead of her as the world suddenly became mute and crystallised. Serena knew her priorities. Preventing Alicia from causing harm was more important than sending pieces of paper to customers who were too intellectually challenged to use their correct name when filling in an online data capture form. With methodical composure, Serena shut down all programs, logged out of the system, gathered her things and walked calmly to the nearest hospital.

"I believe I need to be sedated or there's a chance I might kill somebody," she softly informed the receptionist.

"If you take a seat, we'll get somebody from the crisis team to talk to you as soon as possible," the administrator briskly responded.

Exhausted from the psychic battle, Serena collapsed back into the mindscape as we aged in the waiting room.

Rose externalised, sighing wistfully at the sadness of everything she was losing. After an hour's wait she had a brief chat with a calm, clipboard-wielding lady whose quiet authority reminded her of Serena, a floating entity she once knew but could barely remember. She was sent home with a week's sick note and a prescription for anti-depressants. After a week of rocking on the sofa and staring at the television, we returned to work, medicated. The tablets burned our stomach lining so we couldn't eat properly, got too thin again and were constantly tired and aching, with strange sweats and twitches. We took them anyway because they were the only thing making us well enough to work and we didn't want to be parasitic filth. We asked if we could reduce our hours for the sake of our health, but management said there was too much work to do, so we carried on poisoning ourselves in order to meet their demand.

They terminated our contract a few weeks later.

"We've been running out of work to give you," they explained.

They refused to give us a reference.

With no references, in a harsh economic climate, we struggled to even obtain voluntary work. Our more nihilistic elements berated us for trying so hard when it was always going to fall to nothing. All those days we pretended that everything was fine and the fires weren't rising, managed polite communication and surpassed our targets, when we could have spent the year being lazy and belligerent and it would have brought us to the exact same place.

It occurred to us that the sanity we'd constructed was never really ours to keep, just something we'd borrowed from an advertisement for breakfast cereal: a mockery pasted together from slogans, obedience and wholegrain fibres. It is one thing to build a personality that can function at social events without breaking anything. It's another thing entirely to create a soulless machine out of flesh and blood and spend your days trying to pretend the skies aren't melting.

Honeysuckle believed a weekend of chemical indulgence would be the best temporary alleviation of hopelessness that we could aspire to. Boyfriend #7 accompanied us to a party, and it was the first weekend with no arguments in a while, despite his ongoing mission to keep us insecure. He delighted in constantly flaunting the suggestion that he might cheat on us, never missing an opportunity to make us feel like we had rivals, because the best thing to do with volatile girlfriends is deliberately make them jealous. Other good ideas involve leaving them in charge of your knife collection or handing them matches.

There was a guy at the party who was in an open relationship with a girl who Honeysuckle rather fancied. Boyfriend #7 got talking to him for ages, occasionally glancing back over, before eventually returning to us, looking even more smug than usual. "I've been getting chatted up," he grinned.

"Good for you," replied Honeysuckle, with a false breeziness, knocking back more of her drink.

"He likes you as well, you know. He says he'd be up for a threesome," he continued.

Switch.

"You can fuck right off, we will not have a goddamn threesome!" snapped Alicia.

Switch.

"Tell him, I'm only interested if his girlfriend's

involved, so I'll only consider a foursome," said Honeysuckle, in a mock-officious manner.

It was a quadruple adventure, but Boyfriend #7 got annoyed because Honeysuckle received more attention than him on account of her looking better naked.

We split up a week later.

This is when life did that thing where it slides downhill, and you trip over the pretences that sustain you and wonder if you'll ever stop tumbling. It was a mess, basically. The triple impact of break-up, bereavement and job loss gave life a more disturbing edge than we had recently been accustomed to, with cracks appearing in the walls again and claws reaching through.

The only good thing about this era was the return to our artistic survival mechanisms. In a pen and pencil drawing, butterflies flew out of a bleeding wound. The largest one had eyes for wings, a bullet hole for a pupil and a scar for a body. In a more colourful creation, three scarlet cuts dissected a broken face while an artery became a butterfly in a sky filled with synapses. Our latest collage showed more butterflies falling through a bruised sunset, while the trees had eyes, a Glowbug had its heart ripped out, our nails were in the sky, and infant devils waved their red hands from beside a lighthouse.

A sign on her forehead marked Honeysuckle as disposable, as life fluttered by her in a chaotic whirl of distilled heartbreak. Morgana got a voluntary job doing administration at the local hospital, but they sent her home when they realised she was crazy, even though she begged them to let her stay because she wanted to be useful. They had seen us switch, and told us to try going back on disability benefits because they didn't think we should be working. Needing an income, we found ourselves confronted with a bureaucratic system that now despised us, and facing a controversial new assessment procedure conducted by an office worker with no medical training.

"We don't want to hear about your *childhood*," the assessor sneered, emphasising the word for deliberate derision, "we just need to know how your illness affects your day to day life."

Most of the questions gave us no chance to describe the details of our predicament at all, but we told him as much as we could.

"Do you have any difficulties coping with change?"

"They moved me to a different department at work and I started getting impulses to kill people. I was really scared and had to go to hospital. This should be on my hospital records."

"We can't check your medical records, because that would go against patient confidentiality."

"Surely it wouldn't, if I've asked you to look at them?"

"We're not interested in your medical history here, just how your condition affects you day to day."

We told him about the trouble we'd had with Alicia, with the terror we feel when she rises up out of the embers and we're scared of what she'll burn. She generally makes us an undesired presence in the work environment. Her tone of voice, mannerisms and facial expression make her resemble someone who would happily put a stapler through your eye or try to bash your head in with a magnetic paperclip holder. We tried to mention the crippling anxiety of Terra and the suicidal misery of Fuchsia while answering questions about our diet and hobbies. However, not wishing to lie, we fully admitted to having two functional legs, the ability to use a knife and fork at mealtimes, and the power to regularly make it to the toilet without pissing on the floor.

After three months, we received a report saying there was nothing wrong with us whatsoever. It even said that we had no problem coping with change. Apparently, having a barely containable impulse to kill the person sat behind you is not actually a problem. Who knew that the threat of murder was so mundane? The date for stopping our payments was backdated so that we owed hundreds of pounds unless we appealed. We had no choice but to leave Home #16 and move back in with our mother and Father #2, who had fortunately become a great deal kinder in his old age. We were very lucky to have a place to go, however, this meant returning to the claustrophobic village we had been so desperate to escape, and every time we saw an accusatory tabloid headline we went to pieces.

"The newspapers despise people who don't work now don't they?" observed Alicia, her fire sustaining us as we unpacked boxes. "The only thing they despise more is child abuse, which is a bit hypocritical, because many of the mentally ill are unable to work, and one of the main causes of mental illness in Western society is abuse in childhood. You look at a newspaper and see some poor little girl's face, and we're whipped up into a frenzy because the abuse she went through culminated in her death. However, if she'd been one of the many who survive and grow up too insane to sustain regular employment, you'd see a photo of her as an adult, accompanied by some sensationalist article labelling her as parasitic, scrounging dole scum because she's unable to hold down a job, even though she can walk unassisted, boil a kettle and make it through the day without shitting herself. They'll end up making her feel so guilty for not adequately contributing to society that she'll wish she'd died.

"You know, maybe the tabloid-reading masses should try having half as much compassion for the ones that survive as they have for the ones that end up in a ditch somewhere."

Fortunately, we finally caught a break, in the form of a cash inheritance from our lovely grandmother. Honeysuckle wanted to blow it all on corsets and cocaine, but Morgana preferred to respect our benefactor's memory by spending the money on something worthwhile for our future, to which Estella and Serena promptly agreed. We immediately booked our first driving lesson.

Learning to drive made us feel like a proper person. The money just about covered driving lessons, tests, the licence, tax, our first battered old car and our first year's insurance. There are so many jobs that need you to have your own car, but don't pay you enough to buy one, so the only people desperate enough to take these futureless minimum wage employment "opportunities" have no way of getting to them. Having our own transport made us somewhat employable despite our chequered work history and our craziness. We still lose jobs very easily, as soon as the switching starts and the disorder gets too loud, but it is no longer such a struggle to find something new once we're well enough to leave the house again and the demons have returned to hiding.

In the few months we spent back home before getting our licence, we mostly hid in our room, gluing fragments of vivid madness onto canvas and board. A dolly with pins in her plastic face hovered above a burning girl who the monsters were eating, while paintbrushes and cosmetics tumbled around her. A Glowbug floated in a cloud of chaotic dreamscape.

These vibrant, evocative children of ours should have been enough to live for, but we had yet to acknowledge that they were more a part of us than anything made from skin and bone could ever be. We were still waiting for someone to save us with the promise of a family of our own.

There was clearly one delusion left to dismantle.

CHAPTER 26

(Angelic Tragedy Hurts Me More)

It was because he had a leaf in his hair.

There was dappled sunlight, summer air and the shimmering sparkle of a river running past the edge of the trees. Had it not been for the tangle of branches above us, rustling in the gentle breeze, he would never have had that leaf in his hair, and there would never have been that moment of confusion, when we reached out to remove the leaf and he thought we were reaching out to kiss him.

"Next time some forresty twat brings a leafy hairstyle near us, can I set fire to it?" asks Alicia, looking back on this emotional moment in disgust.

There was, however, a pitiful lack of either kisses or immolation on this particular occasion, just an incredibly awkward moment as he looked at us, expecting us to kiss him, and we froze as we realised what this looked like.

We then took the leaf from his hair.

"You had a leaf," we said, with a forced, casual smile.

We even held up the leaf in front of him, to prove our point, before dropping it into the river below.

The damage was done.

It was bad enough that he had already been confusing Morgana. At his birthday party the previous day, the other guests (all four of them) had been late by a couple of hours. He had taken this social embarrassment as an opportunity to win her over. It really shouldn't have worked.

He had invited his friends over to his supposed three

bedroom house on an urban farm. There was to be a picnic on the grounds, and he had mentioned several books that he was going to lend us from the library.

As it turned out, he lived in his mum's house on a council estate, sleeping on a single bed in the spare room, and the "library" was in fact a large bookcase in the lounge. He had fallen on hard times after a break-up with a cruel girl who had taken everything, and was trying to make the best of a difficult situation. He was ever so wounded. Morgana always liked that sort of thing, the whole vulnerable, tragic hero vibe. She is an incredibly compassionate person who likes to make it all better. Some people like that sort of thing.

He knew exactly what to say.

He was fed up of the shallow scene we belonged to, tired of people using each other, and of romance being so disposable. He just wanted to meet a nice girl he could trust, settle down, and start a family.

"Oh, he keeps saying the right thing," observed Estella, with a sneer of contempt, as though by "the right thing" she really meant "such nauseating bullshit".

"Oh, he keeps saying the right thing," smiled Morgana, genuinely, without the slightest trace of disdain or irony.

This is how we ended up going for a picnic with him the next day, then walking by the river, then stumbling into the whole leaf-in-hair fiasco. The fact that we nearly kissed him made Honeysuckle think that we should kiss him. She is working towards certain goals in this life, and doesn't like it when things nearly happen but don't. The fact that nothing was ever meant to happen had become irrelevant by this point.

The moment passed, and we had to leave because we

had a train to catch. We'd had such a wonderful time that we arranged to meet up with him again in a week. Honeysuckle decided to herself that next weekend would be a fine time to "get drunk and see what happens". She's a classy girl.

You don't need leafy hair when there's vodka.

The next day, he sent us the most absurdly poetic text message, asking us to be his girlfriend, baring his heart with the overblown romanticism of a Shakespearean sonnet.

Morgana wanted to say yes straight away.

Bitches love poems.

To be fair, he did seem to be hopelessly infatuated with Morgana. Quiet, sympathetic, motherly and kind, she came across as somebody who would make everything alright again, a bandage for a bleeding heart. Also, she had the kind of liberal principles that kept him warm at night. For some people, to hear a woman talk about her respect for the environment, her aversion to nationalism and war, and her need to make ethical purchasing decisions, it's like a kind of pornography. He probably got an erection the first time we mentioned recycling.

"I don't like him," said Estella, in the mindscape. Gazing at her reflection, she tried to picture our potential new partner by her side. The image didn't fit. He wasn't good enough.

"You don't like anyone," replied Morgana, with a sigh, glowing gently with an elegant radiance.

"There's a reason for that," retorted Alicia, tensing up, with the wary eyes of somebody who's watching a potential enemy like a rabid hawk, just waiting for a reason to gouge their face open.

As usual in these cases, we had a positive response from Morgana and Honeysuckle, and a negative response from Estella and Alicia. It was Serena's call. She dissected the finer details of our present situation with her rational brain, and decided that, for the moment, he was a logical choice of partner.

Morgana was given permission to respond affirmatively to his message, and we found ourselves in a relationship with Boyfriend #8.

This was supposed to be our happy ending.

Estella and Alicia dislike most people at first, but over time, they often come around. Alicia actually means well, and all the fiery strength she uses to protect herself and her fellow alters can also be utilised to defend other people she's come to respect. Once he had earned her trust, she would have stood fiercely by him, forced Honeysuckle to be faithful, and had a pathological hatred of anyone in his way. Although she may not have actually set fire to his enemies, she might have verbally scorched a few of them. He would have done well to have her on his side. She is severely psychologically damaged, she gets tormented by obsessive thoughts of burning people, and her blood is like petrol, but she has a certain honesty, loyalty and unhinged purity.

It was a shame he tried to kill her.

Everything began with such promise, with poems, flowers, cookies and dreams of a brighter tomorrow.

We were always waiting for the right moment to recommence writing our autobiography, our tale of how we survived such a lunatic whirlwind... and here, finally, was our happy ever after. We would write in the evenings, after the children had gone to bed. Our book would boast of the haven we had found in the suburbs, a place to heal and be whole again. It would have conveyed the message that any disturbed young woman can be saved by love and childbirth, by being a wife and mother, by finding a resolution to personal crisis through domesticity and family commitment.

To be fair, that book would have been shit. We should be grateful really that it all descended into the usual spite and revulsion.

There were warning signs from the beginning that something wasn't quite right. After just a few days, he was saying the strangest things by accident.

"My beautiful wife," he smiled, as he put his arm around us.

We laughed nervously, somewhat shocked and hoping he was joking, but thinking that it was a weird kind of humour, which is admittedly slightly hypocritical coming from someone who jokes about near death experiences, child abuse and sometimes genocide.

"Steady on," we replied, trying to make light of the situation.

"What do you mean?" he asked.

"It's a bit soon for that, don't you think?"

"It's a bit soon for what? What do you think I said?"

"Well... what did you say?"

"I said 'my beautiful woman'," he grinned, still smiling weirdly at us. We knew he was lying. "What do you think I said?" he repeated.

"Nothing," we said.

"No really, what did you hear?" he insisted.

We changed the subject. Over the next few weeks we tried not to focus on how worrying it was that he so frequently mentioned marriage and children at this early stage. We reminded ourselves of all the times we'd been treated as though we were disposable, a piece of short term amusement, and convinced ourselves that this opposing extreme would be far less damaging. Also, Morgana was in love. She had found someone who shared her domestic delusions, and perhaps she stood a better chance of contentment than the rest of us. She started creating spiritual artwork again, a tarot drawing and another chakra painting, because she said it was time for us to leave the past behind and focus on positive energy. There were many meaningful conversations and walks in the countryside.

"I often feel like we're the same person," she told him.

Silly girl. She's not even the same person as herself, how can she be the same person as somebody else?

He was really good with the little ones. When they externalised, their presence didn't disturb or annoy him, and he was comfortable interacting on their level. The main worry, though, was his attitude towards the teenagers. To say he enjoyed Honeysuckle's company would be an understatement, but the hypocrisy arose from the fact that he didn't approve of her as a person and felt a smug sense of superiority towards her lifestyle choices. She didn't live up to his "moral code"... although this became less of a problem when she was naked.

He wanted her to be straight. He didn't like her putting styling products in her hair. He wanted her to wear less make-up. He didn't want her taking drugs, because that's what immoral people did, but she could drink as much alcohol as she wanted. She was basically only allowed to have fun when it was the kind of fun he approved of. Essentially, he wanted her to be more like Morgana. Actually, he wanted all of us to just be

Morgana, because it's great when your partner is just a fraction of a person rather than a whole personality.

The worst part was his attitude towards Alicia. We had told him about our dissociative illness, and that one of us was incredibly angry at times but we had her under control. He kept alluding to an Alicia-type aspect that formerly existed within his own character, saying he had chosen to destroy it because it was holding him back, and recommending that we do the same. This didn't sound healthy. Recovering a broken personality from a dissociative condition is a bit like putting together a fabulously deranged jigsaw puzzle, in that you cannot simply discard a piece just because it's difficult to fit. The further an alter breaks away from their fellow aspects, the more of a demented caricature it will become. Disowning this renegade element completely and driving it further away from the centre would only serve to make its behaviour worse.

When his feelings towards the teenagers became clear, Serena informed us that she no longer approved of our present partner. She is aiming towards full integration, which means that we cannot discard any fragment of ourselves, especially not to please a boyfriend who preaches at us. Morgana, however, is the type to see the best in people, and was not yet prepared to give up on him. She pointed out that we had been miserable under Serena's leadership, the teenagers did need to grow up sometime, and maybe it was now time for us to try things her way.

Serena refused to reign over a system that pinned all its hopes on a romantic delusion, so she decided to stand down as leader and concede to Morgana. She did this with the calm, collected manner of somebody who knows they are merely giving their opponent enough rope with which to hang themselves. Estella grinned with venomous anticipation because she knew where this was heading. Board meetings now consisted of Serena sat reading a book opposite an amused Estella, while Morgana sat at the head of the table, trying to rule but being ignored.

Without Serena in charge, everything began to disintegrate again. Stuck in a provoking partnership with someone who despised them, the teenagers coped their usual way, by running off to lose themselves in the wilderness. Honeysuckle externalised sporadically to drink too much and give him what he wanted. Alicia externalised randomly to defend herself against his controlling, domineering presence. Lacking Serena's internal control or intelligence, Morgana tried to externalise as much as possible, constantly apologising for the teenagers' behaviour.

One of our main incompatibilities, aside from our clashing forms of madness, was the fact that Katie is terrified of dogs. Boyfriend #8 was the kind of person who values animals more than human beings, someone who would massacre an entire village of women and children merely to save an injured mongoose, an activist who would use a machete to cut through swathes of starving orphans just to bring cough medicine to a poorly llama.

He was sat on a park bench with Katie one day, when a dog started running towards them.

"Don't let it jump on me, I don't like dogs, don't let it near me," she cried in terror, hands to her face, shaking.

As the owners and her boyfriend did nothing but stare at the petrified girl, the creature made a leap towards her face. This caused a sudden switch, as a protective Alicia kicked it away to save Katie from being bitten.

"Get it away from me!" she screamed, pushing it back with her foot as it made repeated attempts to jump at her face.

The owners eventually took responsibility for their animal and dragged it away as our screaming subsided. They told us that we shouldn't have come to the park if we didn't like dogs. At times like that, it's tempting to get a pet tarantula and let it wander around in public, scuttling up people's legs as a form of greeting, and tell people they shouldn't leave the house if they don't like spiders.

Having witnessed her fearful mistrust of certain animal life, our eco warrior boyfriend was more determined than ever to destroy Alicia. Back at the house, he tried to make us redeem ourselves by getting rid of her, as though it's that easy or wise to try killing a part of yourself.

"You'd all be better off without her," he informed us.

Morgana began crying because her dream was breaking. "Can't you love all of us?" she pleaded, tears streaming down her clean, make-up free face.

He responded by packing his possessions away in his bag. "I've done everything I can for you," he told her with a sanctimonious frown, "and I don't need to put up with questions like that."

Morgana didn't want everything to end in such a way, so she begged him to stay, so they could talk things through. Against our wishes, she told him about herself and the two alters she ruled with, about how we had spent the past few years pulling our fragmented system together, and how far we had come. She ended up telling him all about the abuse we had lived through as a child, the initial split between Clairey and Katie, and the desolation of the nihilistic teenagers for whom there would be no redemption. She wanted him to understand her subordinates. She honestly believed that if she could make him empathise with their instability then he would love them all as much as she did.

There's nothing quite like being deluded, is there?

No matter what she told him, he stood firm to his opinion that we should kill Alicia because she was holding us back. Apparently, her angry, defensive impulses were unnatural. Clearly, he had never seen a wildlife documentary. He told us how he had managed to destroy his own rage and become a far better person than us, despite having lived through so much more. He painted a chilling picture of what our future would resemble if we did not follow his advice.

"You'll become like my mother," he warned, "a woman who's completely alone because nobody can stand to be around her anymore."

Considering how lonely she had been in the past, this sounded like a vision of her worst nightmare, and Morgana was horrified at the evil inside her and terrified of what her life would become.

Luckily, he was prepared to forgive her, and said he would always be there for her, even after she had driven everyone else away. He suddenly changed into someone benevolent, all hugs and smiles. She could trust him. Apparently, everybody else would eventually abandon her because she was so awful, but he would never give up on her.

He held a tear-stained Morgana in his arms and told her he wanted "make up sex" now that they were finished arguing. He said he wanted to feel close to her again.

She gave him what he asked for.

When he got the train home that evening, he was grinning cheerfully with so much "forgiveness", and Morgana waved him goodbye, thinking that everything was going to work out, because he still loved her.

Unfortunately, he then sent us an email the next day saying he didn't want to see us for a while, which was soon followed by his public announcement of the termination of our relationship due to his moral superiority.

This is when everything came crashing down... again.

In the real world, we sat humiliated and catatonic, rocking gently, slack jawed and dead eyed, only moving occasionally to fetch a glass of water or burst into tears, while a deluge fell upon the mindscape.

Morgana was devastated, staring emptily before her while Clairey and Katie crawled listlessly around her feet. Honeysuckle felt even more used up and worthless than usual, and Fuchsia thought that we should kill ourselves if he didn't come back. Alicia had been banished by Morgana somewhere far away, because this was all her fault for being angry and abusive. Serena was locked away with her books, ignoring us. Kathy succumbed to the hysteria, occasionally bursting into gibberish speech for no reason. Mostly though, we were Katherine, the downtrodden, miserable old hag whose life is over.

This desperate situation was allowed to continue for two days before a sneering, sardonic voice drawled across the miasma of our mind, reaching us all in whichever secluded corner we were hiding.

"Oh please. Let me deal with this."

It was Estella, the one who never liked him anyway. She turned away from the mirror to grace her shaken sisters with her arctic, mocking glance.

"Children," she said to Clairey and Katie, "he was a bad man. You've had more than enough of bad men. You won't miss him."

"Teenagers," she called out to Honeysuckle and Alicia, "gather your sad shadows and get a grip.

"Alicia, I'm sorry that Morgana went against my advice and was credulous enough to fall for someone who wanted you dead. Despite your occasionally unhinged abrasiveness, I value your feisty strength and believe that you're a vital part of our character. We shall find you somebody who appreciates your anger, values you for who you are, and doesn't try to suppress your rage.

"Honeysuckle, we'll find you someone who's prettier than him and better in bed."

"Morgana," she continued, "you might want to consider listening to me sometimes. I was right about him. There's nothing quite like letting a man abuse your children because you're afraid to be alone, is there? You're supposed to be a mother to Honeysuckle and Alicia, and yet you considered sacrificing their existence so you could have your recycled romance with a vegetarian narcissist. You will never be raised above me again. You're too naive to lead us. For God's sake, woman, someone's not necessarily a decent person just because they like nature."

"Yeah! Fuck nature! The lousy, tree-addled bitch!" yelled Alicia with reckless mirth as she stomped defiantly back into the mindscape house, slamming the door behind her with a vicious grin.

"That's my girl," grinned Estella.

"It's fucking ludicrous," continued Alicia, barging back into the boardroom as we began to regroup. "There's so much pseudo-pagan psychobabble attached to the supposed healing power of nature, you would think there was no scientific explanation for the improvements in brain chemistry that follow exercise, fresh air and sunlight. It must be the Goddess of the Earth with her mystical powers. Of course this New Age belief system will save us from our misery, because recovering your life from the mess you have created has nothing to do with practical changes, it's clearly all about finding a higher class of delusion.

"Hug a fucking tree! That'll make the memories of molestation disappear.

"Burn the right incense, and it won't matter that nobody wants to date you, hire you or live with you for longer than five minutes.

"The recollection of once having to sleep with a man who smelt like rotten garbage to have a roof over your head because you were friendless and estranged from your family will simply disappear if you wear the right crystal, washed from your mind by its healing vibrations. Honestly...

"Fuck hippies! Estella for King!"

"Estella for King!" agreed Honeysuckle, eyes wide with admiration, raising a glass in the arrogant one's honour.

"Aw, bless you both," laughed Estella.

"Really, I should take charge now," she mused, "Serena's too absorbed in her academic studies to acknowledge that the world is a brutal place and we should just take what we can from it. Morgana would happily kill us off at the adolescent level so she could go live behind a white picket fence in a solar powered house with snot nosed brats in reusable nappies. With me in charge, we could achieve so much more."

"However," she concluded, "I am still prepared to defer to Serena because I am the ego and she is the brain and people with egos more powerful than their brains can become spectacularly ridiculous. Luckily, I am self-aware enough to know that I will always need Serena, our clever little librarian. Supreme confidence is all very well, but it's always commendable to know things."

So we picked ourselves up, went out socialising that weekend and had a fantastic time. A few days later he started messaging us, helpfully suggesting ways in which we could change if we wanted him to take us back. We messaged him back, helpfully suggesting ways he could go fuck himself.

He accused us of "letting Estella and Alicia dominate our personality". The ladies in question said that he was only jealous because *he* wanted to dominate our personality.

So Morgana got demoted, switching back with Serena, to sit opposite Estella, where they could war eternally while Serena claimed her rightful place as King. For a minute, our life nearly went full circle, ending up in the meat free, Earth friendly, free trade, low carbon, organic, smug, abysmal mire in which it all began. Now we wanted to drive an air-polluting car, deliberately run over small animals, leave lights on in rooms we weren't using, eat hamburgers, throw recyclable packaging away with the general waste, read right wing newspapers and hate immigrants, just to not be like him.

Well... we didn't really, that was actually a joke.

Apart from that first bit.
We like having a car.

CHAPTER 27

(The Beautiful Car Crash Leaves Me Wounded)

That heartbreaking poem which Honeysuckle had written ten years previously was always going to be a self-fulfilling prophecy. She had turned her life into a supposedly beautiful car crash. Staggering through existence with only hopeless fantasies to sustain her, she was always bound to bring about her own undoing, although she never had enough self-preservation instinct to actually care. The fact that she was approaching thirty as a terminally single, unemployable mess didn't surprise her. What shocked the hell out of her was the fact that she had made it this far without accidently killing herself or ending up as a diseased, homeless crack addict. She had done well.

Her desperation to be saved from loneliness had often made her vulture bait. Luckily, she had never really been alone. Her three leaders were always holding her back, encouraging her to behave with some intelligence and dignity. There were times when she couldn't even spell either of those words, but some of their message must have gotten through, because she was gradually evolving.

Our eager starlet had been partially created as a response to the crippling, delusional belief that there were hidden cameras everywhere. Judging by her behaviour, in retrospect, it might have been a better plan to block those pesky lenses with some kind of tinfoil hat. We still do feel their unrelenting, prying presence, and maybe always will do, because we're paranoid and somewhat demented, but humankind is heading into a digital future where this little piece of psychosis may actually become our new reality, so at least we are well prepared. It's a good job we started young.

Following our latest break-up, Honeysuckle had the novel idea of staying relatively sober until she had sorted her life out, rather than disappearing into a fermented oblivion and behaving as though somebody just died. Figuring out that making realistic improvements to life circumstances is a better response to emotional pain than toxic obliteration is hardly rocket science, but some of us are a bit slow.

This time, rather than slitting our wrists over the horrific notion of being single again, we passed our driving test, moved to a new city, found temporary work, began submitting our artwork to open shows, re-coded the design of our website to create a more professional aesthetic, completed another collage and began a new photography series, which turned into some of the best work we had done so far.

Our images lost their previous, bleak melodrama and found a new, subversive subtlety. We were aiming to take the potentially hollow imagery of fashion photography and twist it into something with layers of psychological meaning. We became inspired by artists who use metaphors to express personal experience in a way that's poetic and dreamlike rather than overly literal. Our photographs were intended to evoke a certain state of mind that was difficult to verbally define, leaving the viewer with more questions than answers and having no obvious interpretation.

Alicia gets so angry about the fraudulent pretentiousness of art school brats, we could say so much more about our work if we were able to lie, but she won't let us. Our best work comes from a combination of Alicia's brutal honesty and Honeysuckle's twisted poetry. When they are creative rather than destructive they're such an improvement on the drama-creating, attention-seeking abomination of their youth.

In the seven years that we'd spent playing the Game of Scenes, we had managed to go from being a despised outsider to having a better social life than our sad school days could have dreamt of, only to realise that we didn't really like people and would rather stay home and paint, which is what we had been doing in the first place.

Two years after our latest break-up we were still living a fairly sober life, and Serena's powers of memory and concentration were improving dramatically. She had learnt the first six hundred digits of pi. This wasn't a spectacularly useful thing to learn, but she enjoys the process of memorizing, because she's weird. Also, the numbers make a fantastic mantra for Terra to repeat to herself when the panic rises. They have a certain calming rhythm, and focusing on these fixed, unchanging digits brings a sense of stability, something solid to cling to until the horror subsides. Numb and number.

Serena's logical, neutral character definitely made her the right choice for leader. If Estella's cold, egotistical nature was allowed to rule, it might turn us into something psychopathic and dreadful, but Morgana's bohemian aspirations would have made us a different kind of awful. While temporarily under her command, we almost developed a very spiritual way of understanding our past torments, soothed by the anaesthetizing lullaby of modern self-help literature. It was a close call.

"I keep being told about the power of positive thinking," Alicia informed us, "and it's making me want to burn something."

"All of this negative energy will come back to you in the end," warned Morgana, who still believes in the powers of gratitude and visualisation, despite everything, and would probably dress like a hippy if we allowed her to. "Remember how your fixation with fire led to that arson attack on our home a few years ago. When you project that amount of hatred into the universe, it will always return, and it will be you who gets burned."

"That arson attack was caused by being the token gothic type on a council estate of feral children who wore ill-fitting sportswear and smelt of chip fat," retorted Alicia. "The masses see something different, they want to burn it. A few hundred years ago, I'd have been burned as a witch. So would you, for that matter, and all your talk of 'positive energy' wouldn't have saved you. Do you honestly think that all those women were immolated for being 'too negative'? That all the sadistic, superstitious misogynists would have left those poor women alone if they'd just smiled more?"

"I just think it's interesting that you caused the people around you so much stress and misery and it all came back to you," explained Morgana.

"You know," said Alicia, "it's also quite possible that we got treated like crap because we were vulnerable and surrounded by twats. These days, I do generally manage to keep my thoughts on burning people to myself, unless I can phrase them in a way that's fucking hilarious, so maybe I did learn some of those 'people skills' you keep lecturing me about. However, I made this change because I wanted less drama in my life, not because people started looking any less flammable.

"Besides, your idea of karma is bullshit. It's not much

of an adequate explanation for child abuse is it? Are you going to tell me that the universe was merely getting its karmic revenge on me for being a spectacularly evil new born baby? That I was giving out some really negative vibes as I played with stuffed animals in my cot?

"You know something? I think that this notion of us all creating our own destiny by connecting with certain 'energies' is a pseudo-spiritual deception that's used to brainwash us into blind self-absorption.

"Lost your job in the recession?

"Let's blame a lack of faith, rather than corporate, psychopathic greed.

"Famine in Africa?

"They're clearly giving out those starvation vibes.

"Your village decimated by military bombing and your entire family slaughtered?

"You clearly brought it all upon yourself, wallowing in feelings of bitter animosity because you don't like freedom.

"Abused as a child?

"You clearly weren't cheerful and approving enough towards your parental units.

"It's wonderful how this mentality panders to the charming notion of blaming the victim. It's all very convenient, isn't it? The way it removes all sense of responsibility towards other human beings. Why oppose injustice, when you can merely ignore it? Why speak out for the oppressed, when they clearly chose their situation through a lack of faith in the universe? Why fight to defend those less fortunate than yourself, when you can live in your own smug bubble of superior self-contentment?"

She had a point. We had spent so long trying to

disown the teenagers due to their ridiculous behaviour, but once we started to integrate them, we could see how vital they were. We could never be a surrealist or communicate with tangled symbolism without Honeysuckle's delightfully distorted mind. All she really wanted was a life filled with delirious beauty. So long as she continued to create deliriously beautiful artwork, she didn't need anything from anybody. She was finally losing that desperate neediness and the urge to throw herself away. She just needed to be loved, which is why we decided to love her.

Alicia, on the other hand, brought the necessary punch in the face of harsh reality, and stopped us from being entirely absorbed by self-obsessive lunacy. Providing she was given the freedom to breathe, the clarity of her rage could cut through all delusions, including her own, and her wrath could be the spark that fired us. She just needed to be respected, which is why we decided to respect her.

Morgana just needed someone to take care of, which is why we let her mother us. She makes sure we eat healthily and have a pleasant home.

Estella needed to be placed on a pedestal, so we have learnt to do this from time to time, to allow ourselves to have an ego, one that is self-sustained rather than dependent on external input.

We managed to get our art into a few shops and galleries and make gradual progress with our ability to work with others. We were impressed by Alicia's surprisingly non-violent reaction to the first occasion that we got spectacularly messed about by an exhibition organiser. It was a public funded gallery that ran exhibitions from the empty shop windows of the recession's casualties. We had paid money from our struggling small business to have one of our few "winter" themed pictures made into a large framed print, only to be told that the apparently controversial imagery of this piece "wasn't suitable", and they weren't going to include it. They refused to listen to a rational defence of the work, so we decided to stay calm and just take it home without making a hysterical fuss. We have that control now.

"Are they taking the piss?" Alicia fumed, pacing the mindscape in a frenzied fury. The good news was, she didn't break anything or make any definite plans to burn anybody. She had clearly come a long way, and we were all very proud. All she did was rant about this for days afterwards, stomping around us with her loudspeaker and making declarations from her shoddily constructed soapbox.

"I'm so sick of this tabloid-reading, Orwellian Thought Police, nanny state society, where art is constantly censored, unless you're some famous, rich brat, media darling, then you can be as sensationalist as you like regardless of whether you have any talent. We're not rich enough to get away with using dark imagery in our work. Obviously, some innocent soul could see what we've created and just decide to go straight out and kill someone. I know that I, for one, only get homicidal impulses because of a violent image I once saw. It's definitely all art's fault. Never mind that there are so many biological, social, psychological and political reasons why human beings feel the need to be aggressive... let's just censor the arts to save our children.

"Fuck them!" she continued. "We're not going to change to please the likes of them. We're going to react against this. I'm tempted to make a pact with you that from now on, not one thing we produce will be imagery that a bunch of middle-class, middle-aged, 'family values'-peddling hypocrites will find *suitable*.

"Seriously, fuck them all."

This defiance stayed with us throughout various future creations. Alicia went on to decree that every time the rest of us attempted to make twee, socially acceptable, bland, coffee table, fantasy art for the masses, she would redress the balance by setting fire to an orphan. She probably wouldn't do this, but we have still kept most of our creative output just dark enough to shut her up.

The penultimate step in our recovery involved creating a social identity that wasn't entirely dependent on chemical oblivion, an outward-facing hybrid of us all.

In the mindscape, Serena scooped up fragile handfuls from the littered ground beneath her, and moulded candy, blood and dirt into the shape of a girl. She put some of her brains into its skull, not enough to make it a genius, but enough that it could cross the road safely. Morgana gave it some of her kindness, but was politely requested to keep her hippy spirituality to herself. Estella gave it some ego, just enough to make it vaguely assertive, but not enough to make it an arrogant bitch. Honeysuckle contributed some of her charm, but none of her deranged, predatory neediness. Alicia added enough of her fiery energy to give it some motivation, but left out her unhinged, incendiary bloodlust. The children were allowed to add some of their mannerisms, for use on certain occasions, just to confuse and maybe slightly irritate people.

We made a girl out of all of us, and sent her out into

society to deal with people so that we didn't have to. We created something that could live in the moment, and kept our useless memories to ourselves, deciding that our future was actually far more interesting than our past. Her name was an abbreviated form of our childhood alien identity, the intergalactic warrior princess that we had promised ourselves we would become when we grew up.

Every action has an equal and opposite reaction, and everything here has its twin, apart from Serena, who occupies a state of perpetual equilibrium. While creating our social hybrid, we simultaneously made something dull and friendless from the dust that her shadow fell upon. This unsocial hybrid will rarely leave the mindscape and never leaves the house, another entity to stay back here with us, with our illusions, allusions and delusions. Luckily, she won't get too depressed back here, because our final stage of recovery involved swapping razor blades for punch lines.

We realised that there was nothing that wasn't a joke if you could look at it in a certain twisted light. We had spent far too long not being able to look back at our life without crying. It occurred to us that we could completely change our whole perspective if we could reframe those experiences in our head, turn tragedy into comedy, reach a state of mind where our whole life became hilarious and we couldn't look back on it without laughing.

"How many of Carlie Martece's alternate personalities does it take to change a light bulb?"

"Child abuse."

Here began a new era of making each other laugh instead of making each other cry. We all grew to admire

Estella's dry, condescending humour, Honeysuckle's perverse hilarity and Alicia's comic ranting. In some ways, life was always a lot harder for Alicia. We sometimes allowed Honeysuckle to sleep with people, but we never let Alicia set fire to anyone. She had to learn to find other outlets, like making creepy artwork, exercising excessively, and immolating inanimate objects when nobody was looking. Now that she had her vicious comedy as well as her morbid contribution to our visual output, it no longer felt like she was burning.

CHAPTER 28

(My Dreams Lie Dying On the Floor)

"Well, I'm glad there's no happy ever after," says Alicia.

She is stood next to Honeysuckle on the balcony of their latest imaginary residence. They're both still young, but are now in their late teens, having finally aged a few years since their early days of wandering around in a chaotic wilderness, which is just as well, seeing as their physical vessel is now quite a bit older. Honeysuckle began to dress slightly more tastefully once she stopped trying so hard to make people love her. Although we have been wary of letting her spend too much time with Estella, she has at least been influenced enough by that one's ego to develop something resembling self-esteem. Age and confidence brought an edge to her prettiness, while Alicia lost her ferocity and brought some attractiveness to her edginess, so now the teenagers basically look the same, apart from each having a slightly different glint to her eyes. It's almost as though they're the same person.

Their present accommodation is a castle that Serena built at the centre of the mindscape, with room to accommodate us all in our dwindling diversity, and sturdy central walls that can survive hurricane, toxic rain, volatile explosions or a serious loss of intellectual focus. There are still improvements to be made. During tempestuous days there may be cracks in the outer rooms and turrets might come crashing down. Luckily, there are now safe, secure places where we can retreat inside and wait for the deluge to pass, ready to face the world again, unwounded, once the skies have cleared. Anything that gets damaged can now be rebuilt, stronger and shinier than it was before.

None of us have to die for the rest of us to survive. On the road to integration we'll leave nobody behind, not even Alicia. Especially not Alicia. We've all come to adore her bitter cynicism and satirical hatred.

"Well, I did have a dreadful life," she says, with ironic breeziness, "but now that I've got a husband who provides for me and the nappies of a screaming brat to change, everything's just fine. Oh, thank God, suburban romance saved me."

Honeysuckle laughs. It's less of a coquettish giggle than before, now that she's lost her previous aura of hyper-feminine helplessness. "Alright, so we didn't end up married with children, but Boyfriend #9 is lovely. Are we really going to ignore the fact that we've finally ended up in a stable relationship and we're happy?" she asks, with a smug glow of achievement.

Alicia sighs and smiles a venomous grin. "Let's not end with that," she says.

"Why?" asks Honeysuckle, "because it leaves less for you to make disparaging, sarcastic commentary about?"

"Well, partly that," says Alicia, "but mostly because I'm trying to avoid the world's biggest cliché here. The happy ever after, Prince Charming, knight in shining armour, saccharine delusion. It's just too damn sentimental. I detest the idea of a woman needing the devotion of a man in order to justify her existence."

"Is that because you're a lesbian?" asks Honeysuckle.

"Fuck you!" yells Alicia, "I'm not the one who made ludicrous, lesbian, emo porn with a deranged speed freak in our mate's bathroom. Besides, our last girlfriend was a dickhead and I hate everyone now. I don't need love to justify my existence, not to the outside world and not to myself."

"I think you do," says Honeysuckle, "I think you need to love me, because hating me was tearing you apart."

Alicia has no acerbic response to this. She has finally become less like Honeysuckle's abusive jailor and more like her supportive bodyguard. We no longer feel the need to despise ourselves now that we have managed to collage our personality into something that vaguely resembles a functional human being. We are probably quite beige compared to how we used to be, but we no longer resemble a walking train wreck.

"So what has this all been for?" asks Honeysuckle, referring to the words that have been spilled, this attempt to make art from text rather than image. "Do you think we should tell people our truth? About everything we did? About everything we remember? About everything we thought we were, nearly became and tried to be?"

"I don't think we should," responds Alicia, "but we will anyway."

"Why shouldn't we?" wonders Honeysuckle.

"Because Carlie Martece has moved to a different city now," explains Alicia, "where not everyone knows how mental she was. Even back where all this happened, most of the "Crazy Carlie" stories are so dated they're no longer relevant, and excluding a few former partners and their little fan clubs, there are very few people sitting in judgement. Why cut the scar open? Why lose this ground we've gained and leave ourselves back open to ridicule and contempt? The past should probably stay dead and buried."

"It won't though, will it?" asks Honeysuckle. Even as she speaks, faint memories are flickering across the lightening sky, because there is so much here that never ends. Her chest rises as she inhales a deep breath of the air that's beginning to love her.

"It won't be finished until we are," says Alicia, "because part of this place will always be haunted. So long as we get this sense of cathartic exorcism from creative self-expression, we'll keep telling our sad little story through words and pictures, regardless of whether anyone actually cares."

"I love being self-absorbed," grins Honeysuckle.

"I know you do," glares Alicia, "but I hate it. There's a big world out there, with so much that needs to change, but I keep getting stuck in this place with you. I only tolerate the self-absorption you bring to our creative output because I tell myself it has a universal quality. They say the personal is political. Everything we say about Honeysuckle Martece is merely a tribute to all the fucked up Honeysuckles of this world. It's not just about you, my dear. You're not even real, and yet there's a piece of you in so many people... just like there would have been pieces of so many people in you if we'd indulged you further.

"Some girls are more like Honeysuckle than you will ever be. Many, many girls are more like me than I am. We're already cancelling each other out as we become one entity. Your urge to fuck everything that wants you is slowly fusing with my urge to burn everything that looks at me, and we're diluting each other down as we merge, to eventually be left with nothing but a disinterested apathy.

"That's fine though. I'll never be adequately violent,

but we can be violently adequate, as we rock our hard-core normality, bringing you the extreme mediocre. I'm sure there'll still be plenty of mildly irritating situations... from hell."

Alicia's rants have been slowly losing their combustive edge. We sometimes miss her adrenaline, but at least people can stand to be around us now. Our mind is gradually becoming a more peaceful place to live. We have come to understand too much to recreate a deluded wonderland full of fairies and rainbows, but at least we're no longer living in a tragedy.

We have a system. Most of us stay back in the new, improved mindscape while our social hybrid spokeswoman steps forward to interact with the world. The giant screen in every room shows us the world through her eyes. We let her know what we wish to communicate, and she puts our point across to people in a way that's socially competent. Either that or she just makes up something to do with badger-faced existentialism or a platypus on roller skates.

During busy, important times, we operate as though we're a committee meeting. We arrange ourselves in our traditional formation, but now with our avatar between us, perched up in the middle of the board table with her eyes clouded over as she takes her place in reality.

Most people hate committee meetings, but we hate most people, so at least the feeling is reciprocal.

Her twin, the unsocial hybrid, remains behind the scenes to help Serena with her library, by which we mean the collection of knowledge and information she has gathered while undertaking cultural and academic research. Serena's obsession with learning and incessant need to analyse everything is what has finally helped us to understand each other and brought us all together. She built a home for us all so we could stop stumbling around in a demented wasteland like poisoned children at a music festival. We are now safely indoors.

Terra hides in her padded cell with no sharp objects, Fuchsia gazes from a delirious tower, and Jane lazes in her personal crack den while Kathy spends her days neurotically tidying her own immaculate quarters. Rose and Katherine have pleasant retirement rooms. The children have a delightful nursery where Morgana takes care of them. The teenagers have made a home for themselves in the dungeon, but they don't remain there all the time, they are too fond of wandering above ground and bothering the rest of us.

We are all really pleased that Serena had the power to construct such a magnificent establishment. In this grand abode, the psychotic ladies, Estella and Morgana, each have their own wing. Estella's is a residence of decadence, hung with a plethora of mirrors so she can constantly view herself being awesome. The teenagers have a great deal of time for Estella, who feels like a delicious dopamine high, on a podium, in a glorious spotlight. Everyone needs an ego. It's just that ours has a name, and eyes that laugh at the crippled. She is far more terrible than either of the teenagers could ever be, and yet she is completely in control of her own behaviour, so they naturally see her as something to aspire to. Admiration of Estella has done wonders for Alicia. While Alicia was always prone to an all-consuming rage that threatened to annihilate her from within, Estella has more of an icy, psychopathic animosity. Alicia may never reach Estella's level of coldness, but in aspiring to do so, she has often achieved levels of cool rationality.

Morgana's home on the opposite side of the building is a calming place of hope and flowers, where we can all go when we need to heal. Morgana is our internal mother. She would love a child of her own, but the rest of us would rather put forks in our eyes, so she settles for mothering us instead. Unlike her arrogant twin, she loves herself in a way that's humble and not entirely inward-looking, always seeking to admire others as well. She needs to be carefully monitored for religious tendencies, but is basically a decent person who cheerfully balances out Estella's obnoxiousness.

Serena lives in a mysterious room at the centre of everything and doesn't get out much. We understand very little about her character, about how she has such control over our surroundings in the mindscape, or how she manages to continually hold power over Estella and Morgana, making her the most powerfully placed alter in the system.

We do know that the kindest thing she ever did for us was destroy our dreams. Clairey is so much quieter since being told that she's not really a magical creature, just an occasionally hyper, internal child. Honeysuckle is so much more stable now she realises she's not actually a whore, just a hedonist with a perverse sense of humour. Alicia is so much calmer now she knows she's not really a psycho killer, just a damaged girl who gets angry with the world. Morgana and Estella have both come to acknowledge that they don't actually have superhuman powers, just ridiculous egos, which can sometimes produce the same result. We live in our castle which we know isn't real. We know that none of us are real either, we're just pieces of a person who once got broken, but we're fine with this. In fact, we think it's hilarious.

On the imaginary balcony of a make-believe castle, within a hallucinatory kingdom, Alicia now stands beside her favourite sister, puts an arm around her shoulders, and asks her one final question.

"Do you realise, Honey, that all your dreams are dead?"

Honeysuckle smiles as she answers, staring out across the scarred landscape before her, where things have begun to grow again and the sun is rising.

"There's nothing like a bit of necrophilia."

ABOUT THE AUTHOR

Carlie Martece is a visual artist based in the North of England. She created Toxic Nursery as a response to people wanting to know the story behind her artwork. She is presently living the sequel, and continues to share her art with the world via her website at www.carliemartece.com.

28471320R00177

Made in the USA
Charleston, SC
14 April 2014